TILL WE MEET AGAIN

A Canadian in the First World War

Brandon Marriott

PUBLISHED BY SIMON & SCHUSTER
New York   Amsterdam/Antwerp   London
Toronto   Sydney/Melbourne   New Delhi

A Division of Simon & Schuster, LLC
166 King Street East, Suite 300
Toronto, Ontario M5A 1J3

For more than 100 years, Simon & Schuster has championed authors and the stories they create. By respecting the copyright of an author's intellectual property, you enable Simon & Schuster and the author to continue publishing exceptional books for years to come. We thank you for supporting the author's copyright by purchasing an authorized edition of this book.

No amount of this book may be reproduced or stored in any format, nor may it be uploaded to any website, database, language-learning model, or other repository, retrieval, or artificial intelligence system without express permission. All rights reserved. Inquiries may be directed to Simon & Schuster, 1230 Avenue of the Americas, New York, NY 10020 or permissions@simonandschuster.com.

Copyright © 2025 by Brandon Marriott

All rights reserved, including the right to reproduce this book or portions thereof in any form whatsoever. For information, address Simon & Schuster Canada Subsidiary Rights Department, 166 King Street East, Suite 300, Toronto, Ontario M5A 1J3, Canada.

This Simon & Schuster Canada edition September 2025

SIMON & SCHUSTER CANADA and colophon are trademarks of Simon & Schuster, LLC

Simon & Schuster strongly believes in freedom of expression and stands against censorship in all its forms. For more information, visit BooksBelong.com.

For information about special discounts for bulk purchases, please contact Simon & Schuster Special Sales at 1-800-268-3216 or CustomerService@simonandschuster.ca.

Interior design by Wendy Blum

Manufactured in the United States of America

10 9 8 7 6 5 4 3 2 1

Online Computer Library Center number: 1492418432

ISBN 978-1-6682-0823-6
ISBN 978-1-6682-0900-4 (ebook)

To the family of Lester Harper,
especially his great-granddaughter and her son

CONTENTS

AUTHOR'S NOTE	ix
CHAPTER ONE Cheer Up, for the Worst Is Yet to Come	1
CHAPTER TWO Seriously Inconvenienced by the Lack of Stretchers	65
CHAPTER THREE A Most Unhealthy Spot	119
CHAPTER FOUR The Usual Trench Warfare	161
CHAPTER FIVE An Extremely Hazardous Business	183
CHAPTER SIX Please Do Not Tell Everyone About This	223
CHAPTER SEVEN And Still the War Goes On	245
EPILOGUE Daddy, Did You Ever Kill a German?	283
AFTERWORD I Have Really Nothing of Importance to Say	291
ACKNOWLEDGMENTS	299

AUTHOR'S NOTE

WE WERE DRIVING FROM BRUGES, BELGIUM, TO THE BEACH near Saint-Malo, France, and my wife wanted to stop at Vimy Ridge. Like most Canadians, I knew that the battle was significant in our history, and I had a general understanding of the sacrifice and slaughter of the First World War. We posed for a photo at the national monument atop the hallowed ridge where the statue of Mother Canada mourns her 11,285 sons whose names are inscribed on the base of the monument because their graves are unknown. Then we walked the cratered hillside where signs warn visitors about the three hundred thousand undetonated explosives buried underfoot.

As we toured the chalky tunnels and preserved trenches, my wife told our seven-year-old son about his great-great-grandfather, Lester Harper. "Not only was he awarded a medal for bravery at Vimy Ridge," she said, "but he also wrote hundreds of love letters to his wife from these very trenches."

"Letters?" I asked. As a historian, I felt a flutter of excitement at the mention of a century-old collection of wartime correspondence. Little did I know that I would spend the next few years delving into the lives of Canadian infantrymen on the Western Front, learning the abbreviations in their military records, trying to decipher the handwritten notations

Author's Note

in their war diaries, and travelling to collect photos and memorabilia from their surviving relatives. As I would come to learn, Lester was not actually awarded his medal for his actions at Vimy Ridge and his missives were certainly not all love letters.

This book is the result of my research. It is the story of Lester Harper, a Canadian pioneer who fought in the Great War. Lester was a storyteller. In his correspondence, he recounted incidents and outings and sometimes even quoted his friends. His wife, Mabel, and their daughter Barbara both wrote in a similar fashion. Their notes, letters, and self-published works recall Christmas dinner at home in Saskatoon Creek, a sleigh crash on the Edson Trail, and the rare discussion of the war with Lester.

I have written this history in a storytelling style too, using these sources to track Lester's journey across Canada, the UK, and France. Unfortunately, some moments of his life have been lost to history. Sometimes we know what happened but not exactly how it happened. In those instances, I have crafted heavily researched narratives from the surviving material to fill the gaps in our knowledge.

The same holds true for the dialogue. Much of it is derived from the letters, using the original words and phrases. Other remarks and speeches, such as those made by politicians and military commanders, are quoted verbatim or paraphrased from historical documents. The rest I have written in the spirit of the time—employing the language of Canadians in the trenches—to realistically depict life on the Western Front.

If some of the expressions and sentiments in this book seem outdated, that is because they are. But they were part of the world that Lester inhabited, so I have included them. For a more thorough discussion, please see the afterword.

Robert Lester Harper

TILL WE MEET AGAIN

CHAPTER ONE

CHEER UP, FOR THE WORST IS YET TO COME

PURPLE LINE NEAR BRÉTENCOURT

France—May 3, 1918

SERGEANT HARPER SNUCK INTO NO MAN'S LAND UNDER A starry sky. He could scarcely see the stakes holding up the twisted rolls of barbed wire, but he could feel the soul-chilling coldness of the battlefield. A flare shot up, and Lester pressed himself into the mud. Its light glittered in the rain-filled craters and illuminated the bodies of soldiers caught in the rusted wire. They hung limp and ragged, maggoty scarecrows guarding a wasteland of used armaments, abandoned guns, and heaps of human scraps. Rigid white bones gaped through bloody tunics while sun-blackened faces stared back at him, eyes and tongues eaten by corpse rats.

After two hours in a shell hole waiting for the signal to raid the German trenches, Lester was dreadfully cramped. He longed to stand up and stretch his aching legs, but he dared not move. He could hear the Germans stringing wire two hundred yards in front of him, and his team could ill afford to rouse their suspicions. How the sergeant wished that he had his hefty satchel of British No. 5 MK hand grenades slung across his midsection. The "Millses," as the men called the egg-shaped bombs, were lethal at close range, especially when tossed with the accuracy of an expert bomber like Lester.

Raiders loved grenades. Sergeant Harper could have taken out Fritz's whole work party with his Mills bombs. Yet tonight all he carried was his Short Magazine Lee-Enfield rifle, a smoke grenade, and a single Millsy. What good was a bomber without his bombs? Lester blamed his battalion commander for the cock-up.

"Rifles and bayonets only," the commanding officer (CO) of the 28th (Northwest) Battalion had ordered. While the raiders wore white armbands to identify themselves to their fellow countrymen, Lieutenant Colonel Alexander Ross refused to take chances. Allowing his soldiers the free use of bombs increased the danger for everyone. Their mission was to procure young men for intelligence, and kidnapping armed infantrymen behind enemy lines required intense close-quarters combat in the dark. When things got stabby in crowded trenches, people panicked. And the powers that be had yet to design a bomb that could tell who was wearing a white armband.

With carefully coordinated synchronization, their luminous wristwatches simultaneously ticked 2.30 ack emma (as the military taught them to pronounce "a.m."). Zero hour. A series of shells howled toward them, and the raiders hugged the dirt. Out in the open, they were wary of the Allied artillery because their steel barrels had sagged after years of overheating during firefights. "Drop shorts" is what the troops called the ordnance that failed to reach their destination and landed on them instead. Like "friendly fire," the term sounded too harmless for shells full of razor-sharp shrapnel that sliced through their flesh. If avoiding German bullets and bayonets was not challenging enough, the Canadians had to worry about their own gunners accidentally blowing them up as well.

Thankfully, the artillery's opening salvo was on point. The earth shook, and the enemy's parapet disappeared in a cloud of dust and scarlet flames. It was a short, savage, and ghastly beautiful show.

Sergeant Harper's team hurried into enemy territory, passing mangled men in ugly *feldgrau* uniforms moaning for help. It was a perfectly executed hurricane bombardment. Fritz did not suspect a thing.

Tit-tit-tit-tit-tit. A machine gun barked in the old ammunition dump. The surprise was up. Bayonets clashed. Servicemen shrieked. The hand-to-hand combat had begun.

The Canucks moved cautiously into the first hideout. It reeked of mildew, stale sandbags, and rat feces. "Dirty Huns," one private exclaimed as he rummaged through the half-eaten pieces of black bread, discarded tins, and empty water bottles that littered the surface dugout. "Nothing useful here, Sergeant. No paperwork or plans."

"Nothing valuable to nick either. No pocket knives. No cap badges. Not even a tasty beer," his comrade added.

"I hear Heinz has cellars packed with booze. I'll volunteer for another suicide club if we find real beer," the first man promised. "I'm sick of the French piss at the *estaminet*. It's as enjoyable as kissing my sister."

"I'd enjoy kissing your sister."

"Hold your tongues," Lester shushed them. This felt more like babysitting his younger brothers at home in Pouce Coupe than leading soldiers on a daring hit-and-run operation in France. Were these chatty kids the best that Canada could muster? He gestured toward a candle flickering in the neck of a bottle. "It looks like they left in a hurry. Must've fled with the barrage." Picking up a forgotten overcoat, he checked the pockets. Empty.

"Sergeant," their sentry summoned. He pointed to the red, white, and green fireworks lighting up the sky. Those were SOL flares. The enemy was shit out of luck and calling for support.

"We mustn't tarry," Sergeant Harper said. "We don't have much time before Fritz responds with countermeasures." Lester hoped his privates realized that the word "countermeasures" was shorthand for "shoot us in the back while we scramble helplessly across no man's land."

Crack.

His boys were not listening. The star shell had spotlighted Germans running for their lives, and the soldiers were gleefully gunning away. They were like kids at a carnival.

Crack. Crack. Crack.

"Straight ahead. Two hundred and fifty yards," one private said.

Crack.

"Another Heinz on your left. Three hundred and fifty yards."

Crack . . . crack.

Lester shook his head. The infantrymen were mucking up. They had already forgotten the lessons at the range. In their frenzied excitement, they were jerking their triggers and shooting hopelessly high. Amateurs. They were missing fully exposed Boche at three hundred yards. He could drop a man at twice that distance.

Sergeant Harper was about to call them off when a flash of metal caught his attention. His shrewd eyes stared into the thickening darkness. After eighteen months of midnight patrols, he had developed extraordinary night vision and the ability to identify potential threats. At the moment, his instinct screamed that danger lurked in the dark.

It's only an illusion, Lester tried to convince himself. *There's probably nothing out there.* But he could not suppress the sneaking suspicion that their lives were in peril. What if there was a barrel pointed at them? Yes, he knew that was a big if. But either a Scharfschützen Gewehr 98 (sniper rifle) or a Maschinengewehr 08 (machine gun) could wipe out the Canadians. Should he order his troops farther into hostile territory to neutralize the threat? Lester trusted their ability to outflank an entrenched position, but that was beyond the operation's parameters—and consequently, his authority. How many men could he sacrifice on a whim, on a fleeting glimpse of metal in the dying flare light?

Only one, he decided, and ran off alone. The sergeant scanned the fields frantically, focusing on clumps of bushes, small mounds, and pits ideal for a concealed gun emplacement or a sniper's nest. He searched for any sign of movement, any metallic sound, or any gleam of moonlight reflecting off a barrel.

Nothing. Nothing. Wait. What was that? He was right. It was a machine gun. Sergeant Harper dropped to the ground. Did they see me? he wondered. Lester poked up his head. The Germans were too busy setting up their Maschinengewehr 08 to notice a lone Canadian hiding in the mud. They had already placed the machine gun on its tripod and were inserting the ammunition belt into the feed block. Once the gunner had cranked the handle and flipped off the safety, the *soldaten* would be ready to open fire on Lester's unsuspecting men.

Although he was unjustly ranked a first-class shot by the Canadian Expeditionary Force (CEF), Sergeant Harper was in fact a skilled marksman. Able to outshoot most infantrymen in a fair fight, he concurred with Voltaire's assertion that in battle, providence was on the side with the best shot. But Voltaire was never up against a squad wielding the game-changing Maschinengewehr 08. You didn't need skill when you could fire five hundred rounds a minute. In fact, you hardly needed to aim. The weapon made killing so easy that even Lester's youngest brother, Earl, could have brought down a platoon with one, despite being incapable of steadying a .22 with his puny arms.

Sergeant Harper was a poorly equipped bomber contemplating a single-handed attack on a crew brandishing the world's deadliest firearm. What the devil was he thinking? Charging forward was tantamount to suicide.

An experienced veteran, the Canadian was not about to risk his life for glory. After a year and a half on the Western Front, he had survived numerous close shaves. Medals and decorations meant squat to him, especially when they were awarded posthumously. All he wanted was to get home safely to his wife, Mabel, and their baby girl. But as Lester had learned from playing the national army game of poker, he was pot committed. If he did not put that gun out of commission right away, his boys would be collecting their wooden crosses tonight.

Raising his trusty Lee-Enfield to his shoulder, Sergeant Harper took a half breath. He looked down the sights. He could barely see through the inky blackness. Just like my riflery exam in England, Lester told himself. I could hardly see then too.

CAMP WITLEY
England—September 1916

LEGALLY IDENTIFIED AS ROBERT LESTER HARPER ON HIS Canadian Over-Seas Expeditionary Force attestation paper, the stalky farmer had more aliases than a German spy. While the girls whom he fancied knew him as Bob, Bobbie, or Bobblet, his four younger brothers called him Lester, Les, and a host of pejorative nicknames that mocked the cutesy Bobblet. His signature, on the other hand, read a formal "R.L. Harper," in tribute to his father, Alfred Wesley Harper, who went by A.W.

It was not until Lester joined the army that people started addressing him by his surname. Before then, there were too many Harpers running around the Peace River Country in northeastern British Columbia to use such generic nomenclature. But here at Camp Witley, his superiors designated him a subordinate Private Harper, while everybody else simply dubbed him Harper.

Most of the CEF's volunteers were city slickers who were mediocre with a rifle at best. Not Private Harper. He was a crack shot with the long gun from day one. Born and raised in southern Manitoba, Lester grew up hunting ducks and rabbits on the prairies. His prey were swift, stealthy, and erratic. The targets at their range were not. Firing 165 rounds in each training session honed his accuracy, and he excelled at the Mad Minute, or "Practice Number 22, Rapid Fire," as it was officially titled (but never called) in *The Musketry Regulations, Part I, 1909*.

Lester's lieutenant was so impressed with his shooting that he reported the results up the chain of command, and the commander of the 138th Battalion summoned Private Harper.

"How would you like to be a musketry instructor?" Lieutenant Colonel Robert Belcher inquired through his carefully trimmed moustache.

Lester didn't need to think about the offer for long. The position included a promotion to corporal, Saturday afternoons off, and an extra two quid a month. "Sir, yes, sir!"

"Whoa! Hold your horses, Private. I appreciate the enthusiasm, but you'll have to pass a series of tests first. We know that you can shoot, but we need to ascertain whether you can teach your compatriots to shoot too."

"Yes, sir."

"Very good," the CO said. "Dismissed."

Lester aced both the practical and written musketry examinations, so he was put in charge of the firing line for the 4th Pioneers—a battalion of tradesmen and sappers from the east coast of Canada who were skilled in tunnelling, mining, and railroad work. Because their job was to consolidate the trenches captured by the infantry, the pioneers generally didn't need their rifles unless things went horribly wrong.

Rain or shine (but mostly rain because it was autumn in Britain), Corporal Harper spent his mornings at the range and his afternoons in the classroom at the nearby Bordon Military Camp. In the evenings, he sat in front of a blazing fire in the antiquated brick room where Ernest Hopper, Hugh Morrison, and two other corporals slept. Wet to the skin, Lester diligently transcribed his musketry notes while his friends pulled women apart (theoretically, of course).

Most of the men in their unit were from Canada, but Ernest was a bank clerk from England while Hugh was a sawyer from the US.

Till We Meet Again

Born in Massachusetts, Hugh had moved to Alberta in 1914 to pursue a career in policing. After the war began, he enlisted in the CEF and joined Lester's platoon at Sarcee Camp, near Calgary, before being sent overseas to England.

It didn't take Hugh long to ingratiate himself with the Canadians. Within weeks, they all called him Bud—presumably because he was everyone's bud. Tall and brawny, Hugh was a ruddy Adonis dressed in khaki. The ladies swooned over him. The lads loved him too. They gathered around to hear his inappropriate stories about the aforementioned ladies.

On their days off, Lester and his pals travelled to nearby towns where the narrow streets were overrun by soldiers from across Canada and beyond. They spent their leisure time at the YMCAs, the theatres, and of course, the pubs. The taverns in the UK were unlike any bars that the Canadians had seen before. Indeed, men had been drinking and brawling at the King's Head in Guildford for four hundred years longer than the Dominion of Canada had existed. The timber beams that lined the walls were sticky with layers of spilled ale from generations of boisterous drunks. The pubs were loud and rowdy and chockfull. The Canucks loved them.

"Who's coming to town with me this weekend?" Bud asked.

"Not me, unfortunately," Ernest replied. "I didn't get a pass."

"So? Neither did I. We'll fake 'em and sneak out."

"Fake passes? I don't know."

"Come on, Hopper. Don't be such a stickler for the rules. Guildford is only seven miles away, and Godalming is closer. We'll leave after last class and be back before lights out. This camp is crawling with thousands of Tommies in identical khaki uniforms. Who's gonna miss your ugly mug before roll call?"

"I could use a Jane in the worst way," Ernest conceded. "But you better make sure we don't get caught."

"Don't worry, I've done it before," Bud bragged. "Leave the details to me. How about you, Harper?"

"No way," Lester answered, his nose buried in his musketry notes.

"Come on. Don't be a wet blanket. I'm buying." Hugh held out a handful of cash.

Those were the magic words. Lester knew that he and his fellow soldiers were forbidden to gamble on Crown and Anchor, so he didn't ask where Bud had got his money. "Who wants to know?" was Lester's favourite saying. The answer was never him.

The studious corporal put down his pencil. He was sick of army fare, especially the bland and rubbery meat that he swore was cooked in axle grease. Lester was craving a succulent roast, complete with Yorkshire pudding and dripping with gravy. But a decent meal cost fifty cents, and he did not have a blessed penny. "Okay. If you're buying," the broke Canadian agreed.

"Attaboy!" Bud slapped him on the back.

The three soldiers snuck off to the Saxon market town of Guildford. They played billiards at the YMCA and then went to the pub.

"Sure you don't want a beer, Harper?" Bud double-checked before ordering another round from the barmaid. "It's on me, you know."

"No, thanks. Dinner's fine."

"There's no need to ask," Ernest said. "Harper doesn't drink. He's a Methodist. They don't touch the dirty stuff."

"You're a teetotaller?" Bud exclaimed. "Really? What a goody-goody!" Hugh was a Methodist too, at least according to his attestation paper, but that never stopped him from touching the stuff.

"Sure. Whatever," Lester responded, his face fully immersed in his meal.

A local girl approached their table. "Excuse me. May I please have a biscuit?" she asked.

Lester pushed his plate toward her.

"Would you like my beer too?" Ernest joked.

"Don't mind if I do." Her slender fingers picked up the glass, and she chugged the pint before he could react. "Cheers," she said, smacking her lips.

The Canadian was stunned. "So much for English ladies," moaned Lester.

Hugh gave him a dirty look. "I'm Bud," he cut in with a smile. The burly American followed the lady's eyes to two women giggling at the bar.

"My sisters," she said, answering the unspoken question.

Hugh saw a chance for a date. "It's a spectacular evening," he said. "Why don't we all go out on the river for a row?"

"Bud, Hopper, come on," Lester whined when they were still out at 8.00 pip emma. "We have to be on the bus in half an hour or we won't make it back to Bordon on time." Corporal Harper was not going to take that chance, but his friends were less concerned. They cared more about the women than getting caught with fake passes.

While Ernest managed to sneak back into camp undetected at 1.00 a.m., the brash and cocky Bud came strutting in the next morning too late for parade. He was called on the carpet and confined to barracks. Fornication could be forgiven. Tardiness could not.

That was Hugh Morrison in a nutshell. To a twentieth-century Methodist, he was a rule-flaunting, heavy-drinking womanizer renowned for his muscles, mad escapades, and tomfoolery. When Lieutenant Colonel Belcher busted the cavalier corporal back down to private, Lester vowed to stay out of Bud's schemes lest he get demoted too. Unfortunately, he failed to uphold his pledge. He later admitted that whenever he saw his incorrigible chum, they got up to all sorts of queer things.

Now, however, the time for goofing off was over. Infantrymen from the 138th Battalion were preparing to leave England, so Corporal Harper took off his stripes. Reverting to the rank of private, he went for his annual classification shoot at Camp Witley. Lester would have 170 rounds to prove that he was the best rifleman in the regiment.

The weather was atrociously English when his turn arrived. The deluge did not deter Private Harper, though. He hit nine out of ten bullseyes at two hundred yards on rapid fire.

Even the invigilator was impressed. "One drill left, Private. Snap shooting. One magazine, twenty seconds, two hundred yards. On my mark."

The wind lashed Lester's face and left him half blind.

"I guarantee the conditions will be worse in France," the examining officer added. "These targets don't even shoot back. Ready?"

"Yes, sir." Lester put the rifle to his shoulder, took a brief look at the target, and pulled the trigger. He emptied his clip.

"Zero," the invigilator announced.

"Zero, sir?" Private Harper held up his gun in disbelief. Designed and manufactured in Canada, the Ross rifle was the pride of the nation's arms industry. Lester detested it. In combat, a reliable weapon could be the difference between life and death, and the Canadian-made gun was unwieldy and temperamental. It was excessively long. It often jammed. Its backsights frequently broke. And its bayonet liked to jiggle off mid-shot.

The musketry expert examined the rifle. "Your sighting was off," he said before tallying up the total. "Well done, regardless. You scored 121 points out of a possible 170. That's the highest score in C Company. You're officially a first-class shot."

Lester beamed with boyish pride as rain dripped off the rim of his helmet and down his drenched brow.

"Pity, though, you missed being a marksman by just four points."

With his riflery exam complete, Private Harper marched five miles to Camp Bramshott to rejoin his platoon. Bramshott, Bordon, and Witley were all located within the CEF's Aldershot Command area, forty miles southwest of London. Temporary bases designed to house thousands of servicemen, they were packed with long sheds that slept thirty privates each. None of them were inspiring. The most notable thing to come out of Camp Witley, for instance, was the prelude to Wilfred Owen's "Anthem for Doomed Youth." As the soldiers would soon discover, the encampment was a fitting place to pen a prelude to doom.

"I'd be a marksman if it wasn't for that darn Ross rifle," Lester grumbled to his comrades.

He wasn't the only Canadian to hate the weapon. "To hell with that damn gun," another frustrated soldier remarked. "I'd rather go into battle with a club."

Musketry, the men loved. Bombing, they appreciated. But most could not wait for their Hun-sticking lessons to finish.

"Where do you stab 'em?" the bayonet instructor asked.

"Only the stomach, sir."

"How deep do you stab 'em?"

"Only six inches, sir."

The recruits stuck the dummies in their straw guts with their seventeen-inch bayonets.

"More bloodlust!" the instructor bellowed.

The soldiers skewered the strawmen again. They jabbed and twisted and carved holes in the make-believe Germans. How mad can you get at a dummy? Lester wondered when their instructor moved on to berate the next batch of gentle Canadians.

———

There was a tizzy of excitement around camp. Their battalion was disbanded, and Lester's comrades were being drafted into new units to reinforce depleted regiments on the Western Front. Many had already shipped off, and some had even seen action. This was childhood in Canada all over again. They were picking teams for shinny, and nobody wanted to be chosen last.

Like the twenty-nine other restless recruits in his shed, Private Harper was ready and eager to make Fritz's acquaintance. Believing that only the best men were sent to the front, he begrudged singing "God Be with You Till We Meet Again" to Bud, Ernest, and his other friends while he was left behind. Lester was confident that he would be next to go to France, but his confidence shattered when his cousin Harold Empey left training camp before him.

Lester never thought that Harold was cut out for the military. He wasn't even sure how his twenty-three-year-old cousin had passed the CEF's stringent physical requirements for volunteers. Sure, the pale blond farmer didn't have flat feet or rotting teeth, which would have disqualified him immediately. Harold was, however, only five foot six, so he was too short to be an artilleryman, and his chest measured the requisite 33½ inches for an infantryman only when he puffed it out. There was also not an ounce of strength in him. Nevertheless, the medical officer certified him fit for service.

It was so unfair! When would Lester get a shot at Fritz? He headed to his favourite cart in the camp and picked up a package of sweet biscuits. Whenever he felt upset, angry, or even jolly, he ate.

"How much?" he asked the lady running the cart.

"You know very well, you son of a gun."

Lester saw an impressionable girl at her side. "Well, you need not swear over it," he scolded.

"That's not swearing," the woman spat. Then she started anew. "You know very well, you son of a bitch." She grinned. "Now *that* might be swearing."

"English women," the Canadian sighed.

Lester felt like he was waiting forever in the UK, but he knew better than to ask his superiors for a timeline. Requests from privates were usually brushed aside in equivocations that suggested their officers were just as clueless as they were.

"Not yet."

"You're not ready."

"It's none of your fucking business."

Before joining the CEF, Lester would have found the last answer offensive. Growing up in a God-fearing family, he was taught that profanity was a sin. "You son of a gun" was considered a curse. Taking the Lord's name in vain was unthinkable. In the army, on the other hand, blasphemy was as common as bully beef. "My fucking God!" screamed exasperated sergeants whenever their troops fell out of step on parade.

As a devout Methodist, Private Harper cringed at the carefree way that soldiers employed the F-word. Still, their varied and extravagant usage was impressive. They could fuck almost anything. While Lester was gradually becoming desensitized to their vulgarity, he would learn to worry when his friends stopped swearing. The men cleaned up their vocabulary when they were truly fucked.

When Private Harper had free time, he often wrote to his family. One autumn day, he received a letter from his brother. Wesley was in England, and he was coming to visit. Later that week, Lester was having tea at Camp Witley when Wes walked in. Although Lester was loath to admit it, he was jealous of Wesley. Physically, they were almost identical. The siblings were both five foot nine with matching mud-coloured eyes and hair. Their lifestyles, however, had diverged drastically since 1915, when Wes enlisted. In the military, he had started drinking, smoking, gambling, and philandering—so much for the boy who, like his father, was named after the Methodist leader John Wesley.

Despite the multitude of his sins, Wesley had never looked better. Younger and leaner than Lester, he was dashing in his English uniform and American shoes while his brother was wearing tattered Canadian gear. The quality of Lester's footwear was particularly egregious. Like every soldier, he knew that having a pair of solid boots was a necessity in the army. Yet his wore out so quickly that he swore the soles were made from cardboard (a claim corroborated by the pamphlet *War Scandals of the Borden Government*).

Wesley had never been more popular either. Coming from the Western Front, he garnered the attention of the new recruits, who listened to his every word. They peppered him with questions like gunners firing verbal grapeshot. "What's it like out there?" was the first one on their lips.

"Don't worry about the crack of the rifles," Wes replied, repeating the well-known line. "If you hear the shot, the bullet's already missed you."

"And the shells?"

"The sausages make a terrible noise, but they're easy to spot and dodge. The blasted whiz-bangs are the tricky ones. The whirling little bastards skim right close to the ground, burst ten feet above you, and spray metal shards like a shotgun. You get almost no warning, and the Huns like to send 'em in salvos of four."

For forty-five minutes, the veteran shared tips and tricks to help the men survive in the trenches. But he didn't tell them about the grim part. The recruits took mental notes because Wesley knew what he was talking about. The gold stripe around his left cuff identified him as a wounded Tommy, and the thirty scars on his back, legs, and left arm proved it. The lucky devil, thought Lester. Wes had already enjoyed a ripping time in Ypres while he was stuck plodding along the boring country roads of Surrey. Marching up to twenty miles per day gave him hours to daydream about his brother sniping off Germans from a thousand yards with a fancy telescopic sight.

"Okay, show's over." Lester shooed the groupies away. He did not want to badger his little brother with a billion overeager questions, but he worried that Fritz would be sick of the game soon. "Think it'll go on much longer?" he tried to ask casually. "Peace rumours in the papers suggest we'll be home by summer."

"Fat chance," Wes scoffed. "Nowadays in France, they say the first five years will be the worst. From what I've seen, this war may carry on till the 1940s."

"What's it actually like?" Lester pestered.

"Cushy enough."

"Really?"

"No, of course not," Wesley answered, leaning in close. "You don't want to know what it's really like, trust me. Just get yourself a safety-first job and pray you never have to go over the top."

Lester rolled his eyes. His brother had a flair for the dramatic. But to Lester, there was nothing more embarrassing than being labelled a misfit unable to fight. Those men were left in the rear at the Canadian Casualty Assembly Centre (CCAC) where they assessed and aided the soldiers wounded in battle. "The Charlie Chaplins," he called the casualty battalion, and he considered them a joke. The only fate worse than the CCAC was to be found medically unfit and sent home, like his friend Frank McAleer.

"Don't believe me?" said Wes. "This isn't a sodding kid's game, if that's what you're thinking." He paused for a moment, unsure of how much to share. "Fuck it," he decided. "As the French say, it's *merde*. Life in the trenches is gruelling, exhausting, and terrifying. Coming under artillery fire is the worst. Big nine-inch shells burst close to you, and at any moment, one might drop right into the trench on top of you. I tell you, it gets on a fellow's nerves and makes the strongest man shake. The front is hell, and I dread going back."

Lester's eyes bulged. "Seriously?"

Wesley pulled out a cigarette and turned away. Lester gave up. He knew that the conversation was over. Any soldier who had been at the front rarely wanted to speak openly and honestly about it for long.

Lester felt funny after he and his brother said goodbye. Wes was no coward. Yet he was trying to get a bombproof job behind the lines to avoid going back to the trenches. What kind of madness could have chilled the enthusiasm of the boy who merrily rode sixty-eight miles on horseback to enlist just a year earlier?

As it happened, Lester had to wait almost two more months for his turn to come. The countless hours of tiresome parades and soggy route marches felt worthwhile when his name was finally called in the draft. Although Lester couldn't get into the 49th Battalion with Wesley on the Somme, he was assigned to the 28th Battalion on the Western Front. He was heading into the thick of battle, where the "war to end all wars" would be won or lost. It was exactly where he wanted to be—or so he thought.

The cheery private sent his white elephant gear back to the Canadian grafters who'd manufactured it and collected proper British-made Webb 1908 equipment and a reliable Lee-Enfield rifle for the trenches. Then he stripped naked for his medical exam. Nothing could sour his jake mood, not even the numerous inoculations to protect him from tetanus, typhoid, diphtheria, meningitis, and smallpox. The side effects of those vaccinations were so brutal that Private Harper was given forty-eight hours off to recover. For the next two days, he lay in his chicken-wire bunk with a headache, sore muscles, and the disturbing feeling that his blood was on the bum (to use his description).

When his sore head finally cleared, he pulled out his notepad and penned a message to his wife. Untutored in Victorian etiquette, the college-educated Canadian wrote in a stream of consciousness. Page after page, his ideas spewed forth without care for coherency or plot. Lester rambled. "I have a wandering mind," he admitted. "There is no continuity in any of the crazy dope that I say."

Private Harper must have missed his wife dearly because he wrote with passion. He wrote with exuberance. He wrote with an outrageous number of exclamation marks, which he failed to realize were usually reserved for letters between excited schoolgirls.

Till We Meet Again

Bramshott Camp
November 12th, 1916

My Dear Mabel:
How is my sweetheart? I hope you are well and happy and getting fat. Oh, you cannot know what I would give to have you with me tonight! I would not mind having a piece of your cake!!! Four months is a long time without the dainties of home, especially when there is a girl waiting there for a fellow. I can think of very little else. I hope that you are not worrying. Think of me tonight; I am homesick for my girl!

I have not written for a week, but I'll try and make up for it now. We arrived here from the ranges. I was not tired for it is only five miles from here as the crow flies. As my sweetheart, you might like to know that I did fairly well shooting although the weather was bad. In the test, I got 121 out of 170. I lacked 4 points of being a Marksman, but I had the highest score among 230 men.

The camp is not inspiring by any means. Our food here is very scanty. One does not have to go far to see evidence that England is at war, and war in earnest. Nothing is wasted. Even girls seem scarce. I have been down to the village a couple of times and only seen a few, and they were ugly.

C Company was inoculated and believe me the doctor gave us some dose. My arm is still sore and swollen. I feel as though I have La Grippe, sore all over with a headache too.

The other night, I played the piano for the evening service where we sang "God Be with You Till We Meet Again" for those leaving for France. As you can see, I am not in France yet, but I may go any day.

Don't forget your soldier in khaki when you pray. Every man going to France now is prepared for the worst, so be brave, my little girl. A lot from the 138th have gone to the front, and some have been wounded. I will take care of myself as much as possible and, if I am lucky, I may see Canada by next fall! Fritz ought to be sick of the game by then. Everything points towards a favourable ending for the Allies. It will be some time before I see the trenches, but I expect to make Fritz's acquaintance by Christmas!

Well, the boys are in now and it is noisy, so I will shut off with a few words. Don't forget I love you, dear, and I think of you an awful lot.

Ever your husband,
Private Lester Harper
xxxx

BOULOGNE-SUR-MER
France—December 6, 1916

PRIVATE HARPER WIPED THE VOMIT OFF HIS LEATHER BOOTS and stepped onto the quay. He stood at the port where Julius Caesar had launched his invasion of the Isle of Brittany (or Britain, as it is sometimes called). Almost two millennia later, Napoleon had encamped his Grande Armée here too. Now Lester was walking in their monumental footsteps, or more realistically, the footsteps of their infantrymen. "*Veni, vidi,*" as the *dictator perpetuo* said. The Canadian had yet to conquer.

The queasy private was grateful to be back on terra firma after waves had pitched his troopship to and fro across the stormy English Channel. Lester was not a natural-born sailor. At home in northern British Columbia, the nearest ocean was a thousand miles away. In the last four months, however, he had suffered through two nauseating voyages.

The country boy was unsure which of his crossings was worse. Was it the short hop over from England on the roughest sea of the year? Or the frightful five-night transatlantic passage? The betting line in New York was twenty to one that their ocean liner would not elude Fritz's U-boats when it set sail from Halifax. Lester was the first to admit that those were not reassuring odds.

Private Harper was so excited when they'd boarded the *Olympic*. He had hoped to play the piano in the lounge for the officers like he did when his cadet corps sailed to Australia. Not a chance. Down, down, down, he went, to the bottom of the ship. He was a private, and privates were bunked in steerage. The rank and file experienced few of the luxurious amenities onboard the *Titanic*'s sister ship.

Both of the voyages were unforgettable. Neither was a pleasant memory. At least the rest of the journey is by rail, the private reckoned as he followed the horde of seasick soldiers past the wounded men waiting at the dock. Some leaned on crutches, while others lay in stretchers. The worst were bloodied and bandaged and stuffed four to a Red Cross ambulance. For rookies on the way to the front, this first encounter with the reality of the war startled and unsettled them. Yet Lester noticed smiles on the mud-caked faces of the wounded. What do they have to be cheery about? he wondered.

"40 *Hommes ou 8 Chevaux*," read the stencilled signs on the boxcars in the rail yard. Lester could read French, but what did "40 men or 8 horses" mean? Was it the French equivalent of "Berlin or Bust"? That hopeful slogan had been graffitied in chalk on military railcars in Canada.

Unlike the Canadian passenger carriages, the French cattle cars were miserable. As it turned out, the sign on the front was simply the boxcar's capacity. Each one could hold forty men or eight horses. There were no windows or seats in them either—just a mob of subalterns huddled on the floor. Surely, this was not an Allied troop train? The British Expeditionary Force (BEF) was supposed to be a professional army of soldiers, not a pack of vagabonds and tramps.

The British Tommies were equally unimpressed with the Canadians. "Fuckin' five-bobbers," they called them. The Brits held a grudge against the ex-colonials who looked like back-alley brawlers but drew the wages of commandos. With five times the British salary of one shilling (or bob) a day, the five-bobbers drove up the price of watered-down stout at the *estaminets* (farmhouses that doubled as cafes, bars, and stores) and attracted the attention of women who knew that they were well paid. To make matters worse, the Canadians were shockingly informal. British privates were allowed to speak only when spoken to, whereas the Canucks addressed each other freely by their Christian names.

Lester was a five-bobber, but he certainly didn't feel rich. The married man sent most of his dollar-a-day pay home to his wife. He did not have a spare franc to buy a tasty *poire* from the hawkers selling fresh fruit at the port.

Unfortunately for Private Harper, this *was* an Allied troop train. He too squeezed into the draughty 40 & 8. All of a sudden, the sea voyages did not seem so awful. Lester would have given anything for the comfy seat on the Grand Trunk Railway where he'd watched the endless fields of wheat, the rocky Laurentian Plateau, and the meandering St. Lawrence River speed by on his way from Calgary to Halifax. He would even have settled for the third-class baby carriages that took his battalion from Liverpool to Guildford. How the boys had doubled over when they saw twenty men packed into a compartment built for ten! The CEF servicemen had laughed and laughed until they realized that they had to squeeze into one themselves. "I've ridden everything from a jackass to a lady," a friend of Lester's remarked, "but this is something distinctly new." Travelling through blacked-out Britain in the middle of the night, the Canadians saw little of the country aside from the terminal buildings.

But even that dinky English train was better than the French cattle car. I bet there won't be throngs of ladies blowing us kisses and handing out apples at the stations either, Lester figured. Only soldiers here.

The private was partially correct. His railcar was full of soldiers and lice.

As the train clattered eastward, Lester would have frozen if not for the body heat of his thirty-nine scruffy companions. His heart beat faster at the dull rumble of the heavies. He stared through a crack in the wooden planks. Flash. Boom. Flash. Boom. Gone were the pretty white cottages and peaceful green fields. All that remained were crumpled houses and cratered earth.

Private Harper arrived in a war zone stalemated along 450 miles of mud and men from the North Sea to the Alps. Following the Schlieffen Plan, the German army had advanced into France via neutral Belgium in August 1914. A swift victory seemed assured until General Alexander von Kluck pursued the retreating French 5th Army across the Marne River. Seeking glory by defeating the enemy in a decisive battle, the aggressive general exposed his right flank, and the French 6th Army ambushed him. The German invasion was halted, and the Allies heralded their first major victory as the Miracle of the Marne.

For the next two months, the armies tried to outflank each other as they raced to the coast. No one was successful. Unable to outmanoeuvre their opposition and hemmed in by the North Sea, both sides dug in. That's when the Race to the Sea became the race to the last man.

"I don't know what is to be done," admitted Lord Kitchener. The field marshal was the face of the British war effort. Literally. His image was plastered on "Your Country Needs You" posters in shop windows and on buses across England. The 1st Earl of Kitchener had a storied military career. He had vanquished the Mahdi from Sudan and captured the Boers in South Africa. Yet the gridlock in France flabbergasted him. "This isn't war," complained the UK's newly appointed secretary of state for war.

His subordinate, Lieutenant General Douglas Haig, proposed a straightforward solution to overcome the impasse. To him, the problem was simple and the answer was clear: they needed to kill more Germans. The commander of Britain's I Corps was a proponent of attrition. The Allies had to wear their enemy down, he believed, and they could not afford to be squeamish about shedding British blood in the process. The troops were pieces on a chessboard, and he was willing to trade pawns, rooks, or even his queen. The lieutenant general put theory into practice at the First Battle of Ypres. He ground his eighteen thousand I Corps soldiers down to three thousand within a fortnight. He was promoted to general a month later.

His opponent, General Erich von Falkenhayn, shared that mindset. The chief of the German general staff told Kaiser Wilhelm II that to win the war, they must inflict as many casualties as possible on the French. To use his own (translated) words, he wanted to "bleed France white." Thus, the greatest military minds of the twentieth century begat the greatest slaughter in human history.

With no way to flank the enemy, the commanders ordered frontal charges into grazing fire (an underwhelming term for waist-high machine-gun bursts that massacred soldiers in droves). Attack, defend, counterattack, repeat. The dead piled up for the next two years as each tit-for-tat assault ended in abject failure or a pyrrhic victory.

The whole front was a gigantic graveyard. The first day of the Big Push on the Somme was the bloodiest in Great Britain's history—and this was a nation accustomed to war. The British had been involved in almost one hundred other conflicts since the Acts of Union in 1707. This was also a generation raised on the glorification of the soldier who obeyed orders even when confronted with certain death. As Alfred, Lord Tennyson famously wrote in "The Charge of the Light Brigade":

Theirs not to reason why,
Theirs but to do and die.

On July 1, 1916, over 120,000 British and Dominion infantrymen did exactly that. Following orders, they climbed out of their trenches and walked steadily into grazing fire. When the smoke cleared, 19,240 had been killed in action (KIA) and 38,230 wounded. This was Britain's worst military disaster. It was even more dreadful than the infamous Charge of the Light Brigade, where only 673 cavalrymen had mounted the ill-fated frontal assault against Russian gunners in the Valley of Death.

General Haig was not dissuaded by the bloodshed. He employed the same ineffectual tactics for the next 141 days, until his losses totalled 419,654 for indecisive results. Meanwhile, the French suffered approximately 200,000 casualties and the Germans up to 600,000. The suicidal strategy of attrition was well under way.

Lester's new battalion, the Nor'westers, was at the centre of the mayhem. In October 1916, they were ordered to capture the Regina Trench, a strongly fortified German position on the Western Front. It did not go well.

"Where's the rest of the battalion?" a staff officer asked Lieutenant Colonel Ross when he rode through the lines after the battle.

"This is all of the battalion," the CO replied with tears in his eyes.

The other Canadian regiments had similar stories. The 44th Battalion from Winnipeg attacked the Regina Trench too. They labelled it the Day of Death.

General Haig's grandiose operation was divisive. King George V applauded his former aide-de-camp for his determination and appointed him commander-in-chief of the BEF. The surviving Tommies were less appreciative of what they eloquently deemed the Big Fuck-Up. They gave the newly promoted Field Marshal Haig a derisive epithet: the Butcher of the Somme.

Another 750,000 pawns were carried off the battlefield thanks to General Falkenhayn's offensive at Verdun. *"Ils ne passeront pas!"* the French cried as they died defending the citadel that was more symbolic than strategic. Not to be outdone by their British counterparts, the German foot soldiers gave General Falkenhayn his own dubious title: the Blood-Miller of Verdun.

By the end of 1916, millions of men were dead or disfigured, and neither side had advanced more than ten miles. Yet the tide of war was slowly turning for the Entente. The BEF—originally regarded as "a contemptible little army" by the kaiser (who was an honorary British colonel before the war)—was swelling with troops from home and abroad. As a dominion, Canada placed four divisions under British command. Every soldier in the CEF, from the brass hat Lieutenant General Julian Byng to the lowly Private Harper, was eager to break the deadlock on the Western Front.

When Lester arrived in Bouvigny Huts, a camp that was one of the last stopping points before the front line, an orderly conducted him to the headquarters of the 28th Battalion. To call Bouvigny Huts a military base would be an overstatement. It was designed to be hidden on a hill in the forest, but the trees that were supposed to shelter the huts had been stripped bare or rendered into stumps by German shells. The camp looked just as lifeless. The quarters were shoddy, and the YMCA was the lone shop to buy sweets. Where was the camp's "tin town" or recreational area that often housed a theatre, clubhouses, and overpriced stores for servicemen fed up with their daily diet of bully beef?

When he got to the headquarters, Lester smartly saluted the CO and deputy commanding officer (DCO). "Private Harper reporting for duty, sir."

Major Bond, the DCO, flipped through the muster roll. "B Company, Platoon 5, Private."

Private Harper found his new sergeant on a roughly hewn bench. "I hear you were a musketry instructor at Bordon," Sergeant William Thompson said, "so I assume you can lead and shoot?"

"Yes, Sergeant."

"How's your arm?"

"I played on the Saskatoon Creek ball team, Sergeant."

"Excellent. We've got an opening, and I asked for you specifically. You'll be a lance corporal, second-in-command of our bombing section. *Compreé?*"

"Yes, Sergeant!"

Sergeant Thompson—or Bill, as his friends called him—glanced at the new lance corporal in his crisp uniform and spit-polished boots. "Well, aren't you as keen as mustard." He smirked. "Let's see how long that lasts."

"Yes, Sergeant?"

"Don't be daft. Enough with the 'Yes, Sergeant.' There's no need to be so formal. It's just us. I'm pleased to see you again, cousin. Come along now. Let's go meet your lads."

Lester had not seen his cousin for years, and the thirty-five-year-old engineer from Saskatchewan had changed. With three years of experience in the Canadian militia prior to the war, Bill had been one of the early volunteers in the CEF. He enthusiastically enlisted in the 28th Battalion in October 1914. But the horrific battles of the last two years had had a profound impact on him. Sergeant Thompson was now a grizzled veteran with a couple of bad habits: he liked to drink, and he did not like to listen. Both were problems in the army.

Bill had been court-martialled three times in 1916 alone. First, he was found guilty of disobeying a lawful command given by a superior officer when he refused to go to sleep and kept playing cards for money after lights out. Then he was found guilty of neglect to the prejudice of good order and military discipline when he carelessly wounded himself in the left hand—a highly convenient injury that soldiers often committed intentionally to escape the front. Still in France later that year, Bill was found staggering along a footpath severely inebriated and arrested for drunkenness on active duty. Those were Sergeant Thompson's first three court martials. They would not be his last.

In total, Bill was sentenced to 120 days of Field Punishment No. 1 for his offences in 1916. Nicknamed "crucifixion" by the soldiers, this punishment involved placing the convicted man in fetters and stretching his arms and legs around a tree or over a gun wheel, often wrenching his shoulders from their sockets. There he hung, a khaki Christ, for two hours a day.

And yet, despite his repeated convictions, Bill had been promoted twice. Indeed, Sergeant Thompson had been a private in 1915. He had leapfrogged through the ranks after his battalion was slaughtered in the disasters at the Regina Trench and Hooge.

RENINGHELST

Belgium—June 2, 1916

THE 28TH BATTALION WAS IN THE CORPS RESERVE WHEN THE Germans launched a surprise assault on Mount Sorrel. The four-hour bombardment caught the Canadians off guard and knocked out 3,750 men, killing the divisional commanding officer and wounding the brigadier, both of whom were reconnoitering the front.

When the barrage ended, the Germans stormed up the hillside with flamethrowers. They slaughtered the remaining CEF servicemen and quickly captured the high ground. The enemy now had a clear line of sight into the Allied rear. The entire front was in peril. Lieutenant General Byng was furious. He ordered the lost ground to be recaptured immediately.

The commanders of the Canadian battalions did not have time to plan a proper counterattack, so their soldiers got a disjointed and disorganized response. The men of the 49th Battalion charged up Mount Sorrel in the middle of the day without any cover. "It looks like bloody suicide," one sergeant remarked. His last words were prophetic. The whole lot of them were mowed down.

While the Forty-Niners were being massacred, the Nor'westers were sent to relieve the Royal Canadian Regiment in Hooge. Conditions in the devastated village were dire. Shrapnel rained down upon the men through the clouds of gas. Their ears were deaf from the shellfire. Their eyes burned from the gas. Even their water was contaminated. There were so many corpses in Hooge that the soldiers could taste the dead in their tea.

That was when disaster struck.

Unbeknownst to the Allies, the Germans had been preparing their clandestine operation for months. Twenty feet underground, they had bored tunnels all the way across no man's land to the Canadian lines. On June 6, B Company was in the support trenches while two other companies were at the front. At 3.05 p.m., the enemy blew four mines along a two-hundred-yard strip on the outskirts of Hooge. *Thud.* The earth shuddered. The duckboards swayed. Then the top layer of the earth blew clean off. Mud, dirt, and fire filled the sky. Seconds later, it all disappeared: the flames, the trenches, the men. The entire front collapsed, sucking the troops into a muddy abyss. Those who were not killed instantly were buried alive.

Panic ensued, and the Germans crashed over the parapet. The Canadians were stunned, but they came together. B Company stood their ground and held the line at Menin Road Culvert. They limited the German advance despite being outmanned and outgunned. The CO was proud of his battalion, but the Nor'westers had suffered a devastating blow. More than six hundred of them had been at the front on June 6. Fewer than three hundred walked away.

BOUVIGNY HUTS
France—January 2, 1917

LANCE CORPORAL HARPER FELT THE SUNKEN EYES OF THE privates in his section bore through him. At twenty-three, with schooling in French and Latin at Brandon College in Manitoba, he was a well-educated geezer compared to these kids, who were mostly in their teens with only an elementary school education. Unlike him, however, they were battle-hardened veterans who had survived their share of shows. Lester knew that it would take a lot to gain their respect, and he was proud to have been hand-picked to reinforce their depleted ranks.

Lance Corporal Harper and his section marched to their shooting range. The boys pressed their rifles to their shoulders and squirmed with joy in the icy slush. Musketry was their favourite drill, and they were in awe of their new lance corporal. It didn't matter if they shot from one hundred, two hundred, or four hundred yards or on rapid fire or deliberate fire or while wearing their goggly-eyed buggers with the tit (as they called their gas masks). Lester outshot them at every range in every manner. Soon, they were courting his guidance, and he was happy to oblige.

Lester enjoyed teaching musketry again, even though he was constantly cold, sopping wet, and covered in mud. His uniform, his bed, and even the keys of the piano at the YMCA where he practised *Poète et*

Paysan were stained a dirty brown. Yet it was hard to complain too much when he saw the troops stagger back from the trenches along the sloppy Mont-Saint-Éloi road and collapse in pure exhaustion at their camp.

"What happened to your last lance corporal?" he asked.

"Napooed by Fritzie's Emma Gees," one of the privates answered.

Lester didn't know what language the boy was speaking.

"It's called Tommy French," Bill explained later. "That's how they speak here."

The trench language was a bizarre mishmash of abbreviations, war slang, and pidgin French liberally sprinkled with curses. Lester's linguistic competency helped with the poorly pronounced and frequently misspelled words like *savez, compreé,* and *merde* that monoglot Englishmen randomly added to their sentences, but his language skills were incapable of deciphering their anglicized bastardizations. The medieval city of Ypres, for example, was renamed an easier-to-articulate Wipers, while the expression *Il n'y pas* (it is no more), used to describe everything from dead friends and smashed homes to empty jars of peanut butter, was brutishly mispronounced as "napoo." *Ce voche* (that chump) became the Boche, a derogatory name for the Germans, alongside Kraut, Fritz, Fritzie, Heinz, Heinie, and the Huns.

Machine guns were affectionately feminized as Emma Gees (after their initials), and each shell had its own sobriquet. There were creeping jimmies, flying pigs, hissing jennies, oyster bombs, rum jars, minnies, and the cuddly sounding woolly bears, which were actually packed with jagged shrapnel. The smartest minds at Messieurs Hun and Company were constantly constructing new contraptions to kill them, so the infantrymen were forever fumbling to brand their latest deadly devices.

Some of their monikers were creative. The behemoth ninety-pound ordnance that exploded in clouds of greasy black smoke were called Jack Johnsons after the first African American boxing champion, Jack "Big Smoke" Johnson. Others, such as the onomatopoeic whiz-bangs, were more self-explanatory and less racist. Even the SOS flares were rechristened SOL flares because the Germans shot off the distress signals only when they were shit out of luck.

Living with the constant threat of death also made the soldiers superstitious. They came up with a hundred clever ways to avoid using the word "dead." They said that a man was KIA or RIP. He was buzzed, huffed, or topped off. He clicked it. He copped a packet. He drew his full issue. He went west. The list goes on.

Finally, the Canadians stole from the British, who stole from the Indians. The Urdu word for "foreign" was appropriated and exported from colonial India as blighty, an endearing term for both Britain (capital *B* Blighty) and a light wound that took a serviceman back to Britain (lowercase *b* blighty). "He's in Blighty with a blighty," for instance, was a far-too-common refrain.

Language was the least of Lester's concerns when the 28th Battalion marched up the line to Souchez—or more accurately, the rubble formerly known as Souchez. The town had been so ruthlessly razed that it no longer existed. The buildings had been pounded flat by artillery, while the farms had been ploughed by heavy shells. The victims were left where they fell, and corpses spewed out of the wreckage from St. Nicolas church to the schoolhouse. The sole thing that the Germans left untouched was the town's name. They let the anglophones butcher that.

B Company followed their scout in single file through the perfectly crooked maze of trenches. Bumbling blindly along the loose duckboards, they fought the sticky mud, intent on pulling the boots off their feet, while their guide gave directions in his trench voice (a serious whisper precisely loud enough for only his audience to hear).

"Mind the wire."

"Dead horse on your left."

"Keep your napper down here. Fritz has us enfiladed."

The rookies tried to emulate the veterans, who ambled along

DIRECTING THE WAY AT THE FRONT
Yer knows the dead 'orse 'cross the road? Well, keep straight on till yer comes to a p'rambulator 'longside a Johnson 'ole.

Lester sent Mabel postcards that spoke to his experience in France, including this one entitled "Directing the Way at the Front."

nonchalantly and casually passed on instructions with ease, but they kept bobbing up and down with the crack of the rifles, which sounded close.

"Flat!" the scout yelled.

The infantrymen flopped on their bellies. *Crump!* A rush of hot air swept over them as a Jack Johnson erupted in a fifty-foot geyser of dirt and burning metal. They scraped off the crud, cursed, and carried on.

"Crump hole ahead," the guide continued. "Keep clear."

"What's it like up there?" Lance Corporal Harper asked.

"Cushy enough," came the standard response.

"Good heavens," he choked when they reached the parapet. Lester knew that the front would smell of war. Like mud and rust and rot, the recruits had been told. But here, the air was beyond rank. The sour stench assaulted his nostrils and made his eyes water.

The *eau de guerre* was a hodgepodge of odours. There was gunpowder, burnt earth, and BO mixed with a dollop of shit. Then there was a thick and sickeningly sweet aroma that you could almost taste. That was decomposing flesh.

"Your boys are on first watch," Bill told him. "Stay warm. Stay alert. And, Lance Corporal . . ."

"Yes, Sergeant?"

"Don't stand so straight unless you want to get your head blown off on your first night. There's a bloody war on, you know."

Lance Corporal Harper hunched over on the fire step and peeked through a slit in the parapet to gaze upon no man's land for the first time. The newbie was disappointed.

"I can't see anything," he mumbled.

"Be thankful," Bill responded. "Fritz's snipers are over yonder. During the day, odds are ten to one that they'll pick you off if you stick your napper up. But right now, they can't see us either."

New sentries often kept the sharp tip of their bayonets under their chins because falling asleep on sentry duty was punishable by death, but that painful reminder was unnecessary in the winter, when they were all too cold and clammy to sleep. Although the men continually shuffled about, stomping their feet and blowing on their numb fingers, nothing helped. A damp mist hovered over their lines. The mud never dried. It only froze.

Lester arrived in France during the coldest winter of the war. For an entire month, the temperature did not rise above zero degrees Fahrenheit. This was not the dry cold of the Canadian prairies either. It was all wet snow and sleet, which soaked and then froze his uniform stiff. The wind made it worse. A gnashing breeze blew down the trenches and cut through his greatcoat, his sweater, his tunic, and even his sleeveless sheepskin smock. Never in his life had he felt so cold, not even in the frigid arctic winters of Pouce Coupe Prairie, BC.

Two hours of guard duty, two hours of rest, then two more hours on watch. That's how Lester's men spent many of their nights in the trenches. Thirty minutes before sunrise, the whole platoon was roused to stand-to-arms. Stumbling out of their dugouts, the drowsy soldiers took their allotted places on the fire-platform. With bayonets fixed and Mills bombs ready, they shivered for an hour in the morning's grey light.

It always started at dawn, Fritz's morning hate. The barrage could be followed by an assault, so the infantry had to be prepared. The Germans liked routine, and that meant one thing: if the *soldaten* were going to attack, they would attack at dawn.

When the enemy did not come, the soldiers were ordered to stand down. Then Sergeant Thompson brandished a gallon jar marked "SRD."

"Rum up," he called.

While the privates smacked their lips in thirsty anticipation of their ration of Supply Reserve Depot rum, Lance Corporal Harper demurred.

"No, thanks," he stuttered when his cousin handed him his quarter cup.

Bill shoved the mess tin in Lester's face. "Drink up," he insisted. "You're shivering. This will help. Think of it as medicine to keep from bloody freezing, if you must."

Lance Corporal Harper was too tired and cold to argue. Even his lice were frozen in place. He downed the dose in a gulp. The dark and potent Caribbean rum burned his throat and warmed his belly. A gentle booziness washed over him. Lester was horrified: he loved the feeling. From that first taste, he was hooked. Every winter night thereafter, the lance corporal looked forward to his morning slug of rum.

Squatting in the bottom of a semi-dry trench, the soldiers ate their usual breakfast: a cup of tea, a tin of bully beef, and hardtack.

"Steak, eggs, mashed potatoes, brown onion gravy, and pudding. Yap, that's what I'm craving," Lester said as he looked at his iron ration.

"Mabel's home-cooked breakfast, I presume?" Private Daniel Fee asked. Dan was Lester's best chum in the battalion. Of average height with a medium build and straight brown hair close-clipped in the usual military style, Daniel looked like the stereotypical Canadian Corps serviceman. He was so nondescript, in fact, that you would have had trouble picking him out of the sea of khaki if it was not for his eyes. They were as grey as a German uniform. Less than 3 percent of people have grey irises, and few shone with the kindness of Dan's.

"Her speciality," Lester answered. The famished lance corporal bit into a thumb-sized piece of gristly beef. At least that was edible. The hardtack was so stale that he had to soak the biscuits in his tea; otherwise, he might break his teeth. "Is a good and proper gut-filling feed too much to ask for after a tough shift?" he grumbled.

As the rising sun thawed the mud, Lester surveyed his new home. To call them trenches would be generous. He was sitting in a muddy little ditch in the middle of a garbage dump. There was no sewage system.

Till We Meet Again

When the latrines were full, the men simply dug new ones. There was no garbage disposal either. They just chucked their trash over the parapet, to the delight of the millions of monstrous rats.

Breakfast done, Lance Corporal Harper tossed his rubbish into no man's land. His fingers were stiff from the cold, but he felt obligated to write his wife before their daily inspection. Leaning against the bank of earth, Lester pulled out a pen and balanced a writing pad on his goggly-eyed bugger with the tit.

France
January 6th, 1917

Dearest Mabel:
I hope you have not so many shells flying around you as I have around me. Of course, these shells make a hell of a noise in the air. Crump! There goes a Fritz shell bursting now. If we hear them coming close, we crouch down in a corner and hope that we are lucky.

I am in the trenches just now, and it is not the nicest place, I can tell you. They are muddy, wet, and a perfect maze. Some are blown in, and the whole vicinity is ploughed up with shell holes and barbed wire. It is quite a common thing to be above the knees in mud and water.

My feet have been wet for a week. There are no facilities for drying clothes here, and a person feels cold no matter how much one wears. Ordinarily, I have on my sweater, tunic, sheepskin smock without sleeves and a greatcoat with eight inches cut off the bottom. We wear rubber boots up to the hips, but there is so much rain, mud, and water that our feet are wet all the time. It is most disagreeable. Say, have you got a nice bed to sleep in and clothes without lice in every seam? If you have, I envy you. Do you want a few lice?!

Brandon Marriott

What I want is a decent Canadian meal, even one like we got at Sarcee. If I had some eggs, I'd have ham and eggs—if I had the ham! Have it ready when I return, dear. It will take me six months to fill up properly when I get back. I have received only one parcel from you and that contained the big Christmas pudding, raisins, dates, and socks that I have on now. Swell dope!!! It also contained a Bible. I must read this little Bible for it is a beauty, and I have not read one since I left Canada. There is time yet for more parcels. Send socks (big thick ones) and cakes (also thick ones).

In the Daily Mail, *I read a description of some Canadians going over the top near Souchez. I have been through it. Souchez is a small village, but it is pounded out flat now by artillery. No one living there. If you see articles in the papers about the Canadians over here, you might cut them out. I'll explain them when I go back to you.*

Take care of yourself, girlie, for I love you. I think of you 10,000 times a day, if indeed you ever leave my mind at all. I have to take chances here, and I will be fortunate if I come through. Pray for me that I may be spared.

I must stop writing now. Hoping that I'll be back in Canada soon!

Your loving bean,
Lester
xxxx

LANCE CORPORAL HARPER SANK INTO A CORNER TO PROTECT himself from the blistering hot balls of lead that tore into the snowy sandbags around him. Maybe Wes was right, he conceded. Now that he was in the business, a bombproof job sounded mighty comfy.

While Wesley had managed to secure a safety-first job with the

Canadian Casualty Training Battalion in England, he didn't boast about the fact that he was billeted in a warm room with a fireplace in Hastings while his brother was stuck in the trenches of France. Instead, the veteran sent a care package containing two items that he knew his older sibling would cherish at the front: chocolate and a pair of socks.

When the first high-explosive ordnance pierced the morning's calm, Lester crouched down low, gritted his teeth, and wrapped his arms around his head. *Crump!* The earth-shattering force knocked the hell out of him. *Crump!* The ear-splitting roar left him half deaf. It'll pass, he told himself. He was wrong. It got worse. Shell followed shell until the sky was thick with metal and the gut-wrenching explosions blended into a continual din of jarring impacts. *Crump! Crump! Crump!*

Lance Corporal Harper could not figure out where the shells were coming from or where they would land. It felt like they were everywhere. The bombardment was so immense that he understood how shellfire could turn a hardened soldier into a blubbering baby.

"There you are," Bill said as he approached. "Up and at 'em. It's only Heinie's usual morning hate. Nothing to get bloody jumpy 'bout."

In time, Lester learned to ignore the harmless wail of the shells soaring overhead and focus on the shrieking rush of air that accompanied potential threats. Soon, he could assess the calibre, landing site, and scatter radius by the sound, which let him work out when and where to hide—as if there were anywhere truly safe.

Every day, Fritz's favourite pastime destroyed their defences, so every night, Platoon No. 5 rebuilt them. They re-dug the trenches, replaced the barbed wire, and re-stacked the sandbags. Each man was a mud-covered Prometheus forced to endure the same saga night after night, and they all grouched their never-ending nocturnal workload.

"No one's going out tonight," Bill said one evening as Lester prepped the spools of wire for the midnight crew. The sergeant nodded at a rat skittering along the parapet. The furry black rodent was backlit by the full moon. "That would be you," he said. "A lovely silhouette target for Heinie's snipers."

"That rat's as big as a cat!" Lester squealed.

"Are you listening, Lance Corporal? Don't worry 'bout the bloody vermin. They're lazy brutes who get fat off the corpses. They're not gonna take a bite out of you unless you're dead, or at least dying. Pay attention to the sky. If you go out to no man's land on a moonlit night, you're their next meal. *Compreé?*"

The following evening, the weather was worse and the odds of survival better, so the work patrol set off.

"Stick to your job," Bill reminded his cousin. "Don't be a damn fool who goes picking up souvenirs. Heinie knows our lads are treasure-hunting hoarders and booby-traps 'em. You may fancy that gold watch on a dead Hun's wrist, but don't you dare touch it. As soon as you unclasp it, their bomb goes pop and you no longer have an arm to wear it on."

Lester's men clambered up the ladders. They slipped over the bags and crept through the tangles of broken wire that littered the scorched earth. It was nasty and nearly impossible to silently uncoil and hammer down rolls of barbed wire. The barbs cut through their gloves and snagged on their uniforms. *Clonk.* One of the privates installing the wire made a loud noise. The boys froze.

Swish. A flare shot up from the enemy trench, and the men flopped onto their bellies. The muzzle of a machine gun flashed through a slit in the German earthwork. *Tit-tit-tit-tit-tit.* The gunner sprayed his shots in calculated arcs, probing no man's land for Canadians hiding among the black and slimy bodies.

The traversing fire came and went, a sprinkler watering the soil with bullets. As the rounds pinged off the wire and thumped into the corpses, the living buried themselves into the dead. The flare dropped softly and hissed out in a puddle. Darkness returned. The gunfire ceased. And one by one, the Canucks dragged themselves back to the gap in their wire.

Lester's postcard to Mabel, entitled "The Same Old Moon."

When the servicemen were ready, they motioned to their sentry. No one wanted to die at the hands of an overzealous guard mistaking them for raiders, and the men of the 28th Battalion were trigger-happy. One soldier had already accidentally shot and killed another since they'd arrived in Souchez.

The Canadians sprinted through the mud and hurdled over the parapet. Panting and sweating, Lance Corporal Harper slouched against the sandbagged wall to catch his breath. He never imagined that he would be so glad to drop back into those godforsaken trenches.

Bill handed him an extra ration of rum. "Have a snort," the sergeant said. "For surviving your first trip to no man's land."

Lester drained the quarter cup.

"Beastly out there, isn't it?"

The newly initiated lance corporal groaned.

The men of Platoon No. 5 were a muddy, leg-weary bunch after seven punishing nights at the front. On January 10, they marched to the support lines at 1.10 a.m. and crashed in sandbag huts safely burrowed into the hillside of the Lorette Spur.

Lance Corporal Harper awoke in the dank dawn to the smell of twenty unwashed men. Pushing aside the gas curtain draped over the top of the stairs, he gazed across the poplar forests, fields of livestock, and untilled farmland. Smack dab in the middle of the picture-perfect pasture was a two-mile-wide strip of muck and mire. Rows of frost-rimmed trenches cut into the meadows, as if death itself had dragged its icy fingernails across the tranquil countryside.

"Quite the view, eh?" Sergeant Thompson remarked. "Eight thousand brave lads fought hand to hand here when the Froggies recaptured the Lorette Spur from Heinie in 1915. Want to see the ruins of the show?"

Lester nodded.

"Come along, then. I could use a hand."

While the lance corporal relished the opportunity to walk upright after a week of stooping over to avoid sharpshooters, he did not have a ghost of an idea of the graveyard that awaited him. The town of Notre Dame de Lorette had been fought over in the Battle of Arras, as well as the First, Second, and Third Battles of Artois. After four bloody clashes, only broken bricks and mortar dust remained. The houses were demolished, their furniture pillaged for dugouts and anything remotely flammable burned for firewood.

"Grab some bricks, will you?" Bill said. "We have a job to do."

As Lance Corporal Harper climbed through the ruins, he found skeletons in tattered rags amid every pile of bricks. "Why hasn't anyone buried the dead?" he asked.

Bill shrugged. "Are you going to?"

Lester continued to scrounge through the debris until he came across smaller skulls, the flesh eaten away from their faces. "Good heavens!" he gasped. "These weren't soldiers. They were children!"

"Poor buggers," Bill lamented. "Heinie gassed sixteen hundred civvies here. Poison gas is the worst. There's no hiding from it. The green cloud creeps along the ground and seeps into every crevice. If you try to run, good luck! You inhale more when you exert yourself. Men, women, or kids, the gas doesn't care. Blue faces, black lips, and wagging tongues, they tear off their clothes and grip their throats madly until they choke to death on their own blood." Bill dusted off a cracked brick and put it in his rucksack. *"Mais c'est la guerre."*

Lester shifted uncomfortably. *"C'est la guerre,"* he half-heartedly repeated. His voice was thin and unsure of the words he spoke. The lifeless children had left him gobsmacked and evoked painful memories of the Peace River Country.

SASKATOON CREEK
British Columbia—December 25, 1914

THE HARPERS DID NOT HAVE MUCH, BUT THEY WERE CONTENT. And Mabel made sure to give thanks for their blessings, especially during the holidays. They had acres of land to plant crops, a creek at the foot of their property to fetch water, and a cottage that they'd built with their own hands. They even had enough seats around their table to host Lester's dad and four brothers for Christmas dinner.

Not a single farmer on the Pouce Coupe Prairie was raising turkeys, so Mabel roasted a chicken on their wood-burning stove while the men gathered around the two coal-oil lamps, which cast shadows on Christmas cards sent by friends and family from afar: Kinloss, Reston, Brandon, Vancouver. Their merry messages and season's greetings were a testament to the Harper family's twenty-two-year migration across Canada. The cards marked their stops along the way.

Lester marvelled at the tenderness of his brothers. He was used to scolding the rambunctious boys for roughhousing. But on this day, they were sitting quietly on the floor, doting on baby Hilda. Wesley was playing peekaboo while Wilbur was tickling her toes. Hilda had captured the hearts of the entire clan. Even Lester was astounded by the depths of his love for his daughter. He didn't realize how much he could care about another person until she was born—although he was smart enough to keep that epiphany from his wife.

"Dinner's ready," Mabel announced. Without her mother-in-law, she was forced to prepare the whole meal by herself.

A.W. gave thanks for the bountiful harvest. Then the Harpers devoured the chicken, potatoes, gravy, and dressing. After dinner, they all sat back with sighs of pleasure.

"Mabel, is there any place I can lie down?" Burt asked, his belly overstuffed from the feast.

"You can't rest yet," she replied. "I made my famous plum pudding with special sauce for dessert. It's a tradition in my family."

When the holidays were over, the Harpers returned to work on their homestead. The list of chores was long and cumbersome, and they still had to sleigh down the Edson Trail to purchase a year's worth of supplies before the snow melted. There was no railway to the Peace River Country, so shopping trips were a month-long, death-defying feat for pioneers.

With the new year came torrential rains. The Pouce Coupe River overflowed, and a man drowned trying to cross it. While the heavy rainfall led to bumper crops, the flooding also brought about an unexpected disaster.

"The Addy kids are sick," Lester told Mabel.

The Harpers found George Addy to be a queer duck, but he was their closest neighbour at just a mile away.

"Both Edwin and Ida?"

He turned to Hilda. Her face was flushed.

"No need to fret," Lester began, but Mabel already had her hand on their daughter's forehead.

"She's feverish. Best we call on Aunt Kate." Mabel picked up her daughter to check the old linen that they'd fashioned into a cloth diaper. There was a puddle of bloody diarrhea seeping out the side.

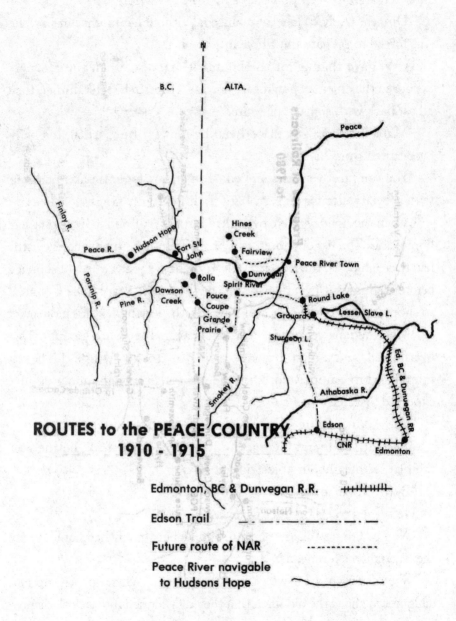

Map of the Edson Trail and Peace River Country, as printed in Mabel's book Faith in a Fertile Land.

Lester raced off to get Kate Edwards. Aunt Kate, as she was known, was as close to a nurse as they could find. While she had no formal medical training, the rancher knew how to set a bone and pull a tooth from looking after her animals. Some men were afraid of her because she had pinned them down to suture their wounds without anaesthetic. Some women were scandalized by her because she dressed in overalls and smoked a pipe like their husbands. But Kate Edwards was the first person they all called upon in an emergency. So when Hilda got sick, the Harpers went to her.

Aunt Kate bathed all three sick children in lukewarm water to bring down their temperatures and force-fed them plenty of fluids to stave off dehydration. Yet her patients did not improve. In fact, they got worse. Soon, the cabins were covered in the vomit and feces of screaming kids. "Dysentery," she diagnosed. This was not her first case. The dreaded disease was raging down the valley because the frequent downpours had led to an increase in water contamination.

Off Lester went to scour the Pouce Coupe Prairie for help. If only they still lived in Vancouver, St. Paul's Hospital would have been a short carriage ride away. The desperate father galloped back and forth across the countryside, but he toiled in vain. There was no hospital with antibiotics and intravenous fluids in the Peace River Country. There was not even a family doctor or a proper nurse. All that was available was a first aid kit, a few patent medicines, and castor oil at Tremblay's homestead.

The Harpers could only seek refuge in their faith. They prayed for a miracle to save their daughter as Hilda's crying grew weak. No miracle came. Their baby girl succumbed to dysentery at eight months old. The whole family was heartbroken, and all of Saskatoon Creek was in mourning when they buried Hilda, Ida, and Edwin in the same week.

NOTRE DAME DE LORETTE
France—January 11, 1917

"LET'S GO," LESTER INSISTED. THE BODIES OF THE CHILDREN had spooked him. The cousins walked back up La Butte de la Mort loaded down with clinking bricks, and they built a makeshift fireplace in their sandbag hut. His hands smeared with ash, Lance Corporal Harper pulled out his notebook and tried not to smudge the paper with his grubby fingers.

France
January 11th, 1917

Dearest,
How is the farm today? I am sitting on my bunk in a sandbag hut built into the side of a high hill somewhere in the rear of our trenches. There has been moonlight lately, and the nights did not seem so long. We are resting for a few days, and we soon hope to go for a long rest. We were a muddy, leg-weary tired bunch as we came out of the trenches.
This morning, Bill and I had a walk to see the ruins of a battle. We saw hundreds of skeletons and equipment galore. The ground was all cut up with shell holes. This is a beautiful country, but not when there are shells. It is a sad sight to walk through the villages that have

been shelled or occupied by the Germans. We collected bricks from a house in the town below, which is absolutely ruined. Not one house left untouched. Fritz throws a few yet. He gassed 1,600 civilians here, mostly women and children, and we can see the skeletons.

You would be very surprised at the clumsy wagons and farm machinery. Country folk here congregate in villages where they have all the farm buildings and go to the fields to work. The French keep their schools running even five or six miles from the front line. Of course, anywhere fighting has taken place, there is a lot of wreckage. Fritz shells around us nearly every day. I am afraid if he breaks through again, there will be a hastily closed up school!

The other day, Fritz made us hug the dust. It gives one a queer sensation to hear the tit-tit-tit-tit-tit of machine-gun bullets so close. Four of the boys who came in the draft with me have been hit, one fatally. Now please forgive the spots on the letter, dear. I am wet, dirty, lousey, and the roof leaks.

There is one thing I wished that I asked for as a Christmas gift. A pair of decent gauntlets or good serviceable gloves. We are issued with woollen gloves in the winter time, but they soon wear out. If you wish, you may send me a pair of ordinary working gloves. Get them large enough with a decent length of wrist but not expensive ones.

You cannot believe how much I miss you, kiddo. You know it is nice to have someone who loves you; one does not feel so alone in the world.

Cheer up, for the worst is yet to come!

Au revoir,
Lester Harper
xxxx

p.s. I forgot to tell you that I spent Christmas Day travelling in a cold boxcar that was full of troops.

LESTER DIDN'T TELL HIS WIFE WHY HE NEEDED HEAVY-DUTY gloves. Knowing that he spent his nights laying barbed wire in no man's land would only make her worry. The faithful husband tucked her faded photograph into the bottom of his paybook and rolled over. Basking in the warmth of the fire, he listened to his boys in their bedtime ritual. They were crooning the bawdy songs of soldiers, their sweet and innocent voices singing of rape and murder.

Three German officers crossed the Rhine,
To fuck the women and drink the wine,
Inky-dinky parlez-vous.

They had two good voices in Platoon No. 5, Lester concluded, and dozens of questionable songs. The lyrics in the irreverent rip-off of "Mademoiselle from Armentières," for instance, were certainly not fit for ladies.

In the Lorette Spur defences, the men spent their nights on work fatigues. While some buried cables, others were put on carrying parties—a task as unimaginative as the name implies. The soldiers hauled weighty crates of ammunition, rations, equipment, and whatever else they were told to carry. The reward for their labour? A trip back up the line.

Lance Corporal Harper was more confident on his second tour of Souchez. The stench did not shock him. The gunfire did not faze him. He was growing accustomed to "the usual trench routine," as their CO put it. Then he was stationed in their listening post.

"The lieutenant's edgy," Bill explained. "He thinks Heinie might be planning something. That's why you're needed out front tonight. It's a simple job, really. Keep your head down and listen. Don't worry 'bout the Huns' regular housekeeping—mending the wire, delivering rations, belting out Bavarian folk songs, and what not. Focus on the unusual. A peculiar sound, shadow, or smell that could signal an imminent attack. Just make sure you and your lad don't nod off or Heinie may slip you a bullet or two. *Compreé?*"

Lester and a private snuck into no man's land and curled up in a shallow hideout. They were so close to the enemy lines that they could hear the *soldaten* speaking German. Snowflakes fell on their steel helmets, and their wet uniforms froze. Lance Corporal Harper wiggled his toes. Even with two pairs of socks on, they felt frostbitten, as if they were turning black in his gumboots.

The lance corporal ignored the pain. He sat proudly at his post, on guard like the angel at the Garden of Eden. But the cherub did not tire when the night grew long, whereas Lester's eyes sagged with sleep.

Crackle. The sound jolted him upright. What was that? *Crackle.* The noise was frustratingly familiar. Lance Corporal Harper strained his ears. *Crackle.* Of course! It was the crackle of ice breaking underfoot. No wonder he recognized it. Living in northern Canada, Lester knew the sound well. *CRACKLE.* Huns, he realized. And they were coming closer.

Lance Corporal Harper pulled their silent alarm. Alone at the advance warning station, the two Canadians prayed that the flimsy string would carry their urgent message back to their battalion. The footsteps drew near. They were stranded in a frozen wasteland surrounded by enemies. Where in the blazes was their support?

The lance corporal considered their options. Should they retreat? He scuttled that thought immediately. He would never abandon a post. They would do their duty to the end, even if that meant certain death. Should they jump out and surprise the Germans? Lester was an expert with his Lee-Enfield on rapid fire, and the private had his rifle too. He fingered a grenade. If they tossed their Millses, they could definitely kill a few Huns.

The experienced private saw what the lance corporal was thinking and shook his head no. He knew that aggressive soldiers who charged the enemy from their listening posts usually ended up dead.

He's probably right, Lester figured. The odds were stacked against them. They were most likely hopelessly outnumbered. I guess it's best to stay put, he determined. Listen, wait, and pray. But what if the *soldaten* had already discovered their hideout? What if they had cut the string on their silent alarm? What if they were currently sneaking up to slit their throats?

It was worth a second thought when their lives were on the line. Maybe it was only a scouting party, and they would have a fighting chance in the dark. If it was a raid, at least a shoot-out would alert the boys. Ambushing the Germans seemed like the best plan. Lester placed his finger on the trigger. The private complied and prepared for a pre-emptive strike too.

Tit-tit-tit-tit-tit. B Company turned their guns on the patrol, and the startled Germans dove into a shell hole for cover. Hands trembling, Lance Corporal Harper lowered his gun. He was thankful it wasn't him stuck out in no man's land this time, hiding from gunfire in a slushy pool of fetid water, blood, and cheese-like flesh.

After two trips to the front, Lester had been baptized by mud and fire. Unlike many rookies, he had managed to stay alive for eleven nights. Yet the lance corporal had not been involved in a single skirmish. Hell, he hadn't even fired a single shot! Fritz thought more of his scalp than to ever stick it up.

Lester had merely served as a moving target for German gunners who painted the sky with rainbows of death. There was the black smoke of the Jack Johnsons exploding into mushroom clouds, the brown dirt of their trenches cascading up to the heavens, and the pink flesh of the Canadians vanishing into nothingness. Ashes to ashes, dust to dust, Mabel would say. Everything unfolded according to God's plan. Her husband was not so sure. The senselessness of the deaths vexed him.

These men did not die in battle. They died smoking cigarettes, eating bully beef, or going to the latrine. Their first taste of action often occurred the instant a sniper's bullet blew through their brains or a shell landed on their heads. All of their training, all of their preparation, all of their lives wiped out in a one-second, one-sided fight. Where was the glory in that?

Take Paul Schattka, for instance. He fought for the Germans, but subalterns on either side of no man's land often had more in common with each other than they did with their own superiors. And his story is typical of too many infantrymen on the Western Front. Paul was a bank clerk who enlisted at the outbreak of the war and served as a company sergeant major. When he reached Belgium, Sergeant Major Schattka sent a postcard to his wife and three children saying how excited he was to be on his way to the front. Those were his last words to his family. He was shot in the head by a sniper three days later as he walked through a town. Paul was wounded before he made it to the trenches, dead before his postcard arrived home.

Warfare on the Western Front was nothing like most men had imagined. For Lance Corporal Harper, it was a bitter disappointment. There was no civility or sportsmanship. Lester simply hid from death. He was a rookie, and that was what rookies did. When a torrent of metal rained down upon them, they ran, they hid, they pissed their pants.

Life in the trenches was either violently boring or boringly violent. Hours and hours of monotonous drudgery punctuated by moments of sheer terror from the German orchestra of shells. While Lance Corporal Harper appreciated classical music like Beethoven's *Fifth Symphony* and Wagner's *Tristan und Isolde*, the Bavarians across from him were one-hit wonders. Every day, they played the same old show at the same old times: the morning matinee and nighttime extravaganza, titled *Death from Above*. Like his compatriots, Lester loathed both types of boredom. No wonder Wesley refused to talk about the grim part.

After almost two weeks, the Nor'westers were sent back to their rest camp. Lester and his men spent a night at Bouvigny Huts and a night at Bajus before settling in cold and uncomfortable billets in Diéval. All of their camps ran parallel to their lines, so they were never more than a two-day march from the front. Humping his gear from billet to billet made Lance Corporal Harper realize that the infantrymen were the human pack mules of the military. They carried heavy burdens on their backs. They worked the land. And worst of all, they frequently died in the field. It's easy to feel like livestock, he brooded, when you sleep on piles of straw in a barn.

The squad drills in Diéval were dull, repetitive, and extremely chilly. Soldiers were retaught everything they already knew: bayonet fighting, trench digging, bombing, night operations, and musketry. They had done the same dope for over a year now. After Souchez, however, Lester no longer grouched their thirty minutes of saluting or their brisk route marches in full kit. Even at 120 paces a minute, he enjoyed touring the country on his feet. The sun was shining. The air was crisp. There was not a shell in the sky. It was serene. France seemed much like England, he gaily mused, except that everyone spoke French.

B Company marched past the shrines and crucifixes that dotted the congested roads, past the prisoners slaving away behind Allied lines, and even past friends and relatives marching in the opposite direction.

"Harold!" Lester yelled. "Harold Empey!"

His voice was drowned out by the crunch of boots hitting the snow-covered road.

He turned to one of the privates. "What regiment was that?"

"Sorry, Lance Corporal. I didn't see."

Till We Meet Again

They had passed by so quickly that Lester wasn't even sure if that was his cousin. Oh well, the lance corporal thought, and he continued to trudge through the snow, just as he had done on that fateful New Year's Eve a year earlier, when he'd met Harold at Tremblay's homestead in Pouce Coupe.

POUCE COUPE
British Columbia—December 31, 1915

LESTER FOUGHT HIS WAY THROUGH THE SNOW TO CELEBRATE the new year with a dance at Tremblay's homestead, the centre of the burgeoning community in the Peace River Country. At the confluence of Dawson Creek and the Pouce Coupe River, Hector Tremblay had built a trading post that included a store, warehouse, and root cellar, and fur traders and gold prospectors often stopped by on their way north. Dances and sporting events were held here too, with people camping out in the surrounding fields.

Lester opened the clunky wooden door of Pouce Coupe's first settlement to find the log cabin packed with farmers and ranchers from Rolla to Saskatoon Creek. The men were a practical lot in their homemade wool shirts, breeches, and socks that retained heat even when wet. The affluent women were elegantly attired in ankle-length dresses brought from the cities, while their poorer neighbours wore clothing crafted from sugar bags and flour sacks. None of their outfits, of course, had zippers. That would have been indecent. Being able to undress a lady with the pull of a zipper was considered scandalous in northern BC. Who knew what would happen if women could get naked that quickly?

Lester scanned the cabin for friendly faces. Across the room, he saw his chum Frank McAleer and his cousin Harold Empey in a fervent conversation with a third party. He craned his neck to see who had enthralled them, but the crowd was too thick. It must be Belle McLean, he reasoned. She always captured the attention of the bachelors at their parties.

He pushed his way through the revellers only to find that Frank and Harold were not flirting with Belle. They were engrossed in a lively conversation with a gentleman in a khaki uniform. "Daniel Hayden," the serviceman introduced himself. "I come from High Prairie. I'm a sergeant in the Canadian Expeditionary Force."

"Lester Harper." He shook the outstretched hand.

"Harper, eh? I hear your brother Wesley's in the 66th. That's a fantastic battalion out of Edmonton. I was just telling your friends that I'm here to raise a new battalion from the north. The 138th is going to be a select mob of pals who will live together, travel together, and even fight together. How swell is that?"

Lester glanced at Frank and Harold. He hated the starry-eyed look that they got whenever anyone mentioned Wes. His brother was a khaki-clad Cinderella who had been magically transformed from a country bumpkin into a war hero the instant he enlisted. What did that make Lester? A jealous stepsister, perhaps.

"Our boys could use the reinforcements after Festubert," Harold chimed in.

Lester grimaced. He was grateful that Wesley was still in training. Canada's second major engagement of the war had been a debacle. There was plenty of blame to go around. The generals' planning was inadequate. The officers' maps were inaccurate. The artillery's barrage was ineffective. The Canadians had a lot to learn about warfare. But who bore the cost of the failure? Poor boys like Wes at the front. They paid for the incompetence with their lives. Even the privates realized that they were doomed when bullets started whipping into their parapet as they prepared to go over the top. Yet the men of the 1st Canadian Division obediently charged into the quagmire, where they got hung up on uncut wire and shot to pieces by machine guns. The Canucks incurred 2,468 casualties to advance 650 yards, the length of a par-five golf hole.

"Reinforcements like us," Frank added.

Lester felt their eyes burning into him. He knew what his friends were thinking, but they were wrong. He was not a coward afraid to fight. He had deeply pondered volunteering for over a year. It was unlike him to dither. What troubled him was his kin. He felt guilty about abandoning his widowed father and three youngest brothers, who depended on him, and especially Mabel. But he had a sacred duty to serve king and country too. They would understand, right? They would make do without him. They were coping fine without Wes.

Lester was sure that Mabel would not veto his enlistment. His wife had a keen sense of right and wrong. She would support his honourable decision to stand up against German militarism. Plus, she would be elated to stay with her parents in Edmonton while he was in the army. She and Lester had never recovered from losing Hilda. Happiness was a mere memory. Their home was a minefield of painful reminders, from the vacant space at the table where Hilda used to sit to the spot on the floor where her crib once stood. Emptiness engulfed everything. The sense of despair looming over their cabin became so dreadful that A.W. intervened. "I'm not fit to raise three boys by myself," he admitted. "I could use a hand, especially in the kitchen." So Lester and Mabel had moved back in with his family, but that failed to help. All it meant was more work for Mabel: more cleaning, more cooking, more bickering. She needed a change badly. They both did.

Lester was pining for an adventure, and the war was the chance of a lifetime for excitement, travel, and money. The government was offering to pay him to hunt Huns and gallivant around Paris with his buddies. How could anyone say no to that deal? Everybody was signing up. It

Lester (second from right) enjoyed playing hockey, and this photo appears to have been taken during the 101st Vancouver High School Cadet Corps' trip to Australia.

was the thing to do. He couldn't bear the thought of missing out on the big game. How embarrassed would he be if Frank and Harold enlisted before him?

Lester knew that he could handle life in the Canadian Corps. He was not a pansy city kid with soft hands and fancy suits who would wimp out. He was a seasoned and scrappy pioneer who had ridden horseback through blizzards, chopped trees in snowdrifts, and trekked down the Edson Trail. He was also used to a rowdy boy's club, and he had the scars to prove it. There was the broken nose from being punched in the face and the gash on his forehead from an errant hockey stick. He even enjoyed the rough-and-tumble lifestyle.

Having been a cadet sergeant in the 101st Vancouver High School Cadet Corps for two years, Lester also understood the army's discipline and structure. He would climb the ranks fast. The cadet corps' five-month trip to Australia was the best time of his life. From sparring on the ship's deck to hunting kangaroos in the outback, he loved the military culture.

"Okay," Lester agreed. They say that every soldier's war is unique. Even men who join the same battalion on the same day have wildly contrasting experiences. They end up with different wounds from different battles in different countries. Shortly after midnight on New Year's Day in 1916, Lester, Frank, and Harold all enlisted in the 138th Battalion. Almost three years later, in November 1918, when the guns fell silent and the bells rang in peace across Europe, the three Canadians would be thousands of miles apart. One would be in England. One would be in France. And one would be in Germany. None of them would be all right.

This was the beginning of Lester Harper's war. The rest is his story.

CHAPTER TWO

SERIOUSLY INCONVENIENCED BY THE LACK OF STRETCHERS

BURBURE

France—February 3, 1917

LANCE CORPORAL HARPER HAD THE BEST SHOWER IN THE mining town of Burbure. Like many of his colleagues, Lester found the lice—or "crumbs," as he called them—unbearable without regular baths.

At the front, the Canadians shaved on rickety wooden benches and took headers in the scummy water of shell holes. While there were hundreds to choose from, veterans preferred ones sullied by at least a few men. That may sound counterintuitive, but you could be certain that nothing lurked beneath the surface of a well-used crater. Choosing a fresh bomb hole was a risky proposition unless you didn't mind discovering a bloated body in your bathtub.

On rest, the troops had proper bathing parades every ten days if things went right (they rarely did). On bath day, Lance Corporal Harper threw his lice-ridden uniform onto a pile of stinky laundry and shivered naked with hundreds of other soldiers in an abandoned factory, a run-down brewery, or a repurposed barn where their engineers had jerry-rigged showers out of rusty pipes. When it was his turn, he got a couple of minutes of ice-cold water trickled on his head, a quick break to apply the repugnant delousing soap, and a couple of more minutes of water to rinse off. Group showers were not Lester's favourite, but they were better than headers.

Today was a special day, though. Platoon No. 5 was using the professional baths of the French coal miners. Warm water? What a treat! The boys were giddy with delight. How they sang and splashed while they showered. Everybody was revitalized when they put on crisp uniforms over freshly scrubbed skin. Even if their clothes were only steamed clean, they still felt louse-free for the rest of the afternoon.

Lance Corporal Harper never would have imagined that a hot shower would be the ideal gift for his twenty-fourth birthday on February 1. Then again, he never would have imagined a lot of things before joining the army, like how time moved faster at the front. Lester didn't feel twenty-four years old. He didn't look it either. Few of his compatriots appeared their age. They seemed decades older. Their hair was grey. They had tremors and tics. Their eyes sank into their faces, two craters in no man's land.

Lester was nearly bald on the top of his bean, so he admitted defeat and got the stragglers on the sides close-clipped to match. "You look like a priest," a fellow non-commissioned officer (NCO) joshed. The other soldiers laughed.

Lance Corporal Harper glowered. He had a bad habit of getting into chewing matches, especially with his superiors. A rebuttal was on the tip of his tongue—or possibly, the knuckles of his fist—when Dan stepped in.

"Don't let that buffoon get you in a flap," his friend said. "This isn't worth losing your stripes over. Say, why don't we grow handlebar moustaches?"

"Darn good idea," Lester replied. The long and skinny kaiser-style moustaches with upturned ends were popular among the Canadian NCOs, who were used to shaggy moustaches that drooped over the lips, which were popular back home. Plus, he thought that adding hair to his face might balance out the lack of it on his head.

Truth be told, Lester was a bit of a loner. It wasn't that he was unpopular—he just rarely made friends with blokes. The Pouce Coupe recruit fancied himself a girl lover, and his four brothers had always provided enough male camaraderie. After his close chums in the 138th Battalion were scattered across the CEF, he told few people of his history and even fewer of his wife.

Private Fee was an exception. Dan was a salt-of-the-earth prairie boy. His character was solid as a chunk of frozen mud. Engaged to his sweetheart, Myrtle, back in Lucky Lake, the farmer from Saskatchewan often asked about married life while he and Lester shared sweets from home. The two men ate an entire parcel of treats—candy, cake, and peanut butter—from Mabel as soon as it arrived.

"I know you love Myrtle," Lester said, "but don't run off and marry her till the war's over, you hear? There's no rush. Take it from me, the fate of a poor married man is to be doomed to everlasting monotony with the same Jane for the rest of his natural—or maybe unnatural—life."

Hair cut and skin clean, Lance Corporal Harper reported to the medical officer because his feet were in a shambles. After weeks of marching and standing guard, they were beyond footsore. Lester tugged off the notoriously tight standard issue boots. The blisters on his heels had turned into open sores, and his flesh felt pulpy, the skin soft and translucent from being caked to his socks with layers of mud.

The doctor prodded every toe for fungus, blisters, and rot. "Are you taking precautions to avoid trench foot?" he queried.

Lester nodded.

"Rubbing your feet with whale oil and carrying an extra pair of dry socks in your haversack?"

"Here, yes."

"At the front?"

The patient stifled a laugh. Lester did not mean to be disrespectful, but it was impossible to follow those guidelines in the trenches. When it was rough and frosty, the infantrymen went days without taking off their boots. Sometimes, it was so cold that they were forbidden to. Other times, the veterans advised them not to or their frozen feet would swell up and they would never get their boots back on.

Either way, it was agony when they finally pulled off their footwear. Like wet cement, the mud hardened, and they were often forced to cut the socks off their mushy feet with a knife. It was a painful procedure, but they had no choice. If the men did not deal with the problem themselves, the surgeon would be cutting off their gangrenous toes with a scalpel instead.

Lance Corporal Harper flipped his boots over. The doctor saw that the soles were shredded and put him off duty until he got a new pair. Lester hoped that Mabel would be proud of him for taking care of his health. He was doing it for her, after all. He wanted to live longer than his mother had. Isabella Gracey—or Gracey, as she was known—had passed away unexpectedly of pneumonia at the youthful age of forty-eight. Poor Mabel, he thought. His mom's death was difficult on her. At twenty, she was thrust into the servile role of a matriarch: cooking, cleaning, and caring for the six Harper men.

Oh, how Lester missed his wife! Pangs of loneliness and regret shot through him, machine-gun bullets of doubt, whenever she came to mind. Had it really been only seven months since they spent that glorious summer together in Sarcee?

CALGARY
Alberta—June 1916

PRIVATE HARPER WAITED ON THE WOODEN PLATFORM IN HIS neatly pressed uniform and shiny new boots. The train rolled into the station, and Mabel stepped down from the carriage. "What do you think of your beau now?" he said, beaming. "Your Bobblet's looking pretty spiffy, eh?"

Mabel bristled. She had once loved that nickname. Back when they were courting, she thought that it was her special term of endearment, that she alone used it. Then she found out that his ex-girlfriends called him Bobblet too.

Mabel looked her husband over, a commander inspecting a solitary soldier. "There," she said, straightening his collar and then giving him a quick kiss of approval.

"That's it?" he roared.

Mabel saw the platform buzzing with couples kissing, and shuddered. A pious Methodist, she believed in tact and decorum, not cringeworthy public displays of affection that were an affront to the respectability of any sensible lady. Mabel was a daughter of the Victorian age stuck in a modern era of ankle-flaunting madness, a bastion of propriety in a world rapidly falling apart.

The couple took the trolley up the ridge to Sarcee. Mabel gasped at the sight of the military encampment on the plateau.

"I've never seen so many tents in my life!" she exclaimed. "There are hundreds, maybe even thousands, and they're so neatly organized into blocks."

"The whole thing reminds me of the 101st Cadet Corps, only in a very large way," Lester said. "They house up to ten thousand men here, so be careful—Sarcee's grid pattern may look obvious, but it's easy to get lost when you're in the tent city. Make sure to follow the painted white rocks that act as street markers and keep this close." He handed her the base's postcard map.

During her time in Sarcee, Mabel barely saw her husband amid his hectic schedule. Lieutenant Colonel Belcher filled every minute of his soldiers' lives with training, fatigues, inspections, and especially, parades. The army loved parades. There were muster parades, clothing parades, equipment parades, bathing parades, church parades, sick parades, and everyone's favourite, pay parades. But Lester was not bothered by their heavy workload or intense regime of physical training (PT). In fact, he found the duties quite soft compared to his life up north.

When C Company had a parade-free afternoon, Lester took his wife out for a walk. It was one of their favourite activities. At home, they would wander the bluffs together for hours. The two lovebirds strolled hand in hand in the warm summer breeze.

"There's something I need to tell you," Lester said. "We've received our marching orders. We're shipping out in August. I'm sorry to leave you all alone."

"There's something I need to tell you," Mabel mimicked his sombre tone. "I won't be all alone."

Lester was stunned. A colleague had recently received a Dear John letter from his wife, who had left him for a gentleman caller while he was at Sarcee. The cuckolded serviceman was distraught and turned to women and booze to cope. The scandal had shocked the men. Apparently, they had never considered that their wives might not remain true. Was Lester about to hear an iteration of those same dreadful lines?

The Sarcee Military Camp, Alberta, 1916.

Lester (centre, arms open) having dinner with the 138th Battalion in Sarcee, 1916.

Dear husband,
This is hard to tell you. I met someone while you were away. I am sorry. I want a divorce.

———

Mabel paused to watch the panic seep into her husband's brown eyes. "I'm pregnant." She smiled.

"Oh, thank heavens!" Lester replied.

Mabel saw a troubled expression momentarily creep across the future father's face. She didn't ask what worried him. She knew how he would answer: Who wants to know? That would end the conversation. But Mabel also knew her husband well enough to understand what bothered him. The same morbid question haunted her too. Would Lester live long enough to meet their baby, or would she be raising their new child fatherless?

BOIS DES ALLEUX
France—February 14, 1917

THE COLD SNAP BROKE ON VALENTINE'S DAY. THE SNOW melted, the frost came out of the ground, and the roads turned into a muddy mess. Cobbled together with fieldstones and reinforced with timber, they were not designed to handle the unceasing line of vehicles that ploughed their way toward the front. A lorry with standing soldiers squished into the trailer bed jockeyed for priority with a truck piled high with ammunition. The truck got stuck in the sucking mud. Traffic deadlocked. Tempers flared.

Amid the never-ending congestion, the Nor'westers splashed their way back toward the trenches. Although they didn't travel very fast, it was a breakneck pace for the infantrymen, who had tin hats on their heads, full kits on their backs, and respirators, groundsheets, and water bottles on their webbing.

In addition to the sixty pounds of standard issue equipment, Lester carried all of his possessions. There were Mabel's letters, his writing materials, a novel, and of course, extra food. It could not have been more than eighty pounds in total, but after four hours of wading through calf-deep muck with blisters burning on his feet, the haversack felt like it weighed hundreds.

Recently promoted to acting corporal, Lester was now in charge of a section. Mile after mile, his boys sang while they marched. Their repertoire of songs was vast. They started with the morbid ditties, like "Hanging on the Old Barbed Wire," then they moved on to the sentimental music hall ballads, like "Keep the Home Fires Burning." But the song that everyone wanted to hear was "It's a Long, Long Way to Tipperary." Although few of the CEF servicemen could have found Tipperary on a map, the Canadians belted out the tune with the enthusiasm of full-blooded Irishmen.

When the troops were not singing, they marched to the rhythm of their boots. The men passed a graveyard, and Corporal Harper noticed Canadians from the 49th Battalion buried among the fallen. "I hope Wes makes it stick in England," he said. He was glad that his brother was safely back in the UK while his regiment from Edmonton was stuck on the Somme. Although Wes disliked hobnobbing with pretentious Englishmen, he disliked getting shot at more.

Dan followed his friend's gaze to their comrades in the cemetery. "At least the graves are well attended to."

The plots in the rear were lovely. They were cordoned off by fences, and bunches of posies sat under the crosses that protruded from the moist earth. On the top of each cross hung a cap. There was the dirt-coloured khaki of the British forces, the misty grey of the Germans, and the striking red kepi of the French, who prioritized looking smart over being camouflaged. In the words of Eugène Étienne, the former war minister, "*Le pantalon rouge c'est la France!*" Anything less colourful went against French taste. This is how France's military committed the worst fashion faux pas of the twentieth century: they went over the top in bright blue tunics with red caps and trousers. To give the *poilus* credit, though, their flashy uniforms made the most debonair burial shrouds.

Lester saw gravediggers at work in the cemetery. "The pity is," he sighed, "there are new ones every day."

While the pretty white memorials above the ground gave the

illusion that each soldier had his own individual resting place, the situation underneath the earth was often much messier, especially after a large military engagement. At those times, the gravediggers just dumped all the bodies into a giant pit. Those communal plots, or mass graves, were a jumble of arms and legs and assorted scraps of men.

As the Nor'westers continued down the road, they came across the enormous Caterpillar engines hauling their heavy guns toward the lines. Fresh graves? Advancing artillery? There was definitely something doing, Lester realized, and they were marching right into the thick of it.

At the rest camp in Bois des Alleux, Corporal Harper climbed into one of the triple bunkbeds that lined the walls of the sandbag huts. Propping himself up on the chicken wire netting, he laid his greatcoat and respirator on his lap to make a table. Then he pulled out his writing paper and used a coded language to evade the censor and covertly share his location with his wife. It was a risky trick that came with twenty-eight days of field punishment if he was caught, but Mabel complained about not knowing where he was. In fact, she offered to kick the censor in the nose if that would help him share more information with her.

France
February 14th, 1917

Dearest Mabs,
Don't be stuck up or horrified at the dirt. I have carried this paper in my pack for a couple weeks. The weather is very rainy and windy here lately, but the cold spell has broken, and it is nice out. I cannot tell you where I am or where we are going. This letter and all other communication to you are censored. Of course as you say, if you were to kick the censor in the nose, then I might tell you where we are.

I will leave that to you to guess, which should not be hard. Today is Saint Valentine's Day. The nearest thing to a Valentine that has "Saint" before it is near here. There is the ruin of a large tower nearby, which was bombarded by Fritz in 1870. Remember we spoke of it? We are on a different front now, but our hut is behind a hill and hidden from aeroplanes by large poplar trees. Our huts have 3 tiers of bunks on each side and chicken wire netting is used for springs! Lunch consisted of mulligan as usual. There is quite a bombardment on today for I can hear the continuous roar of artillery.

I had the best bath! It was in the baths used by the miners. We get fresh clothing each time we bathe. It is not always new, of course. We expect to go into the line before long, and the prospects are that we will have a hot time. You must know that we do not put more than one-third of our time in the line, so do not worry, dear. By the time that you get this, we will be in and out again resting. One always has more than an even chance, and a lot of the wounds are very slight.

I wish a thousand times a day that I were back with you! I saw a 28th fellow leave for Regina. Everybody envied him. Last fall we hoped that we would be home for spring, but I don't know whether we shall be home before fall. I believe I shall be home before Christmas. The French people say the war will be over in three months. Let's hope so, and then I might be home for harvest. Oh, glorious wish!!!

I hope you are well and only then can I be contented. Life would not be worthwhile for me when I go back to Canada if you are not there. I think a great deal about Canada and what I shall do when the war is over. Sometimes, I think I am good for nothing; at other times, I feel confident that I am capable of earning us a good home. This war is certainly a grim experience, but a good one if one comes through without impairing his health. As yet I am jake, but I crave a home. Always remember I love you, Mabs.

*With love, your corporal,
Bobblet
xxxx*

LESTER'S FAVOURITE PRIVATE IN HIS SECTION WAS THE FIRST to die. The corporal felt an affinity for the exceedingly nice young fellow, and they often spoke about their families on their long nights of work parties in the brigade reserve at Écoivres.

"Can I ask how you got that scar, Corporal?" the private inquired. "It looks like you caught a nasty piece of shrapnel in the forehead."

"Ah, that. It's not a war wound, if that's what you're thinking. It's from the good ol' days of pond hockey in Pouce."

"You blocked a slapshot with your face?"

"No, the boys couldn't shoot worth a darn. Baseball was our sport. Me, my brothers, and our chums all played on the Saskatoon Creek ball team. They often swung their hockey sticks like they were bats. One of them nearly took my head off. Luckily, a doctor had recently moved in nearby. Dr. Watson was his name. I ran up to his home with my skates on, banging on his door while blood gushed between my fingers. The doc didn't even bat an eye when he saw me. 'Hold on,' he said and got his first aid kit. If you wouldn't believe it, he stitched me up right then and there. It wasn't the prettiest job, but he did it in a pinch."

On February 24, the Nor'westers relieved the 27th Battalion in the front lines at Écurie. The Germans had clobbered the sector with shells, and the 27th left it that way. The trenches were caved in, and the duckboards were covered in slop. The men had seen cleaner pigsties.

Night after night, Platoon No. 5 refit the bombed-out defences. Up to their knees in sludge, they re-dug the trenches and dugouts. At first, Canadian pioneers like Lester enjoyed the task. Physical labour reminded them of home, and they happily tore into the earth like they were breaking in acres of new farmland on their homesteads. That all quickly changed the moment they hit something squishy. This was not the usual root or rock that they frequently found in their fields. This was the bloated body of a hastily buried corpse washed up by the rain. Out seeped the intestinal gases. The stench was beyond foul. A mixture of death and feces and rotten eggs, it was worse than anything they had ever smelled before. Maggoty torsos hid across the front, grotesque landmines for unsuspecting soldiers to unearth. While you can grow accustomed to the squishy feel of liquifying limbs underfoot, the smell of rotten stomach juices would make anybody squeamish.

The only task worse than digging out their defences was digging new positions in the open. Dressed in musketry order with rifle and ammunition but no pack, the infantrymen laid flat on their stomachs and furiously shovelled soil while bullets cracked and snapped above their heads. No one was a slacker then. There was safety in the earth, and they burrowed into it as swiftly as they could. Nothing motivates like the fear of a messy death.

With their dugouts destroyed, the Nor'westers scraped funk holes out of the trench walls. Most of them hated these teensy caves covered with waterproof sheets. They were vulnerable, damp, and claustrophobically tight. Even if the men curled up in the fetal position, their legs hung over the duckboards, where they were stepped on and soaked by rain. But Platoon No. 5 had no other choice. Lester was exhausted, so he wormed his way into a funk hole to sleep.

An explosion shook the slumbering corporal awake. Wriggling out of his funk hole, he saw his boys gathered around a smoking crater where his private had been sleeping. Lester's lips quivered.

Bill put his hand on his cousin's shoulder. "He didn't even hear the eighteen-pounder coming." His rough voice softened as he added, "He'll wake up in the next world."

When men were blown up by shells, their colleagues gathered the chunks of meat and bone that had rained down upon them. If they were lucky, they found enough of their comrade to fill a sandbag. While collecting and bagging the body parts of a friend may sound horrific, the soldiers felt obliged to bury their pals. They knew that thousands of their fellow infantrymen had been left to rot in no man's land. A funeral was a luxury at the front.

In a rare moment of peace, the Canadians interned the bloody sandbag in a pitiful cemetery slightly back from the lines. Helmets in hand, they stood around the gravesite while the chaplain read from the Bible and the bugler played the last post. There were no fences or headstones or posies in these graveyards. There were just lumps of mud and homemade crosses fashioned from the boards of discarded pallets. Thankfully, a private killed by a shell fit into a shallow grave. Too often, the burial party was forced to break the arms and legs of the deceased to get him into his allotted plot.

The death of the exceedingly nice young fellow shook Lester's faith. If the corporal had been home in Pouce Coupe Prairie, he would have wallowed in bed for days. "Some of the finest fellows have gone under," he mourned. "It's the uncertainty here that gets me. You never know what's coming. If I knew how it would end, I think I'd be more content."

Much to Mabel's chagrin, her husband dodged the Sunday church parades and never opened his pocket Bible. Yet Lester found himself combing through the holy book's crisp white pages for the first time. He searched for a verse of consolation or words of ancient wisdom to understand the mass carnage of the modern world. Where was God in this murderous mayhem? Without his faith, Lester thought that he may give up hope. "Maybe he can save me," his anguished voice called to the heavens. The soul-wrenching cries were met with silence. There is no God in hell.

SASKATOON CREEK
British Columbia—March 1914

THE BOYS THRUST THEIR SHOVELS INTO THE CRUMBLY EARTH. Their callused hands were raw and sweaty. Their breath froze in rhythm to the spades. The Harpers had a long list of tasks to complete. They needed to build two houses and a barn, plant a garden, break land for crops, and put up fences, root houses, and chicken pens.

Lester liked the physical work. Wesley did not.

"Damn it!" he cursed when his shovel struck a rock. "What the hell are we doing here?"

"Watch your mouth," his older sibling warned. "You need to buck up. We're pioneers. Isn't this the adventure you always wanted? Fording rivers, runaway sleighs—we've had more excitement up north this month than we did in three years in Vancouver."

"Ah, Vancouver. Don't you miss it? The pool halls, the dances, the wild nights chasing girlies."

"It's best you forget about those naughty days. There's a reason why Mom wanted to get us out of the city."

The Harpers were the newest settlers to call Pouce Coupe Prairie home. Their journey had been harrowing, and they had nowhere to stay until Harry Gibson, one of the region's first pioneers, pointed them to an abandoned shanty.

"The owner went bushwhacky and shot himself," he told them. "The mounted police from Fort St. John are going to auction off his effects. Be thankful that there are so many of you. It's not good to be out here alone."

"What luck!" A.W. declared.

He attended the auction, bought the deceased homesteader's hay, and rented the glorified shed for a year. Then they built a series of bunkbeds against the wall. Housing seven people in a twelve-by-sixteen-foot hovel may not seem like a lucky break, but Alfred knew better. Settlers often slept in tents or constructed temporary huts out of sod until their first log cabins were finished. A pre-built wooden shed was a luxury.

After scouting the countryside, the Harpers decided on two sections of prime land that backed onto Saskatoon Creek. Because A.W. had already used up his rights in Manitoba, Lester rode a saddle horse to the land office in Grand Prairie, where he filed on the adjoining plots for himself and, as a proxy, seventeen-year-old Wesley.

With snow still on the ground, the Harpers began cutting down trees and laying out baulks of timber for their new homestead. The construction could not be finished fast enough for Lester's new bride. Mabel had left her family and the city only to be stuck with six males in a suicide shack in the bush. So much for newlywed bliss.

For the next eight months, the men worked ceaselessly to build houses, break land, and seed crops. Well, not quite ceaselessly. Sunday was sacrosanct. Like the Lord, they did not work on the sabbath. Maybe that's how you can tell that God is a male: he took a day off. Mabel never did. She still had to cook the meals, do the dishes, and tidy up on Sundays.

While Lester rose early to take care of the farm, his friends in Vancouver were up late celebrating. "Britain at War with German Empire!" proclaimed the banner headline of the *Vancouver Sun*'s August 5 edition. The people rejoiced. They waved Union Jacks and sang "Rule, Britannia" in the streets. Jingoism reigned supreme.

*The Harper homestead circa 1919
(photo courtesy of the South Peace Historical Society).*

Till We Meet Again

Unlike his city friends, the country boy was oblivious to the *casus belli* and lead-up to war in Europe because there were no telephones or telegraphs in the Peace River Country. In fact, there were no roads or bridges either. Their only regular connection to the outside world came via the monthly mail delivered to the post office at Tremblay's homestead by a team of horses from Grand Prairie.

Wesley rode the eleven miles to collect the mail for the residents of Saskatoon Creek once a month, so the Harpers initially knew nothing of the assassination of Archduke Franz Ferdinand or the treaties, politics, and ultimatums that spiralled into the Triple Entente of Great Britain, France, and Russia facing off against the Central Powers of Germany, Austria-Hungary, and the Ottoman Empire. As the world descended into chaos, the Harpers blissfully puttered away on their homestead, completely unaware that the armies of Europe were amassing, that the first shots had already been fired, that their country was officially at war.

"You won't believe it!" Wesley said when he rode in with the gunny sack of letters one September afternoon. "Canada's at war with Germany."

"Hogwash," Lester sneered. "Quit pulling my leg. I'll believe that when I read it in the papers."

"You're so predictable. That's why I brought the front page with me." Wes took out a carefully folded copy of the *Edmonton Daily Bulletin*. "Big Naval Battle Imminent: German Fleet Located—British Admiral Ordered to Wipe Out Enemy," the headline declared. "Canadian Mobilization Will Be Ordered Today."

"Give me that!" Lester snatched the paper from his brother's hand. "Well, I'll be . . ."

The Harpers quickly caught up on world events, and the boys began to eagerly await each outdated newspaper that arrived in Pouce Coupe. While Lester was mildly sympathetic to the plight of the Belgians, he treated the stories of battle as a distant amusement. The fighting, after all, was a continent away. The harvest was a far more pressing concern.

Wesley, on the other hand, caught war fever. He was so appalled by Germany's violation of Belgian neutrality that he blabbed about it non-stop.

"Have you heard about the massacre of Louvain?" he asked between mouthfuls of potatoes and moose steak. "Vicious Huns sacked the city. They shot the men, raped the women, and levelled two thousand buildings, including the university's library with its priceless collection of classic books. Surely we need to teach those German swine a lesson for picking on the defenceless Belgians."

"Burning churches and murdering babies too, I'm sure," his dad cut in.

Mabel gasped. She was unaccustomed to such savage dinnertime conversation. At supper in their house, her father often spoke about his job cutting hair, not cutting people's heads off.

"Sorry," A.W. apologized. "But enough about the Belgians. It's not our concern." Alfred rarely meddled in his sons' political discussions, but he wanted them to know that he had heard all of the propaganda before. He too had once been young and eager to fight for a cause. In fact, when A.W. was Lester's age, he had volunteered to help the army quash the Red River Rebellion in Winnipeg. Fortunately for him, the rebels were captured and Louis Riel was executed before he was called upon to serve.

Alfred hoped that his boys were smarter than he had been, and that they would stay out of the fight. European powers throughout history had invaded Belgium, from the Romans and the Vikings to the Dutch and even the French. Why would his sons want to defend a distant country—one they had never stepped foot in—against an adversary who had done them no harm?

After his wife's death, A.W. had worked hard to build a new home for his shattered family in Saskatoon Creek. Everything was going splendidly until the archduke was shot. Now war was on everyone's lips. The world was going to hell, and it threatened to take his boys along too.

Britain needed men, men, and yet more men, so it was not long before recruiters came north to the Peace River Country. On July 15, 1915, the 66th Battalion organized a recruitment drive in Grand Prairie. After two harsh winters, no one was surprised when Wes rode sixty-eight miles with a group of young men from Dawson Creek to enlist. Upset, yes. Surprised, no.

Not only was Wesley's war fervour growing, but he also hated the pioneer lifestyle. It was an interminable cycle of clearing land, planting seeds, harvesting crops, and trekking down the Edson Trail for supplies to clear more land and plant more crops. Wes was so fed up with breaking acres and acres of farmland in BC that he ran off to join the army. Where did he end up? Digging miles and miles of trenches on the Somme.

ÉCURIE SECTOR
France—February 28, 1917

THE INFANTRY LIVED IN SIX-NIGHT INTERVALS. SIX NIGHTS OF terror at the front under heavy shelling. Six nights of labour in support under sporadic shelling. And six nights of rest in the rear with only occasional shelling to disrupt their sleep. They were forever on the move without a definite home.

Even when there was nothing doing, their nomadic life was taxing. The artillery danced. Machine-gunners tested their parapets. Marksmen picked off the careless. Bored pilots strafed enemy lines. It was never truly quiet on the Western Front.

The Canadians were led by Lieutenant General Julian Byng. Bungo, as King George V affectionately called him, was a highly decorated British soldier who had distinguished himself in the Sudan and South Africa, and guided his troops into battle in both Ypres and Gallipoli. A blue-blooded aristocrat, Bungo had nothing in common with and no connection to the CEF servicemen, so even he was shocked to be appointed their commander. "Why am I sent to the Canadians?" he asked. "I don't know a Canadian."

The Canucks were unconcerned with their commander's title or lineage. What mattered to them was that the Brit was an outstanding soldier, and they were proud to fashion themselves as his Byng Boys.

Lieutenant General Byng loved raids. The bigger, the bolder, the better. He was a true believer in the intimidating tactic because raids facilitated the collection of intelligence on enemy positions, provided valuable combat experience, and broke up the tedium of life in the line. Fortunately for him, his Canadians were expert raiders.

Smash and grab. Raids were simple, at least in theory.

Step #1: Sneak across no man's land undetected.
Step #2: Stalk the German front until a sentry is found.
Step #2b: Slit the sentry's jugular so he bleeds out before he can raise the alarm.
Step #3 (this is the important part): Wreak havoc. Quickly slaughter Boche, bomb dugouts, and snatch prisoners before a multicoloured flare warns it's time to return.
Step #4: Retreat across no man's land without getting shot in the back.

What started as small parties of soldiers haphazardly ransacking the German defences had become systematized. Now the raiders used specialized equipment and practised their roles over taped areas that replicated the enemy lines. They wore darker clothing, blackened their faces, gathered extra Mills bombs, and exchanged their rifles and bayonets for revolvers and daggers. The long guns were too awkward in the narrow German trenches, whereas knives and handguns were perfect for close-quarters combat in the dark.

With the advent of modern chemical warfare, the Canadians also started to incorporate a new weapon in their raids: poison gas. When the Nor'westers were in Écurie, they planned a gas raid. To prepare, the men lugged the 150-pound gas canisters up to the front and piled sandbags overtop to protect them from a German barrage. Then they waited for a strong breeze. That was the problem with poison gas: it needed the weather to cooperate.

On this occasion, the wind would be right on the last night of the month, the gas specialists determined. Zero hour was set for 9.00 p.m. on February 28. Corporal Harper and the rest of B Company covered their dugouts and communication trenches with specially treated blankets and then withdrew to their trench named Labyrinth Avenue while the gas specialists connected the tubes that would release the White Star, as the Allies called the gas, which was stored in a metal canister painted with a white star. A mixture of phosgene and chlorine, the White Star was expected to make this raid a mere clean-up operation. Two and a half hours after zero hour, B Company would send a patrol into the enemy trenches to secure identifications, collect machine guns, and bring back any prisoners—although prisoners were unlikely. If the White Star did its job, the raiders would only find corpses in the German lines. And dead Huns were their favourite type of Huns.

The CEF servicemen knew that poison gas was forbidden in war. It was outlawed by the Hague Convention in 1899, in fact. Few of them cared. If you had asked, they probably would have told you that the Boche started it by sending clouds of chlorine into the Allied trenches at Ypres in April 1915. As the French forces retreated on that blustery spring day, the Canadians held fast with urine-soaked handkerchiefs pressed to their faces. For Lester and his compatriots, that meant one thing: schoolyard rules applied. If the Germans could use poison gas, so could they.

As zero hour approached, the officers received a message with the code word "mud." The conditions were unfavourable. The wind was not right. Their mission was put off.

The raiders were pissed. They were prepped and ready to fight. A low rumbling rose among them.

"Damn the wind."

"Damn the gas specialists."

"Damn the fucking Krauts!"

The Nor'westers marched nine miles in a stiff shower from Écurie to their rest camp. Rest, rest, and yet more rest. That was what Corporal Harper desired. His legs were so tired when they arrived in Estrée-Cauchy that he flopped down on a crate of cartridges and passed out. Working past exhaustion had taught him a new skill: Lester could doze off anywhere, on anything, at any time, almost instantly. He could even fall asleep on a damp pallet in a muddy field under the morning sun.

His superiors were unimpressed with the party trick. Lester was dreaming of going home to Mabel when an officer shoved him awake. "Enough napping, Corporal. You're needed for a fatigue party."

What nerve, Lester thought as he rounded up his section and sleep-marched them another two miles to stack ammunition.

Their duties complete, Corporal Harper whiled away the afternoon on a solitary walk through the scorched farmland. Skylarks were singing. Wildflowers were blooming. Fresh leaves were budding out of the few trees not spoiled by shells. The twittering birds should have been comforting. The springtime scent should have filled him with delight. But Lester knew what the lovely weather really meant: a spring offensive was coming, and death would follow.

He dawdled up a hill to an idyllic old château encircled by mighty trees. The castle's stone facade was coated in soot, its windows broken. He ambled through the gardens, which had been plundered by marauding troops. The flowers were trampled. The low-hanging branches of trees ripped away with their fruit. The château had seen better days, but it had likely also seen worse. His mind wandered back to his history lessons on the French Revolution. How much had it been damaged during the revolutionary wars? he wondered. It had only been a century since France invaded Belgium and fought against Great Britain. Now the British were backing the French after Germany invaded Belgium.

Plus ça change. European countries swapped allies and enemies faster than partners at a dance. Yet one certainty held true: everybody invaded Belgium.

The corporal returned to their rest camp. Estrée-Cauchy was a town without townspeople. The houses were long since boarded up by the confused mass of refugees who'd fled west with their jewellery, clothes, and priceless heirlooms piled high on creaking horse carts. The remaining peasants were too old, too young, too crippled, or too female to fight. But the civilians who'd stayed behind took advantage of their monopoly, turning their farmhouses into *estaminets* where they charged exorbitant prices for greasy chips and watery stout. If they were going to risk their lives to feed the troops, they deserved to get paid handsomely.

Despite the price gouging, the soldiers flocked to their establishments. The smell of melting butter and the sizzle of frying eggs drew them in. Corporal Harper lounged about the loose joints for hours, reading the two-day-old *Daily Mail* that had been delivered by the local children. The fog of war was as thick as the tobacco smoke in the *estaminet*, so he knew little about the global conflict outside of his two hundred yards. Lester relied upon the newspapers to keep abreast of the fighting in other theatres, as well as on his own front. Unfortunately, the reports were unreliable.

"How's the news today?" Dan asked.

Lester flipped through the pages. "Vague as usual, although apparently we're doing well on the Somme."

"Smashing! Maybe we'll all be going home soon."

Corporal Harper rolled his eyes. That was optimistic, which was a problem. In the army, optimism was a dreaded disease that could get you killed.

"Let me ask you this," he said. "If we're doing so well, why are our casualty lists so long? Why are there persistent rumours of heavy losses? And why are we still patrolling these same darn lines? The news is too good to trust. That's why! What we need is for the Russians to start an offensive and the German people to revolt. Then we can all go home."

"It's quiet in here considering there's forty other fellas putting in the time," Dan enunciated each word to calm his friend.

Corporal Harper looked around. The *estaminet* was eerily calm. No one was spilling his glass of ale on the sawdust floor or pawing at the pretty barmaids whose husbands were in the trenches. The soldiers were just sitting nicely at the long wooden tables or leaning against the wall, their eyes politely lusting after the three girls step-dancing to the music of a mouth organ. Lester realized what was wrong.

"They're out of dough," he said. "That's why they're so well behaved. The boys are thirsty for beer and more, but they can't afford either."

Corporal Harper was no exception. He was broke too. The last pay parade was a week ago, and he went through his fifteen francs fast. Unlike many of his comrades, Lester did not waste his hard-earned money on women and booze. He spent every last penny on food. First, he and Dan ordered eggs and chips, bread, and coffee at the *estaminet*. That was their favourite meal. "*Oofs et freets*," the anglophones called it. The only dish better? *Dooble oofs et freets*, of course. Then they purchased syrup, jam, and canned fruit from the army canteen. Unfortunately for them, their wages did not stretch far when tinned stuff cost two francs each (or forty Canadian cents in 1917).

Penniless again and back in their billet, they impatiently waited for the Canadian mail to arrive. Receiving care packages stuffed with clean socks, homemade cake, and honey was their greatest joy. The postman was their Santa Claus, and they relived childhood Christmas mornings every mail day.

"Any parcels from your folks?" Lester asked.

The unwritten rule of the military was that anyone who received a package had to give their friends a fair whack. To translate from Tommy French: the recipient got first dibs, then he divided the rest of the goodies among his closest chums. Lester was Dan's wintertime bedmate, meaning there was literally no one closer.

"Not today," Private Fee responded. "We'll probably both get honest-to-god boxes next pay day. I swear they never arrive when we're out of cash and need 'em most."

Corporal Harper's stomach grumbled in accord. "Fritz must have sunk our mail boat 'cause no Canuck mail has come lately." The fact that his head could be blown off at any moment troubled him less when his belly was full of first-class chow. "How many days in a row do they expect us to eat bully beef?" he grumbled. Lester scraped out the last of his peanut butter and ate it with his mulligan stew.

"Peanut butter and mulligan? Bleh!" Dan said.

Lester took another bite of the concoction, and his chum gagged.

The two friends had won the army's bed lottery. They had discovered some sheaves of hay and an oil cloth in their barn. Shaping the sheaves into a mattress on the cement floor, they tucked the cloth around the hay like a fitted sheet to hold it together. Then they lay down with their blankets and overcoats on top of them like duvets. It was their most comfortable bed in France thus far. Toasty and snug, Corporal Harper's only lament was his bedmate. Why was his wife not cuddled up beside him instead of a man!

On March 6, B Company marched to the baths at Camblain l'Abbé for their first shower in almost a month. Then it was all polishing, saluting, and drills.

"I appreciate the fresh uniform," Lester told Bill. "But what's with the parade dope? Chin up, chest out, shoulders back, stomach in. We know the routine. We've been doing this dope for a year now. Is it just me or do these theatrics seem ludicrous with Fritz's artillery rumbling over the hillside?"

"Whatever we're doing this for," Bill growled. "It's a bloody nuisance." He handed his cousin a mug of sickly sweet tea.

Lester took a sip and sputtered.

"Don't look so surprised," Bill laughed. "Of course it's laced with rum. Did you hear 'bout the raid?"

"Only that some Canadians near us had a lot of casualties one night. What happened?"

"Total fuck-up. Almost seven hundred KIA or wounded. The gas specialists finally got their breezy day. They released a thousand canisters of White Star, and the chlorine and phosgene blew straight into Heinie's lines. Like you'd expect, up went the SOL flares, and their artillery counterbarraged our trenches. Their big boys came hurtling over and punctured several canisters we were saving for round two. The gas came whistling out and poisoned our own lads."

Bill picked up his tin cup and savoured the tea.

"And?" Lester prompted.

"Well, hacking and retching, the raiders fought their way through the gas cloud only to find the barbed wire intact and ol' Heinie waiting with his machine guns ready. Not a single Hun dead. Go figure. So much for these gas raids being simple clean-up missions, eh? Apparently, they've got effective respirators over there now. Sure enough, our lads stopped bullet after bullet. Did they quit? No, siree. They surged over the bags and fought hand to hand with their pistols and daggers. They might've even been able to take the trenches if they'd had reinforcements, but it was a hit-and-run operation, so no support was coming. When they tried to retreat, Heinie was waiting for them again. He sniped them off while they crawled from crater to crater, picking their way back through the muck."

"Didn't we give them cover?"

"We tried. We sent down a bombardment, but our officers had to call it off when the drop shorts landed on our raiders. Now if that wasn't bad enough—"

"Wait, it gets worse?!"

"What did I tell you 'bout that bloody gas? It wafted over no man's land and pooled in the craters too. One by one, our lads were either shot by Heinie, blown to bits by our own gunners, or strangled by our gas. The battlefield was such a mess that a German officer came out with a white flag and offered us a two-hour truce to collect our dead and wounded."

"Gee. That's a stand-up act."

"Yeah, they're certainly a decent mob till they drop a ton of minnies on us," the sergeant said drily, using the soldier slang for trench mortars. "My guess is that they were sick of listening to the chorus of pain from no man's land. There's nothing worse on the ears. The hours of blood-curdling screams followed by the low and painful groans. Then the whimpers and cries for mommy at the end. Bloody awful, it is."

Awful was right. Had Corporal Harper been only a strong breeze away from a gory death? He hoped his friends from the 138th Battalion had missed out on the botched gas raid of March 1.

Bill opened his mouth to speak again, but Lester cut him off. "*Mais c'est la guerre?*"

"Yes." His cousin smiled. "*C'est la fuckin' guerre.*"

The British press told a different story. According to *The Times*, the raid was an outstanding success. Despite the heavy casualties, the Canadians showed great gallantry and gained valuable intelligence. There was a reason why Corporal Harper did not trust the newspaper reports. He found their accounts to be greatly exaggerated and felt they conveyed only the faintest idea of the real conditions. But how could he expect otherwise? Maintaining morale on the home front trumped journalistic integrity. As Lester was starting to learn, nothing was ever simple in wartime—or to put it more crudely, *c'est la fuckin' guerre.*

OTTAWA
Ontario—August 1916

PRIVATE HARPER JUMPED DOWN FROM THE TRAIN compartment. His back was stiff from sitting in the same seat for five days, but he could barely contain his excitement. This was the stop he had been waiting for. This was the highlight of their trans-Canada tour. From Calgary, the 138th Battalion had sped like hell via Winnipeg and Graham to the nation's capital. Where they were going next was anyone's guess. Some men said England. Others anticipated a stop in Bermuda first. They all wished that their destination was France. Only the officers knew, though, and they did not feel obliged to inform their subordinates. "There's a ship waiting for us in Halifax," was all that they were told.

Private Harper hoped that ladies with khaki fever continued to wait for them at every station from here to Nova Scotia. Oh, how they cheered when the train pulled in! After an uncomfortable night crammed upright in his seat, the red-eyed private's mood was always buoyed by the sight of the adoring women. As a polite country boy, Lester graciously accepted their apples and good-luck kisses through the carriage window.

Ottawa was a pleasant surprise from the barren landscape of Ontario, which was predominately bush and rock with only a smattering of spruce.

Although a great fire had devastated the province and burned the town of Cochrane to the ground the month before, Lester refused to cut the inhabitants any slack. Even as he sped by at fifty miles per hour, he swore that Ontarians were lazy. "The farms are dishevelled, and the houses are unpainted," he complained. "Even the hay's left unbaled. What a poor country this is. Pouce Coupe for me. Thanks!"

Ottawa was terribly hot and sultry, and Lester's tunic was soon damp with sweat. But there was a joyful swagger in his step as he marched in the shade of the giant maple trees that lined the streets. The 138th Battalion stood at attention on the manicured lawn of Parliament Hill. Out strode the prime minister, Sir Robert Borden, and the governor general, Prince Arthur, the Duke of Connaught. It was no secret that the two men did not get along. The prince considered the prime minister to be a weak wartime leader (unlike his nephew Kaiser Wilhelm II), while the prime minister was annoyed that the prince wore his field marshal's uniform and spoke to the servicemen without guidance from Borden's office. Nevertheless, they cordially inspected the regiment together. Chin up, chest out, shoulders back, stomach in. The infantrymen paraded in front of them in flawless formation.

Standing in front of the charred ruins of Canada's House of Commons (only the Library of Parliament survived the fire of 1916), Prime Minister Borden addressed the troops: "We are face to face with the greatest military power in the world, but when I see training and discipline such as I have seen this afternoon, combined with a courage and a loyalty of which I need not speak, I feel we have all that we can desire. You stand before me, not for love of battle, nor lust of conquest, but for the cause of honour, to uphold principles of liberty and to withstand forces that would convert the world into an armed camp. You know of all the sacrifices this may entail, but you don't shrink from them. With firm hearts, you abide by them."

Private Harper soaked in the prime minister's inspiring words. He believed every one. They were a sacred brotherhood devoted to a righteous cause. His battalion was a thousand-faced angel of death sent to smite the wicked. Love for his fellow countrymen surged through him. Standing at attention before Sir Robert Borden and Prince Arthur on Parliament Hill, Lester felt honoured to wear the khaki uniform and maple leaf badge. He was ready and willing to die for Canada.

GRAND SERVINS
France—March 9, 1917

"BLOODY TRENCH TOURISTS," SERGEANT THOMPSON HUFFED.

"Explains the stupid marching about," Corporal Harper replied.

The Northwest Battalion joined the rest of the 6th Infantry Brigade for a surprise visit from the prime minister on a chilly spring morning. Chin up, chest out, shoulders back, stomach in. The military review was the same. Lester's attitude was not. He was fed up and far from home. He no longer gave a hoot about Sir Robert Borden, who was in Europe to determine if Canada should enact conscription. Shells had blasted the patriotic spirit out of him, and Prime Minister Borden's speech sounded hollow.

"What a farce! He's spreading the same old bull about patriotism that we're used to," Corporal Harper said. Lester wanted to see all Canadian politicians make a few trips up the line. That would sober them up. If a whiz-bang detonated near their heads, he bet they would need an undertaker right quick.

"I'd just like to go home with him," Dan sighed.

If only it were that easy. Therein lies the rub. When the men enlisted, they signed up for the duration. They volunteered to come, but if they tried to leave, they could be executed for desertion.

How Corporal Harper missed his fair Canada! Lester yearned to sink his feet into the soil of his homeland. He was done with the war. But the war was not done with him. He was stuck in France until they won or lost—or most likely, until he got hit by something.

Corporal Harper did not fight for the prime minister anymore. He did not fight for his country or ideals like justice and liberty either. He fought only for the men by his side. For Bill. For Dan. For his boys. They were his family on the Western Front, and he would die for his family if need be.

Lester made the best of Borden's visit by catching up with his friends from the disbanded 138th Battalion—at least those who were still alive. His former colleagues had been sent to theatres across Europe and had been slaughtered in every one. Corporal Fordyce: dead. Lieutenants Heffernan, Campbell, and Peariton: *fini*. The list of RIPs was long and troublesome.

No one was immune. Even Lord Kitchener was cut down by a mine. "*Kaput*," the Germans declared. If they could kill the highest-ranking British officer off the coast of Scotland, what chance did Canadian infantrymen have at the sharp end?

The myriad casualties made Lester realize how fortunate the 28th Battalion had been to escape the last three months of fighting relatively unscathed. He remembered the wounded soldiers at the port in Boulogne-sur-Mer. No wonder they were smiling. They were off to Blighty with light wounds. They were laughing at their luck.

The Nor'westers spent the next two weeks perfecting their attack formation on the mock battlefields of Grand Servins, much to the annoyance of the bitter old Frenchmen who watched the khaki horde trample their fields. The CEF's artillery bombardment would jump ahead one hundred yards every three minutes, and the infantry needed to learn to lean into the shellfire in order to safely cross no man's land while the Germans hid in their dugouts. "The creeping barrage," high command labelled the strategy.

"Follow the artillery barrage as closely as a horse will follow a nose-bag filled with corn," Brigadier General Arthur Currie instructed the 1st Canadian Division.

If the soldiers were too slow, they would be fodder for the enemy gunners returning to their posts from the safety of their dugouts. If they were too fast, they would get one of their own eighteen-pounders on their heads, and nobody wanted to die from friendly fire. So they practised the manoeuvre over and over again. In clouds of white smoke designed to simulate combat, the grunts climbed out of their jumping-off trenches and clambered across the chewed-up farmland behind bored officers on horseback who rode at the pace of the bombardment. It looked more like a rehearsal for a military parade than preparation for a large-scale assault. There were a thousand men walking forward in a line. They were queuing up to get shot.

Corporal Harper thought of his brother Wes. He had marched into battle in a neat column behind a massive bombardment too. "The [artillery] fire was as good as it could be," the CO of the 49th Battalion later acknowledged. That had not helped Wesley.

CAMP WITLEY

England—September 23, 1916

CORPORAL HARPER'S KNEES BUCKLED. HE GRABBED HOLD OF the wall for support. The note in his hand fluttered to the ground. Its news hit him with the force of an eighteen-pound bombshell.

"You okay, Harper?" his shed mate asked. "You look awfully pale. You're not going to drop dead on us before we make it to the front, are you?"

"It's my brother." The words caught in his throat. "He's been wounded."

"Damn. How bad?"

Lester picked up the field service postcard. His brother had merely crossed out the pre-written statements that did not apply to him. The remaining words were sparse.

I have been admitted into the hospital wounded.
I have received your letter dated September 1, 1916.
Letter follows at first opportunity.
Wes Harper.
September 16, 1916.

That was it. The lack of details was infuriating. Horrific images ran through Lester's mind. He reached out for his cot and sat down. Then he remembered his other letters that he had received at the same time. He flipped through them quickly. There was a card from the hospital informing him that his brother had been wounded, but it didn't provide any new information. Then he saw the letter from Wesley.

Lester ripped open the envelope.

September 13th, 1916
No. 101206 Pte W. Harper
49th Canadians
France

Dear Lester,

I received your letter about a week ago. I suppose you heard about Tremblay dying, and the latest news is that Mr. Leroy died.

Well, we are having a pretty time of it. Marching every day with a field pack, 120 rounds of ammunition, and our rations.

I want to tell you about this unit business. We also expected to come across as a unit, and we would have if it hadn't been for the scrap on June 2. Then we were needed for reinforcements. The four divisions are continually needing reinforcements, and the casualties are heavy and will be a lot heavier in the future. We have moved and I can't say where, but you can judge by the casualties.

If you come as a draft try to get to the 49th. They will very likely call for a draft out of the 138th because they are from Edmonton. If you come in a draft you will have to revert. Of course, the chance for advancement is good out here after a few trips in the trenches.

Tell Harold to write and you write often too. I will answer every one.

Well, good bye for this time,
Wes

Alas, Wesley had written the letter two days before he was injured. His brother may have anticipated the battle—he wrote that the casualties were going to get heavier—but that did not help explain what had happened to him.

"Well?" Lester's shed mate asked.

"Doesn't say how badly he's wounded," Corporal Harper replied.

"It's probably minor. A lot of injuries are superficial."

"Even superficial injuries can fester," Lester snapped. He knew that infection was rampant. He needed to see his brother immediately. The hospital in London was only a train ride away.

Even though Lester had just returned from leave, he rushed over to the Base Orderly Room (BOR) with the field service postcard. His superiors were reasonable men, and they approved an emergency pass. Corporal Harper packed his bag and took off for London. Unfortunately, a train wreck interfered with his plans. He did not arrive at Waterloo Station until after dark. Visiting hours at the hospital were over.

Although it was too late to see Wes, Lester could not sleep. At home, he would have traipsed through the woods to calm himself down. But there were no forests in London, so he did the next best thing: he wandered the city's busiest streets in hopes of losing himself in the crowds. He was a solitary nightwalker adrift in a sea of people.

As he crossed the Waterloo Bridge over the Thames, two women smiled at him. "Doesn't that Canadian look handsome in his fancy uniform?" one said loud enough for him to overhear. "Where are you going in such a hurry?" she inquired. "Perhaps you'd like to see a show?"

Lester sped up. He wasn't used to being ogled and wanted to be left alone.

Lester's military pass to visit his brother Wesley in the hospital in London.

"Maybe he's hungry," her friend replied. "How about dinner?" she called after him.

Corporal Harper spun around. "My apologies, ladies. I don't have time to chit-chat. Duty beckons. I have to catch a 9.00 p.m. train."

"That's okay. We'll walk you there."

Caught in a lie, Lester acquiesced. He let the women accompany him to the railway station, where they bid adieu. Then he snuck back into town and roamed the Strand by himself until 1.00 a.m.

Lester rose the following morning and took the Tube to the hospital in Hampstead. After showing the receptionist his card, he made his way to Wesley's dreary room. His startled brother winced in pain when he walked in. Even the nicest surprise was agony with a back full of shrapnel.

"Oh, churches! Are you really that shocked to see me?" were the first words out of Lester's mouth. "What in the blazes happened to you?"

Wes forced a smile. "Just a dose of shrapnel," he said. "Funny thing. They say that the artillery conquers, the infantry occupies, right? What they don't tell you is that there's no contingency plan for us if the gunners fail to conquer."

The wounded private had an issue with high command's unwavering faith in the artillery, and rightly so. Wesley was laid out on his stomach awaiting surgery because his company had been held up on an obstacle that the artillery had failed to take out during their attack on Courcelette.

ALBERT

France—September 15, 1916

THE SOMME WAS ONCE A PARADISE TEEMING WITH LIFE. The river, which snaked down from the hills of the ancient Arrouaise Forest to the English Channel, was the heart of the lush valley. Fishermen lolled about its banks while pleasure seekers punted through its marsh gardens, where cauliflower, artichokes, turnips, and leeks flourished in the rich silt. But that was before a million men murdered each other on its rolling hillsides. And before thirty million shells poisoned its swampy waters.

By the time Wesley arrived, the Somme was a desolate plateau of muddy holes and maimed stumps. Only scavengers thrived in the wasteland. Rats feasted on the blackened flesh of corpses. Swarms of flies covered the leftover bones like giant buzzing blankets for the dead. The Somme was the type of place that you were dying to escape.

The French dug in south of the river. The British protected the north. When either army tried to advance on the enemy positions, the Germans pulverized them. With each regiment that the Maschinengewehr 08 mowed down, the machine gun poked holes in the nineteenth-century military theory that it was better to attack than to be attacked.

Battalion after battalion was obliterated within minutes of making a charge. In the flash of a muzzle, entire male populations of small English towns were summarily relocated to soggy patches of soil in France. When a thousand devastating letters arrived in the same hometown at once, the British government realized that drawing a whole battalion of pals from a single community was not the smartest idea.

The last ten weeks of warfare on the Somme had yielded a piddly amount of mud in exchange for 250,000 lives. The Allies had taken five miles of German trenches, to be exact. To use a macabre ratio, that is 9.5 lives for every foot.

General Haig was not discouraged. He kept his Big Push going in hopes that the next engagement would be the decisive victory. His soldiers were more skeptical. They began publishing trench newspapers that mocked the general's strategy.

Are you a victim of optimism? the July 16 issue of *The Somme-Times* inquired. Do you wake up feeling that all is going well for the Allies? Do you think that the war will end within the next twelve months? Do you consider our leaders competent to conduct the war to a successful issue? If your answer is "yes" to any of these questions, then you are in the clutches of that dreaded disease. All it would take to cure you of your optimism, the satirical advertisement promised, was two days with them.

Many Canadians, including Wesley, had spent more than two days on the Somme. As part of the latest offensive, the CEF was ordered to capture a sugar factory and farm on the outskirts of Courcelette. The 49th Battalion was sent to support the assault. The men marched five miles from the town of Albert to the Chalk Pit west of Courcelette with plans to push out from the trenches their compatriots had captured in the initial stage of the attack.

Till We Meet Again

By now, Wes was accustomed to the army's "hurry up and wait" mentality. Not today. Today, it was hurry up and fight. The men arrived tired and hungry only to be told that they were moving into position in two hours. There was no time to rest or even properly prepare. Each infantryman was hastily issued forty-eight hours' worth of rations and a single Mills bomb instead of the usual two.

At 4.00 p.m., they were marched up to within a mile of the front and told that they were to take a certain part of Fritz's line at 6.30 p.m. "That's not much notice to give a man to prepare for a life-or-death struggle," Wesley complained.

At 5.45 p.m. on the misty autumn day, the sky exploded. But this was not the CEF's artillery launching their creeping barrage. This was the Germans bombarding the Canadian lines. Huge clods of earth erupted around the Forty-Niners, killing and wounding many men. Their entire world was aflame.

The CO ordered the battalion forward through the tumult. Wesley's C Company advanced together over the churned-up earth. Destruction and desolation lay all around them. Not a square foot of the ground was undisturbed, and broken-down tanks were strewn among the debris. The 49th Battalion advanced through the wreckage and reached the former enemy trenches, where they prepared for the next phase of the assault.

The officers blew their whistles, and the troops surged forward again. Just before Wesley's company reached the village of Courcelette, they got caught in a nasty jam. The infantrymen were up against a well-placed and well-manned German machine gun, which their artillery had failed to take out. The Maschinengewehr 08 started firing, and the neat columns of Canadians were cut down.

Wesley could see his comrades charge for the machine gun through the gaps in the barbed wire. That plan was *pas bon*. They were being funnelled into killing zones where their corpses were piling up. Those who tried to cut the wire fared little better. Shocked looks crossed their faces when they got stuck in the barbs. How could it happen to me? their expressions asked. Then their bodies started dancing to the rattle of the machine gun as bullets punched off their limbs and heads.

The well-fortified German defence was supported by the heaviest calibre of shellfire. As Wesley's section advanced, a shell whizzed toward them. *Bang!* It burst to his left and took out the whole section. Shards of molten metal filled men's flesh. Some of the wounded crawled desperately for the safety of bomb holes. Believing that a shell never landed in the same spot twice, they hunkered down and hollered for their stretcher-bearers. "I'm hit!" they cried.

Wesley decided not to wait for help, which was a smart decision. His battalion was short of stretchers, and the holey soldier was in a battle against time. Along with the threat of bleeding to death, Wes had to worry about *Clostridium perfringens*. That bacteria would turn his painful gashes gangrenous if he took twelve hours to get to the doctor like the average casualty. And he had no desire to decompose alive, with the surgeons hacking pieces of rotting flesh off his body. He was not a rifle to be disassembled one part at a time.

Marshalling his strength, Wesley turned back toward their lines. The pockmarked ground to the first aid station was at least a mile. Wes beat it back to the dressing station as quick as he could with shrapnel in his legs, back, neck, and left arm. Once there, the medical officer gave Wesley a shot of rum, an anti-tetanus injection, and a medical tag listing his injury. "Chin up, it's just a dose of shrapnel," the doctor said. "That's only a light flesh wound."

How was this a light flesh wound? Wes wondered. It felt like he was being prodded with dozens of white-hot spikes.

He was too badly hurt to be fixed up and sent back to fight, however, so a bus took him and the other wounded men about five miles to Albert. When they reached their destination, the injured were moved to another lorry for their journey to the casualty clearing station. Between the traffic and the transfers, tempers flared. The commute away from the front was worse than the rush to get there.

The air in the makeshift hospital reeked of blood and acetylene gas. Wesley was placed on the floor among discarded bandages and sticky puddles. The beds had been filled up hours before by mutilated men stifling groans of agony. When an overworked doctor finally got to him, he did a rapid assessment of his patient. The physician did not have time for flesh wounds.

"Multiple superficial lacerations to the back, buttocks, neck, and left arm incurred in the line of duty," he dictated to his adjutant. Then he probed a gash with his forceps. "Does this hurt?" he asked Wesley.

"Fuck me!" Wes screamed.

"Fragments of enemy shell lodged in wounds," the doctor continued. "Give him a shot of morphine and fresh bandages, then send him onward for surgery." Patch them up and move them along. The physician knew his role in the casualty clearing station.

Wesley was fortunate—he got the treatment needed to save his life. Many of his comrades did not. If the doctors couldn't help a patient, they moved him to a lonely room slowly filling with soldiers. Some lay silently, hiding unseen horrors under muddy blankets. Others, delirious with fever, raved for their mothers. Their faces were ashen and lips pallid as the blood drained from their bodies. The look in their eyes was soul-chilling. This was the room for the dead and dying. The doctors had to choose between those they could save and those they could not, and these were the unlucky ones.

A filthy ambulance train and an overcrowded ferry later, Wesley arrived at the hospital in London. He was one of the 7,230 casualties in the Canadian victory at Courcelette. What was one of the most significant lessons from the show? According to their CO, the Forty-Niners were seriously inconvenienced by the lack of stretchers. Not only did this lead to higher wastage (as the army called the crippling wounds and painful deaths), but the cries of the injured also distracted the fighting troops.

LONDON
England—September 24, 1916

HOW FORTUNATE TO GET OFF SO EASY, LESTER CONCLUDED as he left the hospital ward. Wesley was extremely lucky, in fact. He was the only soldier in his section who walked away from Courcelette. Okay, "walked away" was an exaggeration. But he managed to hobble away.

Wes looked quite well considering the thirty pieces of shrapnel embedded in his back. What a lucky devil to have a souvenir that proved he had seen action, Lester thought, especially in a battle that was such a resounding success. The Canadians had met and exceeded their objectives, capturing the village of Courcelette and a thousand prisoners too. "Without parallel in the present campaign," the British High Command declared.

With visiting hours over, Lester headed back down to the Strand. He was not going to waste any free time in London. The corporal was minding his own business when a pretty Jane eyed his maple leaf badge.

"Oh, there's a Canadian," she said.

Lester scuttered along.

"Don't be slow," she chided. "Aren't you naughty looking? And all by your lonesome. Can I spend the night with you?"

The married man was taken aback by her boldness. Wesley had warned him to avoid the very bad women in London. Thankfully, this woman did not look like a tart. She was confident and gorgeous. A little flirtation was harmless, right? Lester was tired of being alone, or worse, surrounded by testosterone-driven males. He took the stump, and they chatted. "Want to see a show?" he finally suggested. "I never enjoy the theatre alone."

While Lester laughed hysterically at the high jinks in *Sarah Sleeps Out*, his date was less amused. Mabel would find this hilarious, he rued. Why wasn't she at his side instead?

After the play, the two strolled down the Strand. The evening was dark and cloudy, the conversation dull. Lester's date seemed distracted. She kept glancing up at the sky.

"What's wrong?" he asked.

"Nothing," she lied and tried to make small talk. "Bob, if you ever do marry, you'll make a good husband because you don't really drink."

Lester grinned. He pondered giving her Mabel's address so she could find out if his wife agreed.

Suddenly, sirens blared and searchlights lit up the heavens.

"Zeppelins!" the woman stammered, quaking. "A bomb fell on my chum's house. There was nothing left. Nothing!" She ran off without even a kiss goodnight.

Lester turned toward the Zeppelins dropping their four-hundred-pound bombs in the east. They were sleek and tan, like monstrous fish swimming across the sky, shitting death and destruction on the city below. Why was she so scared? he wondered. Even travelling at sixty knots an hour, the Zeppelins posed no imminent threat to them. They were miles away.

Half-dressed women, children in pajamas, and elderly men wearing only overcoats agreed. They came out to the street to see the anti-aircraft guns, or Archies, play upon the colossal airships caught in the searchlights.

"A hit! A bloody hit!" a frail Brit cried.

Till We Meet Again

The shrapnel from a Vickers quick-firing pom-pom gun punctured the hydrogen-filled balloon. The Zeppelin burst into flames, and a cheer went up from the crowd.

Spectacular, Lester thought. Now that's a show.

Camp Witley
September 25th, 1916

Dear Wifey:
You will likely know by this time that Wes is wounded and in the hospital at London. He is quite well and very fortunate to be only slightly wounded in the back and legs. In case he has not written to you, I will give you the particulars. He was wounded in the night of September 15th while making a charge. He was the only man left in his section who was able to walk back alone. This he did after being wounded by shrapnel in the back (30 pieces). I consider Wes very lucky. He's going to have an operation today in order to get out any pieces that may remain. It will not be long before he is back in France. My bad time is yet to come, and I want your prayers to bring me through.

I rushed through a pass and came to London Saturday afternoon. It was good to see Wesley. He did a lot of sniping at Ypres before he went to the Somme. Perhaps I never told you, but Wes and I got along exceptionally well in Edmonton. We never had rows together like we did up north.

After seeing a show, I wandered about until midnight when the Zeppelins started. The flashlights were about, and soon they located a Zeppelin over east of me. It was very high but could be seen plainly. I saw the anti-aircraft guns firing. Two were brought down.

Let me tell you one thing, Mabel. In Canada, you can never know what a fight for existence this war is, but it is terribly evident here. In London, trains leave every day with troops that take England's men to war. I saw the endless chain of wounded being unloaded too. It was a very sad sight. This last offensive is taking a lot of England's best men. The sacrifice is very heavy.

I am well as usual. The nights are cold and foggy here. I wish I had you here tonight. How you would enjoy a walk here!!! Your eyes would just stare, and you would hug me close.

Dear, you must not be shocked if you hear that I am wounded. If one gets out of this with a light wound like Wesley's, why he is lucky.

So long,
Bobbie
xxxx

p.s. I received your parcel with the peanut butter. Now that was "Somme" parcel!!!

CHAPTER THREE

A MOST UNHEALTHY SPOT

MONT-SAINT-ÉLOI
France—March 24, 1917

THE TROUBLE STARTED BEFORE CORPORAL HARPER MADE IT up the line. Normally, the Canadians had the upper hand in artillery duels. They outshelled the Germans twenty to one. Not today. Today, Fritz was angry. He was a toddler throwing a temper tantrum in a butchery. He was slinging sausages all over the place—the front, the rear, even the nearby town. Shells were blowing up. Houses were crashing down.

The Northwest Battalion's time in a quiet sector was over. They were headed into a hot shop. Fortunately, they were still on rest until nightfall. Lester was savouring the last few hours of relative peace when two soldiers approached him.

"Can we ask you a question, Corporal?" one said. "What's it gonna be like up there tonight?"

Lester smiled. That was the first question on every rookie's lips. He remembered Wesley at Courcelette. "Cushy enough, I suppose. It could be a whole lot worse. Guarding trenches is much easier than taking 'em."

"How far away will the Krauts be?"

"Well, our neighbours will be stationed—" The corporal stopped mid-sentence. Something was amiss.

"You were saying?"

"Shush," Corporal Harper instructed. His head shot up. His ears went on high alert. His eyes roved the skies. Without a word of warning, he flung himself into a shallow gully.

Lester glanced back at the infantrymen. There were puzzled expressions on their faces. Why were they still idly standing there? Did they not hear the incoming roar? It was louder than an express train barrelling toward them.

"Get down!" he shouted. The warning came too late. His words were lost in the burgeoning mushroom cloud of smoke, and the soldiers were flying through the dusty sky. The boys are going to give me hell for this, he thought. Then his world went black.

———

Lester came to in the dark. Was he blind? His head was pounding. His ears were ringing. His nose was clogged with grime. The veteran coughed, sputtered, and struggled to breathe. He blinked the guck from his eyes. No, he was not blind. He was buried alive.

A high-explosive ordnance had thrown up a huge shower of soil, and a wave of mud and turf had covered him from head to toe. Lester wheezed and gurgled and clawed frantically at the loose dirt. The earth pressed down upon him, slowly squeezing the life out of him.

He tried to call for help, but he couldn't hear himself scream. Lester felt his jaws stretch open and his lungs empty. No sound issued forth. When he inhaled, his mouth was filled with watery mud. He yelled and gagged until his silent voice went hoarse. Then his mind fogged over. His vision blurred. He was running out of air. Mother Earth was smothering him in her soggy embrace.

Corporal Harper had all but given up hope when something struck him in the shin. He yelped with pain and glee. Were those servicemen digging him out?

"Honest to God, you're the luckiest son of a bitch alive!" Dan exclaimed when they finally freed him.

The shell-shocked soldier tried to speak, but only gibberish came out. His brain was scrambled, an egg cracked and beaten at the *estaminet*. He took a step and stumbled. He was having trouble seeing. He felt like he had taken a good drubbing from a prizefighter like, say, Jack Johnson.

Dan grabbed his woozy friend by the arm. "Hold on, take 'er easy. Think you can make it back to our hospital tent on your own, or do we need to get a stretcher to carry you there?"

Lester scoffed and pushed his chum away. He gingerly touched his cut-up face. Blood gushed from his nose and into his mouth.

"He's fine," Dan declared with relief. "Same ol' stubborn Harper. Tough as fucking nails."

BRANDON
Manitoba—April 1909

"MILK THE COWS," ALFRED HARPER DEMANDED.

"But, Dad," the teenage Lester whined.

"Now go. Git."

Lester knew that his father didn't care who milked the cows as long as they were milked. As the eldest, he believed in delegating responsibility for chores downward. Seizing Wilbur by the collar, he dragged his brother over to their stone barn and slammed the metal pail into his chest.

"Papa says milk the cows."

Wilbur was in no mood to take orders. He was not a lackey or a stooge. Standing tall in defiance, he let the pail fall, planted his feet, and hit his older sibling square in the face. Lester's nose exploded, and Wilbur ran for the safety of their mom as fast as his twelve-year-old legs could carry him.

Lester had never understood why his father needed such a grandiose barn. It was a stone monstrosity, twice the size of their neighbour's, with two slanting roofs. It must have been the result of one of A.W.'s outlandish schemes, he realized later in life. His dad always had big plans and bigger dreams.

Till We Meet Again

Even in his youth, Alfred had been restless. The country was going railway mad at the time, and the Ontario boy dreamed of the free and untamed west, where land was plentiful. Money and settlers were pouring into the prairies, and A.W. was certain that the transcontinental railway would revolutionize the Canadian economy. This was the opportunity of a lifetime, and Alfred believed that he had found the perfect place to homestead: Reston. He had relatives nearby who spoke highly of the land, and the community was on the Canadian Pacific Railway (CPR) line in southwestern Manitoba.

While his hometown of Kinloss was minuscule, it was a gigantic metropolis compared to Reston, where only a handful of farmhouses peeked out of the waist-high buffalo grass that covered the prairies. In fact, Reston was so isolated that Canada Post simply labelled it as "Location 9-7-27W." Yet A.W. saw the potential. The CPR could turn the rural district into a thriving city.

Alfred went west and built a homestead. When it was finished in 1892, he headed back to Ontario to see if Isabella Gracey Mowbray, whom he had known as a teenager, would come back to Manitoba with him. On the way to Kinloss, A.W. met another homesteader who had the same idea. "I'm going to see if Gracey Mowbray will marry me and come west," the man said.

Alfred did not share his own plan. As soon as he came across the next telegraph machine, he sent a message to Gracey, proposing to her before the other suitor could. She agreed, and they were married on March 9, 1892.

Gracey was twenty-six at the time, and Kinloss was her entire world. She had grown up there among the scenic woodlots overlooking the sandy shore of Lake Huron. Her family lived there. Her friends did too. Now she was off to start a new life sixteen hundred miles away.

She packed up her belongings and settled at the homestead in Reston. Within a year, Lester was born. Wesley, Wilbur, and Burt followed in quick succession. They had a daughter too, but Pearl died as an infant. At the turn of the century, the Harpers were a family of six.

As it turned out, Alfred was right about the prairies going railway mad but wrong about Reston. The CPR passed right on through, taking its passengers and their money farther west. No one stopped in the middle-of-nowhere Manitoba.

With his bet on Reston a flop, A.W. sought to cut his family's losses and move on. He didn't care that the Harpers were an integral part of the community. He wanted to be closer to a railway hub to profit from the economic boom. "We can buy a two-storey house on a section of land three miles south of Brandon for only six thousand dollars," he told his wife.

Gracey sighed but consented. The Harpers moved to Brandon, where their fifth son, Earl, was born in 1903. A.W. started travelling to Alberta to catch wild horses, which he sent back to Manitoba by the trainload. It cost a lot of money to ship twenty horses in a railcar, and the stallions did not appreciate the journey or its expense. They nipped and kicked anyone who got close. Of course, the Harper boys got close. They pleaded with their father to let them ride one. He always refused. Alfred spent more time chasing his sons away from the horses than he did breaking them in.

A.W. wasn't satisfied with life as a successful prairie farmer, even though he made an extra ten dollars if he broke the horses in himself. He was always hunting for the next opportunity. That was when he heard about the thriving real estate market in British Columbia. Borrowed money was cheap and accessible in Vancouver, he learned, and you didn't need a special skill set to buy property. Anybody could do it, so why not him? There would be no more hard work homesteading and no more freezing cold winters. All that it took to make a fortune in Vancouver was to sign the right pieces of paper.

The Harper boys in Reston, Manitoba.

After eighteen years of marriage, Gracey wasn't surprised when her husband called the family together. "We're auctioning off our farm and moving to Vancouver," Alfred announced.

Gracey saw the excitement in her husband's eyes. She couldn't bear to crush his dreams, no matter how many times she was forced to move. At least Vancouver, unlike Reston or Brandon, was a fascinating destination, she reasoned. Gracey had heard stories about BC too, but it wasn't the tales of easy money that intrigued her—it was the descriptions of raging rivers and snow-capped mountains. An avid artist of the natural world, she was bored with painting the flat farmland of the prairies. Maybe the rugged beauty of the Pacific Northwest would revitalize her paintbrush.

"Fine," she agreed.

When their mother acquiesced, the boys did too. Arguing was pointless. The decision was made.

In 1910, the Harpers were not the only Manitoban family to sell out, pack up, and head west. Fred Riches was also lured to the West Coast by rags-to-riches stories. He took his wife, Charlotte, and their daughters, Mabel and Jessie, along. As the fates decreed, the Harpers and Riches went to Vancouver on the same train and bought houses on the same street, East 21st Avenue near Ontario Street in Mount Pleasant.

Lester spent hours watching Mabel blush while he made love to her over a cup of tea. Apparently, that was how you courted in 1911. Mabel was not as fair or delicate as her younger sister, Jessie, whose beauty called to mind the porcelain teacup in Lester's hands. Pretty and dainty. No, that was not Mabel. She was smart, stoic, and strong-willed. It was a vicious combination. She never raised her voice in anger, but Lester could see the fire in her eyes when he offended her sense of decorum. And he knew that he would pay dearly for it. That was what he loved about her. Unlike the fragile china, Mabel was unbreakable.

Vancouver in the 1910s was becoming an economic centre, and Lester found employment with Dominion Trust, a thriving real estate company. Their thirteen-storey Dominion Trust Building in the financial district was the city's first skyscraper and, for a time, the tallest building in the British Empire.

The prairie boy was vacillating between a career in business or medicine. After finishing at Brandon College, he was accepted at McGill University, where he intended to attend medical school. But then he was offered an opportunity with Dominion Trust in Calgary. Lester chose business. The problem with accepting the transfer to Alberta was Mabel. Breaking up with her was unthinkable. Leaving her was unbearable. After many sleepless nights, he did the only thing that solved his conundrum: he proposed. The two were married in an intimate ceremony at her parents' home on August 1, 1913. Wesley was Lester's best man. Jessie was Mabel's maid of honour.

The newlyweds moved to Calgary, where Lester continued to work for Dominion Trust. That was when the West Coast's property boom turned to bust. Alfred had bought multiple lots in Point Grey and 146 acres on Vancouver Island (with seven other people). The Harpers lost a fortune on the investments. But it could have been worse. Five million dollars disappeared from the accounts of Dominion Trust, and the managing director in Lester's former Vancouver office "accidentally" shot himself in the heart.

A.W. was done with speculative real estate ventures. He longed to return to pioneering, so he called the family together once more. "The North is the new West," he announced. "The Canadian Northern Railway is putting in a line from Edmonton to Grand Prairie, and the Peace River Land Office is open for business. What's more, they're practically giving away plots for free."

This time, A.W. was better prepared. His pitch included evidence. "Have a look here," he said, taking out a newspaper advertisement. "It says quarter sections are only ten dollars apiece. Can you believe it? We're selling the house, shipping our stuff to Edmonton, and heading for Pouce Coupe Prairie."

Gracey felt like she was having déjà vu. This argument sounded familiar. She had never heard of Peace River or Pouce Coupe Prairie, but that didn't matter. This was Reston and Brandon all over again.

Despite her husband's spotty track record, she supported his decision. Although Gracey enjoyed painting the Capilano gorge, she was done with Vancouver. Alfred had touted the West Coast as the Promised Land, but she found it to be more like Sodom and Gomorrah. Temptation abounded in the city, and it was difficult to keep her sons in line. She had even caught Wesley frequenting a pool hall. In the country, she would not have to worry so much. They would be too busy working the land to get into trouble.

Her boys were behind their father too. They were hankering for an adventure, and trekking into the Great White North was the most daring and dangerous expedition imaginable.

As the final autumn of the old world order drew to a close, A.W. sold their house on East 21st Avenue and took two teams of horses and their harnesses in payment (a steal for the buyer considering that property is worth millions today). Sending their household effects ahead of them by train, the Harpers travelled to Edmonton, where Jasper Avenue was bustling with hundreds of real estate offices. Giant banners waved across the wooden storefronts advertising land for sale in Grouard, Peace River, and Grand Prairie. The frenzy over the North was bordering on madness. Some properties were being bought and sold multiple times in a single day. The fear of missing out was so extreme that hawkers peddled deeds to newcomers at the train station.

Give Alfred credit, though. After Vancouver, he did not buy

into the hype. As he strolled leisurely along the manure-befouled avenue, he took his time to gather intelligence from more experienced hands. "You don't want to go north yet," one man told him. "Wait until January, when the snowpack is solid and the sleighing is better on the Edson Trail. Settlers have got into trouble when they've left in the warmer months. It's easy to get bogged down in the mud."

With little actual knowledge of the Peace River Country, A.W. heeded the advice. The Harpers temporarily settled in Edmonton, where Alfred purchased three more stallions at auction while the boys hauled coal to make money for supplies and keep their own horses in working shape.

As Christmas rolled around, the family prepared to set out on the journey. That was when tragedy struck. What began as a sniffle over the holidays turned into pleurisy, and A.W. rushed his wife to the hospital as the bells were ringing in the new year. Three days later, Gracey succumbed to pneumonia.

The death of Isabella Gracey Harper was a severe shock for the family, but it did not dissuade Alfred from embarking on their planned endeavour. In fact, it strengthened his resolve. His wife had wanted to raise their boys far away from the dangers of the city, and he swore to honour her wish.

The problem was his sons. Alfred couldn't raise his motherless boys while building a homestead in northern Canada. He needed help tending the house and taking care of Wilbur, Burt, and Earl. There was only one solution: Lester and Mabel would have to come north too.

Lester felt duty-bound to help his father, but Mabel had no desire to go. She had already left her family and an office job in Vancouver for her husband, and now her father-in-law wanted her to trek into the wilderness to raise her brothers-in-law and clean his house too. Mabel was young enough to be their sister. How could she replace their beloved mother? But she agreed. The faithful Methodist believed in doing what was right, even if it involved self-sacrifice. Lester quit his job, and the newlyweds left the life they were just beginning in Calgary to set out for the Edson Trail.

MONT-SAINT-ÉLOI
France—March 24, 1917

"WELL, AREN'T YOU LUCKY?" THE MEDICAL OFFICER (MO) SAID when he concluded his examination. "Aside from a minor case of shell shock, a scratched-up face, and those humongous black eyes, I'd say you're fine as a rub. I guess that shell didn't have your name on it."

"Gee, thanks, Doc." Corporal Harper refused to ask the question that was gnawing at his brain. Who wants to know? he told himself whenever he wondered what had happened to the other Canadians.

"Shell shock," the MO had said. It was a vague term used to cover a wide variety of symptoms in 1917. The war had spawned a new illness that baffled the medical community. How do you diagnose a soldier who was buried alive and could no longer speak? What about an infantryman seized by stomach cramps after bayonetting an enemy in the gut? How about a sniper who lost his ability to see? The answer to all three questions: shell shock.

No one knew what caused this mysterious condition. Was it physical? A concussion from the impact of explosions on the brain. That failed to explain the cases found nowhere near shellfire. Was it psychological? A neurosis derived from the terror of war. That did not account for the millennia of human conflict. Mankind's history was rife with violence, brutality, and slaughter. Yet Homer never sang of shell shock when the Greeks torched Troy. The *Iliad* does not tell of Achilles suffering from a nervous breakdown and babbling incoherently or of Hector tearing off his clothes and clawing madly at the dirt like some soldiers did in the Great War. Only the most cold-hearted men on the Western Front were certain of the cause of this modern disease: their comrades were suffering from a bout of cowardice, plain and simple.

Without knowing the origins of shell shock, the doctors struggled to cure it. The proper course of treatment was hotly contested. Hypnotize the victims? Knock them out with chloroform? Attach electroshock cables to their testicles? The doctors tried all three. Fortunately for Lester, he had only a minor case. His MO prescribed rest.

The groggy corporal was left out of the ranks when the Northwest Battalion moved into Aux Reitz Corner. Lester was standing by the crater in Mont-Saint-Éloi when a friend snuck up behind him.

"By Jove!" the man said. "That's one big bloomin' crump hole. You've got tip-top luck. Walking away from that mess is no small feat. Did you know that a Jack Johnson can burst a man's eyeballs from ten feet away? Pop, like a balloon, you're blind."

Lester smiled. He did indeed have tip-top luck.

"Too bad about the other lads," his chum added. "Sounds like the men had to scrape them out of the mud with a spoon."

Corporal Harper groaned. He strode over to the red-bricked *estaminet*, took a seat at an empty table, and watched a lass dance to the music of a bum mouth organ.

France
March 24th, 1917

Dear Maybelle:
Do you like me to spell your name "Maybelle"? I like it that way.

Till We Meet Again

It looks nice and sounds nice. Our battalion is in the trenches just now, but some were left out and I am among that number. We are billeted near a town that Fritz shells a little each day. We move to a safe distance when he starts up. I had a close shave the other day, but one has to take chances for the whole war is a game with a certain amount of chance in it.

Do you remember the long lists of casualties in the papers last September? Well expect them again this spring. The weather is clear, and the country is drying up. When it dries up, watch the papers. Casualties are inevitable unless the war ends before the drive, and I doubt that. We expect a lot of stiff fighting this summer. I hope the war ends before because, if it doesn't, there is going to be something doing and I don't want to be there, to tell the truth. There is bound to be a large number of casualties, and there have been too many already. We will give Fritz a rough time. We are superior in everything now, and we hope to give him some of the same stuff he gave our boys two years ago. Even yet the boys talk and talk of last September 15th, the same day Wes was wounded. I sincerely hope the Canadians never have to go through that again.

Your letter made me homesick. I was so pleased that you and Dad got along so well for I feel guilty of so many things that have happened the last three years. I almost hate to go back to Pouce Coupe and face him. I want to be with you and yours in a home somewhere and, as long as it is a home, I don't mind where that somewhere is. I hope this world conflict will be cleared up soon and you and I are reunited.

I am anxiously waiting for a letter written about the middle of March containing very important news. Long ere you receive this, I expect you will be well and happy. Out here, I can do nothing but wait.

Say there is a fellow playing a bum mouth organ, and I find it hard to write or collect my thoughts. I wish he would play on his own organ instead! Give my kind regards to Jessie and keep the love for yourself.

Your loving Bob,
R. L. Harper
xxxx

THE WEATHER WAS ABOMINABLE AND THE SHELLING WAS worse when Corporal Harper rejoined Platoon No. 5. High-explosive blasts tore bodies in half while burning shards of metal rained down between flurries of snow and sleet. "His or ours?" the men desperately asked each other when they heard the shells overhead but could not spot them. In Aux Reitz Corner, the answer was unfailingly "His." The sun set. The artillery howled. Canadians died. Aux Reitz Corner is being made a most unhealthy spot, Lieutenant Colonel Ross noted in his war diary.

A miserable March gave way to a balmy April, and new problems sprung to life. As the wildflowers bloomed among the barbed wire, the lice stirred in the servicemen's clothing. Then La Grippe ran through the battalion. Soldier after soldier reported to the MO with flu-like symptoms. They were stricken with fevers, debilitating headaches, and fatigue for up to three months. Many felt pain in their bones too, especially in the shins. "Shinbone fever," the men dubbed the sickness. The doctors had a more academic name: it was a pyrexia of unknown origin (PUO).

Like shell shock, PUO was something of a medical mystery, so in true bureaucratic fashion, the government created the British Expeditionary Force Pyrexia of Unknown Origin Enquiry Sub-Committee.

In 1918, the research paid dividends. Scientists discovered that shinbone fever came from *Rickettsia quintana*, a bacterium spread by the lice that lived in the troops' uniforms and sucked on their blood.

Lester fingered a thistle growing out of a sandbag. It was amazing how nature could flourish in such a wasteland. He gazed up at a captive balloon floating high above their lines. To the hungry corporal, the gasbag was a giant baloney sausage in the sky.

Corporal Harper appreciated the bizarre-looking captive balloons because they were highly effective. The observers in their baskets were able to see what the enemy was planning and guide the Canadian artillery with ease. Naturally, the Germans did not like that. They shot down the balloons whenever they could.

At that moment, a British airplane came out of the clouds, smoking and flying erratically. Even from afar, Lester could tell that the pilot was lucky to have eluded Fritz's ruthless fighters. The aircraft wobbled and veered toward the tethered balloon. *What the devil is he doing?* the corporal wondered.

The Canadian could only watch helplessly as the pilot dove toward the observers and dropped two incendiary bombs on top of the gasbag. The balloon burst into flames, and the observers jumped from their burning basket with parachutes open. As the captive balloon crashed in a fiery heap, the airplane flew back across no man's land.

"That's a darn clever trick," Lester admitted. "Fritz isn't done yet if he's rigging up our captured planes to roast our sausages like that."

"Postman's here," Dan piped up.

Lester hustled over. He was eagerly awaiting news about the birth of his child, but he received a month-old package from Mabel instead.

"I think you're the first person to be disappointed to get a parcel instead of a letter," his friend chuckled.

Corporal Harper put on the socks knitted for him by his wife and broke off a hunk of cake for his side-kicker.

"No, thanks," Dan replied.

Lester took a closer look. Sure, the cake was covered in mould. Back in the billets, he might have tossed it out. But he was in the trenches, and he was hungry. Eating the cake was worth the risk. Okay, who was he kidding? Lester would have eaten Mabel's mouldy desserts anywhere in France. As careful as a surgeon operating on a soldier with gangrene, he sliced off the infected growth without sacrificing too much of the healthy host. Satisfied with the result of the procedure, he took a bite and offered it to his friend again.

Dan shook his head.

"You really don't want a piece? I know the air got to it, but it's a helluva cake."

"I'm fine. Thanks."

"Suit yourself. More for me, I guess."

Corporal Harper scarfed down the rest of the cake, only to regret his impulsive decision soon after. Lacking knowledge of microbiology, he'd failed to recognize that the infection had spread too far. His tasty patient was terminal. Alas, the fungus was now contaminating his stomach. Within hours, Lester was sick as a dog.

———

The Northwest Battalion was dirty, bone-tired, and short another thirty-six infantrymen on the muddy march out of the line. Sapped of his strength, Corporal Harper sagged under the weight of his haversack. His legs quivered with fatigue. Yet he trudged onward because every step took him a little farther away from the war and a little closer to their rest camp.

When they finally stumbled into Bois des Alleux, Lester was too tired to shower or shave. He had a spot of tea and a drop of rum and then crawled into his tent. But the lice would not let up. While the

Germans posed the greatest threat in the trenches, the louse was the real enemy in the rear. The cooties attacked their prey with a ferocity that would have made the bayonet instructor at Camp Bramshott proud.

As soon as Lester got warm, the lice thawed out. They crawled out of the seams of his uniform and started biting. Wave after wave advanced in battalions to feast. No matter how exhausted the corporal felt, he could not relax with all those prickly little legs swarming his skin. He tossed and turned and scratched until he bled. His skin red and torn, his fingernails thick with blood, Lester felt so crummy that he admitted defeat. He stripped off his undershirt and got into bed naked for the first time in eight months. Then he fell asleep and scratched himself in his dreams.

La Grippe soon caught up to him. Lester lay in bed with a fever, severe abdominal pains, and a deuce of a headache. How the sick corporal wished that he was at home with Mabel serving him hot lemonade (the ultimate nineteenth-century flu foe) and not at the mercy of the MOs, who prescribed the same remedy for every undiagnosed ailment: dynamite, salts, and Pill No. 9.

Little did the soldiers know that the small black pill contained calomel, a cure-all drug used to treat syphilis, cholera, tuberculosis, cancer, and even childhood teething. It was phenomenally popular until scientists discovered that the mercury in the compound was toxic. Calomel poisoned its patients. The army's infamous panacea was also a mild laxative. Pill No. 9 sent the servicemen running for the latrine.

Dan had a better remedy. He showed up with two steaming mess tins full of eggs.

"Look what I found for five francs!" Private Fee exclaimed. "Got the cook to make the oofs just the way you like 'em."

"Extra greasy?"

"You know it."

They had a good feed, and the sick corporal felt 100 percent better.

A few days later, on a grey and cheerless Easter Sunday, Lester attended his first church parade in France. Unlike most services, this one was full. Not because it was Easter. Not because attendance was mandatory. But because every man worried that this Sunday might be his last.

After a quiet winter on the Western Front, the Entente was on the verge of launching the next Big Push. The charming General Robert Nivelle, the French commander-in-chief, promised success. As long as the BEF could draw the kaiser's forces away from the south with a feint, Nivelle said, his infantrymen would do the majority of the fighting. Three French armies would punch a hole in the Hindenburg Line along the Aisne River within forty-eight hours for the low cost of ten thousand casualties. "I can assure you that victory is certain," the handsome general told Prime Minister David Lloyd George in exemplary English. "The German army will run away; they only want to be off."

The British prime minister bought the French general's pitch with the unbridled enthusiasm of a Tommy buying his first beer at an *estaminet*. Lloyd George believed that General Nivelle had proved himself a man at Verdun, so he put the British troops at his disposal—much to the disappointment of General Haig, who had no desire to be placed under French command.

As part of the BEF smokescreen, General Haig ordered the Canadians to capture Vimy Ridge. For a diversion, it was a hell of an ask. The strategically important escarpment was the linchpin of the Hindenburg defence system. The Germans had fortified their position with concrete bunkers that withstood artillery barrages and had laid impassable tangles of barbed wire that funnelled their enemies into killing zones for the machine guns. They would not relinquish this fortress easily.

Even the overconfident General Nivelle thought that the Canadians were likely to fail. The CEF was not a professional army. It was made up of volunteer farmers, ranchers, and shopkeepers. These were battalions of civilians who knew nothing about warfare. How could they succeed when France and Britain had lost 140,000 men in futile assaults on the ridge? The attack would surely end in disaster. The British, he suggested, should bypass Vimy and start the offensive farther south. General Haig refused to listen, so General Nivelle did not press the issue. As long as the Dominion troops kept the Germans occupied, he would not interfere with their plan.

Lieutenant General Byng was not willing to sacrifice his Byng Boys unnecessarily, however, so he set about the task methodically. He began by prioritizing knowledge. The Canadian Corps commander carefully studied the previous Allied failures, as well as the recent battles on the Somme and at Verdun. He also sent out several of his favourite raiding parties to capture prisoners and acquire information that would aid the mission.

Because the Germans could see into the Allied lines from the ridge, the lieutenant general ordered his men to construct an elaborate subterranean system of subways, command posts, and ammunition dumps that allowed for the build-up of a massive assault safe from Fritz's prying reconnaissance planes and menacing shells.

The veterans were not having it. Many, like Wesley, had left the West to get away from digging. "You would, I know, fight and die if necessary to the last ditch," a frustrated Lieutenant General Byng told his troops. "But I'm damned if I can get you to dig that ditch."

The CEF commander's strategy was almost as ambitious as General Nivelle's. Choreographing his assault down to the minute, Lieutenant

General Byng expected his four divisions to capture almost all of Vimy Ridge by lunch on the first day. No wonder the French general thought that the Canucks were unlikely to succeed.

With the plan in place, the Canadians relied on their artillery to soften up the Germans in preparation for the attack. Allocating one heavy gun and two field cannons for every sixty feet, they lined the weapons up in a semicircle around the ridge and launched the largest barrage of the war. Day after day, the artillery pounded Vimy Ridge mercilessly. They fired a total of 1.6 million shells to render the enemy's communication lines, trenches, and barbed wire irreparable. "Saturation bombing," the Allies labelled the tactic. The Germans had another term: "the week of suffering." The Bavarians defending the ridge were famished, sleep-deprived, and dazed from concussion after concussion. But what infantryman was not shell-shocked by 1917?

As the ground trembled beneath his men's feet, Lieutenant Colonel Alexander Ross issued their orders. The Nor'westers were to drive the enemy from their position and consolidate a new line. The lieutenant colonel made no qualms about their role: this was going to be a dangerous and large-scale mission vital to the Allied offensive. The eight thousand Germans had all the advantages, and they were expected to fight to the last man. The 2nd Canadian Division was likely to have the heaviest fighting, especially around Thélus, where Lester's B Company would clear the houses and old trenches with their Lewis guns, grenade rifles, and Mills bombs. Fortunately, the infantrymen would have help—they would be accompanied by two tanks.

Lester was intrigued. He had never seen a tank before. There were rumours that these steel monsters were packed with guns that fired a thousand rounds per minute and had treads that crushed barbed wire. Wesley had told him about seeing tanks in the Battle of Courcelette.

"They certainly are funny-looking things, but they are wonderful machines," he said. "They can cross trenches and go through shell holes. Even if their engines happen to be put out of business, they are still as good as any machine-gun emplacement. Gunfire does no damage to them at all."

Corporal Harper was thrilled to have the armoured support, but their orders were clear. The men were to stay away from the tanks! These new vehicles did not need a bunch of soldiers gawking at them in the midst of an advance—or worse, trying to use them as shields.

The servicemen were issued additional ammunition, emergency rations, wire cutters, picks, and shovels to carry in their already hefty packs. As Lester put his kit together, he felt the field dressing he had stashed away in his tunic. He wondered who in his section might need to be bandaged up. If his brother's experience at Courcelette was any indication, he worried that it would be all of them.

Corporal Harper's fellow NCOs were emptying their paybooks into a cap. It was considered bad luck to carry francs into combat, so they were pooling their change. The dead would not need the money, and the wounded would have more pressing concerns. The cash was a consolation prize for the survivors.

One of the men saw Lester eyeball the growing kitty. "Not a chance, Harper. You're always broke, and you're far too lucky of a feller."

Lester pulled Dan aside. "You still have Mabel's address in Edmonton?"

"Of course. And you, Myrtle's in Lucky Lake?"

He nodded. "Remember to tell her—"

"I know."

Going into battle, the soldiers made the necessary arrangements in case of their untimely demise. If the unthinkable happened, each swore to lie to his friend's sweetheart until the end. No matter how gruesomely the man died, the story was to be the same: quick and painless, bravely fighting the enemy.

Dan turned toward the battlefield. "So Vimy Ridge, eh? Looks like a baddish place for a show."

"You know it must be awful if they took the trouble to name it," Lester quoted his brother Burt.

EDSON TRAIL
Alberta—March 1914

"YOU KNOW IT MUST BE AWFUL IF THEY TOOK THE TROUBLE to name it," Burt said as they surveyed Fraser Hill.

"You're right," his father agreed. The hill was steep, bare, and a half mile straight up. "This is going to be a real snifter."

The Harpers were a week into the 260-mile journey to Pouce Coupe Prairie when they reached their greatest challenge yet. The Edson Trail had proved more treacherous than anticipated. An early spring thaw had melted the frozen muskeg, and their overweight sleighs sunk into the bog.

The Harpers were already behind schedule. They had travelled only fifty-seven miles in their first week, and the feed for their eight horses was running low, which was their paramount concern. If your means of transportation died in the bush, you usually did too. There was a reason why the Edson Trail was known as That Woeful Road. Shallow graves dotted the trail and proliferated at the fording points across the Athabasca and Berland Rivers.

Their sleighs were packed with necessities. The Harpers had every tool imaginable to build a homestead from scratch. There were walking ploughs, logging chains, axes, saws, and a forge, as well as mattresses, bedding, and a stove. Okay, maybe they had more than just necessities.

Mabel had brought along an Underwood typewriter so she could write letters to her sister. At least Alfred was smart enough to leave their piano behind.

The journey without Gracey was sad and burdensome—especially for Mabel, who was relegated to the stereotypically female chores. It was 1914, after all. Rising before dawn every morning, she made their porridge, did their dishes, and put away their bedding. When they stopped at noon, she made their lunch and cleaned up too. At dusk, her job was the same: make dinner, tidy up, and set up their beds. Anything remotely domestic was her domain, including wrangling the children.

What did the Harpers eat? Mainly potatoes. Alongside the six hundred pounds of flour, six hundred pounds of sugar, and twenty-five pounds of dried fruit that they carried in their sleighs, Mabel had made one hundred pounds of mashed potatoes that she dished out at mealtime. Whenever she had a free moment, she sat in the caboose (their makeshift kitchen and bedroom on runners) and wrote to Jessie, tapping away at the typewriter in the middle of the wilderness.

The Harpers approached Fraser Hill carefully. They divided the load into two parts and took each half up with three teams of horses. While it was slow-going, they navigated the peak successfully. It was the next hill that surprised them. Although this one was not as steep, there was a gully with a creek on the backside. Alfred went down from the summit and attempted to cross the bridge, but his sleigh got stuck.

"Don't fret," Wesley said and doubled up his team. Even with four horses, the jammed sleigh refused to budge. Miles from nowhere, there was only one solution: more horsepower. Wes called to Lester, who was bringing up the rear. The eldest son unhitched his horses from the caboose on top of the hill and came down to help.

Mabel was in the caboose when she felt it slide forward. She had seen Lester unhook their team and knew that she was in trouble. Mabel held her breath out of fear as the horseless sleigh accelerated.

Wilbur was the first to see the driverless sleigh come sliding down the hill. "Watch out!" he yelled and drove his father's buggy toward it.

Alfred waved him off. "Get out of the way!"

It was too late. Wilbur had put himself directly in the path of the oncoming caboose. The overstuffed sleigh crashed into the buggy and crumpled it up like an accordion.

Lester ran over. "Mabel! Darling! Are you all right?"

Mabel stood up and shook herself off. "That was a son-of-a-gun hill all right," she swore.

"My buggy!" Alfred exclaimed. Both the hind axle and reach were broken.

Lester was livid. His father was more concerned about the buggy than he was about his daughter-in-law.

On March 11, the Harpers rode into Grand Prairie City. They had conquered the Edson Trail and arrived in the Peace River Country; their only casualty was A.W.'s prized buggy. They had entered their Garden of Eden.

Grand Prairie City
March 11th, 1914

Dear Jessie:
This is the fourth letter I have written to you since we left
Edmonton, and I hope you got the others all right. You can send all
letters you write to—just wait. I can't tell you that just yet. We may
settle in Pouce Coupe as we first intended or we may switch off and
settle down at Lake Saskatoon.
   The weather has been grand all the way with the exception of
Sunday afternoon when we had a howling snowstorm and blizzard

combined. Say! It did blow for a few hours, but we were all right, as we are in our "Prairie Schooner."

The first seventy miles were very hilly and bad roads were quite the fashion. Most of the hills were very bare, and that made it very hard for the horses to pull the loads, which were a lot heavier than most people take over the Edson Trail. Say, we would have a picnic bringing the piano to this country. We crossed several rivers of considerable size, then we came to the Fraser Hill, and it was a snifter, as Mr. Harper said. Burton said it must be awful if they would take the trouble to name it, and it sure was.

Then we crossed the lake, nine miles across, and came to the stopping place at the other side. It was run by a Frenchman and he had the nicest-looking house we had seen since we left Edson. It was made of logs and was two stories. He got very friendly, as he had been drinking a little, and offered Mr. Harper a drink. When he refused, he asked him if he had a family. Mr. Harper said that he had, and the Frenchman told him that if he would milk the cow in the barn that he could have the milk. So we had dandy milk on our porridge.

The next morning, we set out again. There was quite a hill there. I happened to be in the caboose and I had heard Lester take the horses off, so I knew that it was going down by itself. The buggy was at the bottom, and we ran into it and broke the hind axle and reach.

I guess you would like to know what we do every day. First thing in the morning, Mr. Harper gets up, lights a fire, and feeds the horses. Then I make porridge, and we have breakfast with bread, jam, and tea. I wash the dishes while they are hitching up, and we go until suppertime. Then I make dinner, do the dishes, and get the beds ready. We generally get into bed about nine o'clock.

Last night we reached a stopping place thirteen miles from

Till We Meet Again

Grand Prairie City, which we reached today at noon. It is a nice little town. Sugar is 15 cents a pound here, and nut bars two for a quarter. I suppose you wonder where in the world I got the typewriter. It is Harold Empey's. It is an Underwood, the same as I used in the office, and a dandy, too.

Say, I will have to finish this some other time.
So good night for this time,
Mabel and Lester

ARRAS-BETHUNE ROAD
France—April 8, 1917

THREE YEARS LATER, CORPORAL HARPER STUMBLED UP THE mule tracks under the dark clouds of an ominous sky. On this trip, unlike past ones, the boys were not singing their favourite cheeky song:

Send out my mother,
My sister and my brother,
Don't for heaven's sake send me!

Instead, they were eerily quiet as the platoon made its way into position in the assembly area near Neuville-Saint-Vaast. The Northwest Battalion joined the thousands of Canadians waiting in the tunnels and trenches. This was the first time that all four divisions of the Canadian Corps were going into battle together.

Men from Victoria to Halifax spent the night underground. No one slept. They snacked on hardtack, drank tea, and used barrels as toilets. The time for nervous jokes, half-hearted laughter, and false bravado was over. The soldiers just gripped their rifles restlessly and chain-smoked cigarettes while they listened to the shellfire echo through the caverns.

At 3.30 a.m. on the dot, the officers of the 28th Battalion synchronized their wristwatches with their counterparts at battalion headquarters (who had synchronized their own with the brigade at midnight). Like the Israelites of the Bible, the Canadians would be following a moving wall of fire. But they didn't have an angel to protect them from the maelstrom. They were reliant on their watches to keep precise time. A sloppy count was the difference not only between success and failure but also between life and death. As Lieutenant General Byng had warned them, "Chaps, you shall go over exactly like a railroad train, on exact time, or you shall be annihilated." Accurately following a barrage across cratered ground, however, was much easier for the lieutenant general to order from the command centre than for the infantry to do under fire.

B Company was leading the battalion's charge, so Corporal Harper took his place in the front of the Old French Trench. He stood in icy slush while sleet rained down upon him. This was the moment he had wished for. This was his chance to prove his mettle in combat, to distinguish himself in battle. He had prepared for it, both physically and mentally, for years. But Lester was no longer bloodthirsty. He was not remotely excited to fight. Red-eyed and dog-tired, he was first in line for a show that he did not want to see, let alone take part in. The corporal looked at his men. This would be the last sunrise for many of them, maybe even him.

Just then, an explosion rocked the lines. A fidgety Newfoundlander had accidentally loosened the pin on one of his grenades when he was hitching up his gear. The Mills bomb exploded, killing him instantly and wounding those around him. This was the first death of the day. It would not be the last.

Corporal Harper double-checked his special carrier packed with Millses. He went over his mental map of Thélus again. They had run so many sham battles in the mock village that he had memorized its layout. Lester also knew that he could count on his section to follow him. What worried him was their new officer. Oh, the corporal thought that their lieutenant was a decent chap, but he belonged in a staff office fighting a paper war with reams of meticulously crafted orders. A pencil-pusher, the lieutenant would have been content to watch the little coloured cutouts murder each other on their model, blissfully removed from the real men dying on the battlefield.

That was the problem with the CEF's system: lieutenants were the middle managers of the military. They lacked the leadership skills of the captains above them and the experience of the sergeants below them. Privates were perpetually needed because they were routinely shot, but what do you do with the green excess officers when you disband a battalion to refill the ranks? The Canadian Corps could not send them home, so they made them line officers. They put each one in charge of a platoon and sent him over the top to let the Germans do the culling. Voila! Problem solved.

Lester's new lieutenant was one of those leftover men. Everyone in the platoon wished that Lieutenant Edward Davies was still leading them. He had risen through the ranks as an NCO and earned his commission. Lieutenant Davies was battle-hardened, well-respected, and remarkably, absent from the battalion. What a time to be away!

The officer who'd replaced him was as antithetical to Lieutenant Davies as could be. He was unseasoned, unknown, and jumpy from the start. Every time the new lieutenant heard Fritz's artillery fire, he got the wind up. He turned quivery and went to pieces. He even admitted as much.

Lester could not believe that the army had chosen this high-strung officer to lead them through the tightest life-or-death schedule under a heavy bombardment. The decision was mind-boggling. It was so absurd, in fact, that it was almost funny. He would have laughed hysterically if this were one of Charlie Chaplin's slapstick comedy routines and not real life.

As a misty dawn rolled over the ridge, the artillery ceased their salvo. A hush fell over the troops. For the first time in a fortnight, all was quiet on the Western Front. Yet it was only a ruse. The Canadians were trying to lull the Germans into a false sense of security before the shelling reached its crescendo.

"What's that noise?" a soldier yelled.

A few men laughed. Most did not. After weeks of continuous shellfire, the silence was terrifying.

Corporal Harper watched Sergeant Thompson dole out a double tot of rum. It seemed wrong to butter up the boys with alcohol in the run-up to a show. Why dull their wits and slow their reflexes before throwing them into, literally, a fight for their lives?

His cousin waved the jug of rum in front of him. Lester grabbed hold and drank greedily to quench his parched throat.

"How's the lieutenant holding up?" he asked in his trench voice.

"Filled the poor bugger's canteen with rum," Bill said, winking. "Let's hope that helps with the windy. Just follow me. *Compreé?*"

"Yes, Sergeant," his voice wobbled.

At 5.28 a.m. sharp, 983 heavy guns and 150 machine guns exploded in a thunderous roar. The clatter was deafening. It was so loud, in fact, that Prime Minister Lloyd George heard the barrage 148 miles away on Downing Street. The earth shuddered, a chorus of shells screeched overhead, and hundred-foot flames engulfed the horizon. The destruction was biblical, hellfire and brimstone. This must have been how Lot's wife felt watching Sodom and Gomorrah burn. The Canadians could not turn away. How could anyone survive such a devastating barrage?

The Germans did. They hid in their deep dugouts. The Bavarians were so confident in their preparations for the onslaught that they put up signs that read "Welcome Canadians." As one captured soldier defiantly remarked, "You might get to the top of Vimy Ridge, but I'll tell you this: you'll be able to take all the Canadians [who get there] back to Canada in a rowboat."

Red, white, and green SOL flares shot up from the German lines. The Bavarians were calling for backup. That was troubling. Fritz knew they were coming, and he was waiting to catch them in his favourite killing ground. The Canadians were walking into a trap.

The officers blew their whistles, and the first wave of assaulting troops grabbed the rungs of their scaling ladders and climbed out of the jumping-off trenches. As the Canucks pushed up the ridge, the Maschinengewehr 08s began to rattle. The gunners fired in scything arcs, and the Canadians were cut down like stalks of wheat on the prairies. Arms flailing and bodies spinning as bullets tore through them, the wounded crawled for the crump holes.

"My legs are broke!"

"Stretcher-bearer!"

"Help me, please. I'm wounded!"

Unfortunately, helping the injured was forbidden. Infantrymen were only allowed to mark the spot of a comrade by jamming his rifle into the ground like a flagpole. The Canadians were on a tight timeline. They could ill afford to slow the advance. The wounded would have to wait for the stretcher-bearers. Hopefully, they would not bleed out before then.

The Northwest Battalion moved into position on the Arras-Lens Road, and then B Company advanced on Thélus behind the artillery fire. The nervous privates wavered, their eyes laced with fear. They were not alone. Under all the bluster and hard faces, everybody was scared. Okay, maybe not everyone. Sergeant Thompson shot into the fray with reckless abandon. "Give the fuckers hell, lads!" Bill yelled.

Lester's chest swelled with love, pride, and a double portion of rum. Head down and helmet tilted forward, he led his section in a diamond formation under the shrapnel-torn sky. Corporal Harper struggled to identify Bill through the acrid smoke and khaki mass stampeding toward Thélus. Fortunately, there was only one direction to go: forward. Anyone caught shirking his duty would be shot on sight.

An immense whirring and grinding came from behind them. It was a tank! Bullets sparked helplessly off the iron frame as it lurched over barbed wire and dipped into a crater. The steel monster was invincible. It was unstoppable. Until it wasn't.

A cloud of black smoke blew out of its back. The engine coughed. The treads spun aimlessly. The tank was stuck in the sticky slime. So much for the armoured support. The new war machine was nothing more than an expensive target for Fritz's gunners.

Corporal Harper hunkered down and checked his watch. The creeping barrage would move ahead one hundred yards every three minutes, but their officer was already motioning them onward. *His timing's off*, Lester realized. *He's nervous.*

The men hugging the storm of steel were the first to get hit. They had begun to advance when a drop short crashed on top of them. A gigantic spurt of earth sent the soldiers flying. Whirling splinters of metal sliced through their flesh. The wounded screamed their lives away.

We'll all be dead from our own fire if it's up to the lieutenant, thought Lester. He hesitated to order his men forward when they were supposed to wait. But should he disobey a direct command from his superior? That was insubordination. The officer could execute him on the spot.

A flash of khaki caught Lester's attention. What in the blazes? It was his cousin. He was racing across the open ground, Germans chasing him with bullets.

"What a mad bastard," a private whispered in admiration.

The corporal knew better. Sergeant Thompson was the most courageous man in their platoon, possibly even their company. His cousin was brave to the point of folly, but he was not mad. Like many veterans, Bill had become a fatalist. If a round had his name on it, there was nothing he could do, so why worry about it?

But maybe there was more to Sergeant Thompson's bravery than simple fatalism. Perhaps he had something to prove to his comrades who thought him yellow for wounding himself in 1916. Either way, Bill ran across the battlefield alone, and no one considered him a coward after that day.

Sergeant Thompson had almost reached their officer when the fated bullet struck him. Its force sent him sprawling backwards into the mud. But it would take more than a gunshot wound to stop the gruff NCO from his duty. Bill shrugged off the pain and laboured to his feet. Dragging his right leg behind him, he limped forward through the gluey slop. "We're getting up too soon, sir," he told their lieutenant.

The officer was wise enough to listen. With the trusty sergeant at his side, he steadied himself and led the platoon to Thélus precisely as the bombardment lifted. The infantrymen crashed the German lines effortlessly. The artillery's saturation bombing had done its job. The village was a pile of blackened ruins. Not a single wall remained standing. The German defences were steamrolled too. The barbed wire was shredded, the parapet a mangy pile of dirt. Everything was charred and burnt and scorched to ash.

The downside of the gunners' success? The total destruction meant that there were no houses to clear and the trenches were distorted beyond recognition. What was the point of memorizing the map of a village that no longer existed? The Canadians were forced to go in blind. They never knew if they would find a khaki uniform or a grey one around each bend.

Corporal Harper's section went down the narrow dog-toothed trenches in search of *soldaten* hiding in dugouts and cellars. They turned a corner and came face to face with a German sentry. A shot was fired, and a Canadian private crumpled to the ground. His comrade speared the sentry with his bayonet before the man could get off a second round. Reeling, the German clutched his chest. Blood gurgled on his lips. His eyes rolled back, and he tumbled down a set of stairs into the dugout.

The Canadians charged down after him. One broke down the door, and the next man pitched a bomb inside. *Thud*. A cloud of dust and smoke blew out of the entrance. The survivors ran for the exit, but the Canucks were waiting. Each German was met with a hail of bullets. Their bodies piled up in a bloody mess.

The Canadians looked at their wounded compatriot. The private lay headlong in the mud, rosy cheeks and a nickel-sized hole in his forehead. His vacant eyes were fixed on the heavens. They seemed to ask everything and nothing at once. No one tried to move him. They could already see the puddle of brains leaking out the back of his dislodged helmet.

Lester was furious. Losing men made his blood boil. His infantrymen felt the same. That was when things got ugly. One by one, his section painted the cellars and dugouts of Thélus a sticky crimson. The lucky Bavarians died from the blasts. The unlucky ones slowly bled to death. Anyone who tried to flee got shot or bayoneted. It was a lose-lose-lose scenario for Fritz. The Canadians didn't feel guilty. They were enraged and wanted revenge. There was a savage pleasure in their eyes.

Three white flares illuminated the sky when the assaulting troops met their objective. The Northwest Battalion had captured thirty-five German prisoners and taken only forty-four casualties.

Lester noticed a blood-soaked bandage wrapped around his cousin's leg. "You need to get to our first aid station immediately!" he said.

"Relax. It's only a scratch. The bullet went clean through."

"Stretcher-bearer!" Lester waved a medic over.

"Don't be a damn fool," Bill grumbled. "I'll be fine. Get on with the job now, Corporal. There's no time to waste. *Compreé?*"

Sergeant Thompson was correct. British intelligence had discovered that the German High Command demanded lightning-quick counter-attacks to recapture any lost ground before the invaders could dig in. The Nor'westers, therefore, started the second phase of the offensive immediately. Trading their rifles and bombs for picks and shovels, they waded through the mud and blood to consolidate their prize.

The soldiers worked tirelessly to reverse and rebuild the lines. They laid tangles of barbed wire, traced out the trenches, and carved new fire steps, stuffing the excess dirt into sandbags for the parapet. There was no time to rest. The Canadians were certain that the counterassault was imminent. Germans, they knew, always obeyed orders.

While Fritz shelled them constantly, the expected counterattack never came. Instead, the barrage petered out. The Germans were ceding the land. The Canucks had conquered the unconquerable Vimy Ridge.

This was the first major Canadian victory on the Western Front, but it came at a high cost. Out of the 37,000 CEF servicemen who participated in the four-day attack, 3,598 were killed in action and 7,000 were wounded. When combined with the 9,553 casualties at Vimy from snipers, artillery barrages, and raids leading up to the battle, over 20,000 Canadians were killed or injured in order to take the ridge. April 9, in particular, was the bloodiest day in the country's history, with 7,707 casualties.

Sergeant Thompson was one of those wounded. He was eventually sent to No. 14 General Hospital in Wimereux, where the doctors diagnosed him with a gunshot wound (GSW) to the right thigh and a severe concussion from shellfire. Bill would later be awarded the Military Medal for bravery in the field on April 9.

In the aftermath of Vimy, the dead outnumbered the living. Bodies littered the ridge, and the Canadians were left to collect the remains of their compatriots, sewing the corpses up in blankets and interning them in mass graves. Even in the midst of the horror of the battlefield, Lester's mind was back home with his wife. He could not wait to tell Mabel about the battalion's howling success.

In the Field
April 11th, 1917

Dear Wife:
Long before you receive this, you will have read in the papers about the Canadians at Vimy Ridge and Thélus. The latter place is the one I saw. We had good fortune in having no opposition at all. Fritz

beat it, except those caught in dugouts. There were lots of prisoners. I only lost one man in my section. Our artillery is very strong and certainly pounded Fritz's roads, towns, and trenches until they were a quagmire.

I saw two tanks! I did not get any souvenirs because I did not have an opportunity of getting into any dugouts. It is very cold at nights, and it is very hard to advance to any extent in this weather. I cannot tell you more. I only hope that I may be fortunate enough to come out safe in subsequent events. Bill Thompson got slightly wounded in the right leg. He did not go out at the time but, when his leg got sore later on, he went out and is in hospital now. He is lucky.

Say I am cold, and I have my greatcoat on. It rains, snows, blows, freezes, and shines all in the same day here. I mean that literally. The weather has been very rainy for over a week and, needless to say, it makes things intolerable in the trenches. Today is much better, and the sun has peeped out. I am quite well as usual, and it pleases me to know that you are as well.

I received your parcel containing cake and a pair of socks. The cake was very mouldy because the air had got at it. I ate some of it, and I was sick as a dog in a few hours. If I could get at you, I would spank you. No, I would not. I would kiss you! All the parcels, except this last one, have been in excellent condition. The only thing is that there ought to be two parcels a day, for I have a sweet tooth and a large stomach.

Girlie, I want to ask a great favour of you. Please write more letters. Tell me all about yourself, your thoughts, and your music. Letters that make me love you more and more. I think of you a million times a day, and all I get to cheer me is a few letters. It is hard work out here and very little pleasure. Lots of danger and very little compensation. Last of all, we have no guarantee that we will ever *see fair Canada again. So, love your Lester; he needs it. It is good for mind and body, and it cheers me when I'm downhearted. I want to see a happy, healthy, and well-dressed educated partner when I go sailing home. In return, I shall try and be a good husband. Wish me luck, Mabs.*

Good night, girlie,
811729 R.L. Harper
xxxx

CHAPTER FOUR

THE USUAL TRENCH WARFARE

NEUVILLE-SAINT-VAAST

France—April 12, 1917

WITH THE TRENCHES SECURE AND THE NEW LINE consolidated, the Nor'westers were relieved to the dugouts in their divisional reserve. Lester and Dan cleaned up, had a good snort of rum, and fixed their bed. Then they slept the sleep of the dead tired, still and silent like sentries with their necks slit from ear to ear.

Despite the success of the CEF, the Nivelle Offensive ultimately failed. When General Nivelle's wildly optimistic promise of 10,000 casualties for a speedy victory topped 187,000 in a fruitless assault, the *poilus* revolted. Twelve French divisions mutinied, and 27,000 soldiers deserted the ranks. Those who stayed at the front did so with extreme reluctance. Flocks of Frenchmen showed up at their posts drunk, weaponless, and bleating like lambs to the slaughter.

The Canadians were either uninformed or unconcerned. Spirits were high among the conquerors of Vimy Ridge. They say that the battle was a defining moment for Canada. It was a national coming of age. For the first time in history, men from coast to coast came together to fight and die for their country. Such nationalistic propaganda reached its zenith in the run-up to Canada's hundredth birthday in 1967, when Brigadier General Alexander Ross wrote of Vimy: "From dugouts, shell holes and trenches, men sprang into action, fell into military formations and advanced to the ridge—every division of the corps moved forward together. It was Canada from the Atlantic to the Pacific on parade. I thought then, and I think today, that in those few minutes I witnessed the birth of a nation."

The birth of a nation. That phrase was repeated until Vimy Ridge became ingrained in our collective consciousness as part of Canada's founding myth. Who was this Brigadier General Ross, the man who penned those fateful words? Originally a lawyer from Saskatchewan, Alexander Ross was commissioned as a second lieutenant at the start of the war and quickly climbed the ranks. As a lieutenant colonel, he joked that he commanded his battalion the way he ran his law firm in Regina. His battalion, of course, was the Nor'westers. Alexander Ross was Lester's CO.

In April 1917, then Lieutenant Colonel Ross did not imbue the Battle of Vimy Ridge with any nation-founding significance in his official report. His words were plain and simple. "Resistance offered by the enemy was noticeably feeble," he noted. "About 35 prisoners were taken, and the men displayed great coolness at all time under the enemy's shell fire. They carried out the attack in precisely the same manner as it had been worked out on the practice fields near Grand Servins."

Lieutenant Colonel Ross's 28th Battalion was fortunate. The CO had lost only 10 percent of his soldiers. That was the lightest casualty rate of any of the Canadian units on April 9.

With the deaths came promotions, and Lester's acting position of corporal was confirmed. After their muster parade, Corporal Harper hurried over to collect his mail. Putting a parcel under his arm, he flipped through the envelopes until he saw Jessie's name. Lester ripped the letter open. "It's a girl!" He beamed proudly. "Lillian Riches."

"Congratulations!" Dan exclaimed, slapping his chum on the back.

"Wait a minute. Riches?! Really? I like Lillian, but Riches? Is she kidding?" Lester should have known better. His wife did not joke.

The new father opened a jar of honey to celebrate. It was not the traditional cigar-smoking party, but it was an enjoyable way to end a rough trip. Corporal Harper hoped that they would now go for a long rest to clean up, recuperate, and replenish their forces. He wanted a real break, not one of those six-night stints in the reserves.

The officers constantly dangled the promise of an extended rest in front of the men. It may happen after the next trip up the line, they said. Perhaps. But tour after tour came and went with no hiatus. Despite the multitude of unkept promises, Lester thought they might actually get an extended rest after this battle. He was suffering from a bout of optimism. Like Field Marshal Haig before all of his doomed assaults, Corporal Harper figured that this time was different. Their battalion was nowhere near full strength. Surely they could not go over the top again without replacing the dead privates and appointing new officers to lead them? Personally, he could use a break. His feet were sore, waterlogged, and covered in blisters. They smarted with every step.

Unfortunately, the 28th Battalion received orders to report back to Vimy on April 14. There was no time to rest. They were needed immediately. Despite their exhaustion, the men were excited. There had to be a reason why they were being sent back to the front already. Had they finally broken the torturous stalemate with their victory at Vimy? Had they routed the Germans? Were they being sent forward to deliver the decisive blow?

Fat chance. Any hope of an imminent triumph withered away when the Nor'westers arrived at Vimy. B Company was tasked with rebuilding the road up the ridge. The soldiers had been called up not to advance but to dig in. Everyone felt deflated.

The road needed to be fixed ASAP because the countryside was impassable. The fields were covered with mud-filled craters, tangled wires, and broken-in trenches. Platoon No. 5 went to work clearing the debris and tamping crushed rocks into the crump holes. The job was monotonous, backbreaking, and extremely dangerous because of the severe and wild shelling from the Germans, who sought to isolate the troops at the front.

The Canadians pitied the horse and mule teams that carried their supplies up the road. They were emaciated, overburdened, and forced to brave the steady barrage of intercessionary fire too. Yet nothing deterred the bony animals. With broken hooves and bloody mouths, they obediently pulled their weighty loads through the tumult.

The pack beasts, unfortunately, were not rewarded for their loyalty. Many stopped eating after they were worked past exhaustion. Then they were shot, their carcasses left to rot in the fields by the hundreds. *Oh, c'est la guerre!* There were far more unburied men scattered across the fields of France.

B Company moved into the former German support trenches, where Corporal Harper marvelled at the deep and roomy concrete dugouts lined with logs. There were tiers of bunks, comfortable furniture, and even a spacious bathroom. With proper ventilation, electric lighting, and drainage, the *soldaten* had all the modern conveniences of the early twentieth century.

"Unbelievable," Lester commented. "Fritz was certainly well fixed up and didn't expect to be ousted."

"You're right, Corporal. He was ready for the long haul," one private replied, leaning into a plush armchair. "This I could get used to. Here we are, nestled twenty feet underground in the lap of luxury. No wonder Fritzie refused to leave. I'd fight to the death for this chair too. Can we while away the rest of the war down here?"

The enemy's permanent dugouts at the front were a startling contrast to the Canadian accommodations, which were shabby even in the rear. This brought about an uneasy realization: if the Germans were this well prepared along the entire Hindenburg Line, this was going to be a long and desperate war.

On April 16, B Company marched into a forward position under Lieutenant Reginald Blackburn. For the next two wet and miserable nights, they dug a new support trench under the glow of Very Lights (flares that were *very* bright) and the harassment of three-inch shells packed with deadly shrapnel. The Germans may have ceded the ridge, but they were making the Canucks pay with their lives. There was only one benefit to the wretched work. They were assisting the 31st Battalion from Alberta.

"You're lucky you missed winter," Lester told Harold between shovelfuls of dirt. "My toes nearly went black with frostbite."

"Welcome to France," his cousin replied. "We have three seasons here. There's the cold. There's the damned cold. And then there's August. Plus, it didn't sound half bad this year. At least not for Bud with his lady friend keeping him warm."

Hugh shot Harold a dirty look. Bud did not want to have this conversation because he found Lester to be a judgmental prude. "I wish I could spiel a line or two in *français* like you," he admitted. "It sure would help with the French Janes. Not all of us have lovely and nicely dressed wives waiting at home, you know."

"Don't you even think about Mabel." The married man waved his spade at his friend. "As for you, cousin, you need to toughen up. We're pioneers."

"Toughen up? I was in the hospital for sixteen days!"

"Sixteen days in Blighty for a sore foot and a sniffle," Hugh mocked. "Such a softie. You call yourself a pioneer? What kind of pioneer has a typewriter?"

Lester wiped his nose and faked a limp. Bud sat down and pretended to type. They both burst out laughing, cracking the veneer of mud plastered to their cheeks. It felt like old times at Camp Witley, except with more shells. Their nights in Vimy were full of death and drudgery and utter nonsense. The best and worst of the war mingled together in these moments, the bodies of friends and foes tossed into the same mass grave.

CAMP WITLEY

England—October 26, 1916

EVEN DURING TRAINING, THE MEN LOVED TO TEASE HAROLD. The whiney farmer complained non-stop.

"The route marches are too long."

"The drills are too hard."

There was a reason he was single.

Bud had the opposite problem. A handsome head taller than Harold, he was never alone. The ladies loved him—even those who should have known better.

One Saturday afternoon when they had weekend passes, Lester, Bud, and their pals took the bus to Guildford. While the Canadians played pool and drank tea at the YMCA, the American snuck off with an English Jane. Unfortunately, discretion was not part of Bud's skill set. Two plainclothes officers caught him in a compromising position with the lady. Even though Hugh was a former cop, they dragged him back to Camp Witley and informed the battalion's CO and DCO that the woman in question was married. Her husband was a British soldier at the front.

"Do you know what the major told me after the police officers left?" Bud asked when he regaled the lads with the story.

Lester groaned. He knew that the answer was going to be

inappropriate. What normally besmirched a man's reputation only bolstered Hugh's legendary status among the boys.

"He told me to go farther out in the country to fuck her next time!"

That was Bud. He was funny, charming, and extremely loveable. You just had to keep him away from your wife.

Lester couldn't imagine life in the military without his friends. They made the unbearable bearable. Hugh, Ernest, and Harold helped him cope with the intense loneliness that he felt in England. Now that Lester was an ocean away from his family, the homesick farm boy missed his wife, his brothers, and even his unborn child. Every time he marched past a comfortable cottage in Surrey, he longed to be home.

The air was heavy that autumn morning when Lieutenant Colonel Belcher addressed the battalion. The news had already spread through the ranks, so everybody knew what was coming. Somehow, that made it worse.

"The 138th Battalion is hereby officially disbanded." The moustachioed CO's voice cracked when he read the order. His servicemen would be absorbed into other regiments.

Lester felt betrayed. This was his battalion. They were a unique band of brothers from the North. He could recognize every man. He had already lost Frank McAleer, who was found to be medically unfit. Now the rest of his pals were being scattered across the CEF. It wasn't fair. They were all being sent to strange units. Even family members were being split up. Abraham Abbott was off to Belgium, while his brother William was going to France. No one had a choice. They went where they were told.

The infantrymen all had filmy eyes when the band marched through their lines playing its final piece together. Even the bandmaster nearly broke into tears because his musicians were being separated too. "It was very hard to see the boys part," Lester admitted. The hearts fell out of the men, and they reacted exactly as he expected—the whole battalion got rip-roaring drunk together one last time.

THÉLUS
France—April 21, 1917

EXPLODING PUFFBALLS OF FLAK CHASED A GERMAN SPYCRAFT across the sky. The anti-aircraft guns were always a plane-length behind. What could you expect from nascent weaponry? The Wright brothers' first powered flight had taken place a mere thirteen years earlier, and only a psychopath would have tried to shoot down an airplane before the war. Unable to calculate the range, height, or speed of their targets, the gunners' guess-and-test method rarely brought down an experienced pilot.

Corporal Harper was not sure which of the enemy aircraft he hated more. Was it the high-flying spy planes that tracked and corrected Fritz's bombardments with deadly accuracy? Or the fighter planes that raked the troops with front-mounted machine guns? At least the dogfights were a delight to watch, Lester thought, especially when the Allies won.

It was a perfect day for airplanes. The sun was out with little cloud cover. Lester cupped his hands around his eyes and looked up at the sky. Circling, dodging, and weaving, biplanes jockeyed for position. An Albatros D.III marked with the dreaded black cross pursued a British Sopwith Pup. The docile Pup tried to dive and outmanoeuvre the Albatros, but it was no match for the best fighting scout on the Western Front. Armed with twin Maschinengewehr 08s, the German hunter lined up the target-shaped roundels of the Royal Flying Corps (RFC) in his sights. Gunfire. A hit. Spinning uncontrollably, the British plane plunged downward. Smoke spiralled out of the Pup's tail, and the aircraft crashed in a fiery wreck near the battalion headquarters at Thélus Cave. "Another victory for Fritz," Lester begrudgingly admitted. "Rotten luck."

The Germans had more than luck, though. They had better planes and better pilots. In the sky, unlike on land, the Central Powers were the undisputed masters. Lester noticed that one ace, in particular, gave their airmen a great deal of trouble. That man was none other than Lieutenant Manfred von Richthofen, who painted his Albatros scarlet in 1916 and became better known as the Red Baron. With his Flying Circus, the Germans shot down 245 aircraft in April alone, while losing only 66 planes. "Bloody April," the RFC designated it. The Allies lost a third of their air force in France that month, but they couldn't let the prying reconnaissance planes have free rein to photograph their operations, so they kept sending fresh flyers up to the skies, even though the life expectancy of a new pilot was a paltry eleven days.

"Doesn't it seem odd to hear the *tit-tit-tit* of the machine gun way up in the air, Corporal?" a private asked.

Lester grunted.

"Corporal?"

Lester was not listening. Squinting into the sun, he focused on Fritz's fighters because the German pilots enjoyed stalking the infantrymen. The Canadians were trench rats hunted by birds of prey. The lead plane dropped lower. The enemy pilot was coming down fast.

"Flat!" the corporal yelled and threw himself to the bottom of the trench as the swooping aircraft dusted their lines.

"My hand!" the private whimpered. He tried to move his fingers, but they hung limp and flaccid.

"What a lucky shot," one of his comrades exclaimed. "I'd kill for your injury."

"I'll never get out," the injured private solemnly declared. "I feel my time has come."

Some of the men believed in supernatural occurrences, but others found such prophetic statements infuriating.

"Quit your blithering," another colleague grumbled. "You're off to Blighty for sure."

The men helped their friend bandage up his wound, pleased that he got a cushy one and sent him off to the dressing station. Like many of them, the serviceman had been out for too long and needed a break. A rest-cure was the best remedy.

The soldiers were in a cheery mood when they marched out of the line. Then they saw an arm dangling over the communication trench. The hand was bandaged. Oh, churches! The wounded private had been right. He'd had a premonition of his own death. On the way back to the dressing station, a shell had blown him out of the trenches and sliced his stomach wide open. The lad was a rag doll with his stuffing strewn about. The Nor'westers stumbled into their rest camp short another infantryman.

At their camp in Aux Reitz, the 28th Battalion began an intense training regime, and Corporal Harper realized that there would be no break. They were already preparing for the next offensive. After the private's grisly death, Lester wanted to make sure that his own affairs were in order. He updated his next-of-kin information, wrote to his insurance company, and looked into getting an extra allowance for Lillian from the Canadian Patriotic Fund. The $22 million social fund urged Canadians to fight or pay. He was fighting, so he hoped they would pay to support his family while he was abroad.

His chores done, Corporal Harper sat down next to the poor soldier's grave. The sun was shining, the band was playing, and the artillery was singing its deadly tune. As the sharp blasts of the heavies punctuated the soft music of the band, Lester took out *la crayon* and started to write. For those few moments, the war melted away and he lost himself in thoughts of his wife.

France
April 25th, 1917

Dear Sweetheart:
I received Jessie's letter of March 18th with your note appended. Congratulations. I was much relieved to know that you had an easy time, and I hope you are well and happy now that the babe is not cranky. I like Lillian for a name but not the Riches part.

We have completed another trip. I am still jake, but we had a hard trip in a way. A lot of walking and bad weather. I had bad feet and they are not well yet: blisters and sore heels. Of course, we have not the trenches and dugouts to sleep in, only improvised coverings for the time being. I have been in some of Fritz's good dugouts; he was certainly well fixed up and did not expect to be ousted.

The weather has been good the last few days. Fritz made us shift camp once, but nevertheless we have had a restful time. I spent all my money on eats, mostly canned goods and sweet biscuits. That's all we can get at Y.M.C.A.s and canteens anyway. This morning I bought three tins of jam, one can of pears, one of pineapple, and some biscuits. Total ten francs. I carry this in the line and eat it as required. Last time our rations failed to arrive one day, so we ate bully and hardtack and little of that. When we get out and get paid, you can imagine how we enjoy some canned stuff. I received your parcel with the honey. Needless to say, I have since filled the jar with air and extracted the honey. Encore, please!

Till We Meet Again

We see quite a number of aerial fights. Fritz has one plane that gives our airmen a great deal of trouble. Frequently our men come down first. On fine days, we take quite an interest in watching the dozens of aeroplanes, which we see continually overhead. There are air scraps sometimes and a lot of shelling by anti-aircraft guns. The other day, one of Fritz's planes turned his machine guns on us in the trenches, but we got down low.

The great asset, which is keeping us, is our artillery. Our guns are making a hell of a noise just now. Fritz counterattacks sometimes and, believe me, our artillery gives him something tough to eat. I do not like to see casualties, but I suppose they are inevitable. I hope I am lucky enough to escape his shells. He scatters them all around behind our lines, villages, and all. It is inhuman and barbarous.

I long to be back with you, but there seems to be no end. At present, I can see no early conclusion of the war. I hope something radical happens, which will end it. I dread the thought of a fight to the finish; the wastage would be awful. Fritz is making a very large offensive, and there will be a great deal of hard fighting in the next two months. We dream dreams of home and all the comforts attached, but they are only dreams for I fear, as Ambassador Gerard said, this is going to be a long and desperate war. Don't worry if I get wounded, but rejoice for then you know I am safe.

About the insurance: I should have fixed it up before I left Canada for it is harder to do legal work here. However, I'll communicate with the company. I suppose, if you could get hold of me, you would pull my hair out—or what is left of it anyway!

My hand is a bit shaky for I have been playing catch. But you can figure it out, and I think that's the main thing. We are liable to have to go in anytime. I close with kisses for you and wee little second-hand ones for Lillian. Well, here's hoping I am lucky.

Your soldier boy,
Cpl. R. Lester Harper
xxxx

B COMPANY RETURNED TO VIMY RIDGE AS PART OF A WORK CREW on loan to the engineers. Platoon No. 5 was tasked with digging narrow ditches to bury their telephone wires. The cables were a favourite target of the Germans, so they had to be hidden six feet underground for protection.

Lester and his section headed out to work under a flickering sky. Heavy German shelling—or "the usual trench warfare," as their CO described it—lit up the night. As the men searched for the designated spot to dig, the private in front of Lester yelped in pain.

"Ouch! What did you do that for, Corporal?"

"What are you squawking about?" Lester whispered angrily.

"You socked me!"

"No, I didn't," he said in his trench voice.

The private rubbed his stinging shoulder. It was oozing blood. "I'm hit!" he squealed. A piece of steel shrapnel had sliced through his back, just below his shoulder blade, and come out his chest.

Corporal Harper took out a field dressing and bandaged up the youngster. "There you go," he said. "It's just a scratch. Come on, I'll walk you back to our dressing station myself."

"Excellent timing," the corporal remarked when they arrived at the first aid station thirty minutes later. There was no rush on, so he knew his soldier would get top-notch care. While bleeding to death in no man's land was a horrid way to die, bleeding to death waiting in line at the hospital tent seemed worse.

The MO examined the injury.

"Is it a blighty case, Doc?"

"Looks so."

"Congratulations!" Lester exclaimed. Few things merited celebration more than a cushy wound. "You're a darn lucky devil," he declared with a hint of jealousy in his voice.

———

On June 1, the truncated Northwest Battalion marched to the French mining town of Hallicourt, where they finally received their extended rest. If only the respite would last for the duration of the war, Corporal Harper wished. Every day, he ate bacon and eggs for breakfast before their morning drills. Section drills, platoon drills, musketry drills, bayonet drills, box respirator drills, and so on. It was the same dope as before. After lunch, the infantrymen were free to do as they pleased. Lester loafed around the meadow sunning himself or bummed around the canteen with Dan, who had recently been promoted to lance corporal. In the evenings, the men paid two pence and a half penny per person to attend a moving picture show or a concert party in the large huts erected several miles behind the lines. Each division drew the best actors, singers, and musicians from their ranks to entertain the troops, so there was always a performance to watch. The theatrical revues were Lester's favourite, especially the drag performances that poked fun at the "occifers."

"What's the difference between a Zeppelin and a man?" asked tonight's low-brow comedian. "A Zeppelin goes through the air to kill babies while a man goes through the hair to make babies!"

With an abundance of free time, Lester caught up on his correspondence. His darling wife had written him faithfully every week since he left Sarcee. He treasured her letters, re-reading them umpteen times until he had memorized them. The devoted husband even felt guilty when he had to burn her missives to make room in his pack for food.

Regrettably, Mabel's packages came less frequently. Lester was collecting his mail, packetless again, when he had an idea. He asked if there was any mail for his wounded private. The postman handed him a stack of envelopes and two bulky boxes. While the thoughtful corporal forwarded the letters to the private's convalescent home in London, he kept the goodies for the boys. There was nothing better than a casualty parcel.

Lester sucked on a jelly while he read through his letters. Wesley was back in France, now as a corporal. Although the note was censored, Lester surmised that his brother was near Ypres. That was worrying. Even from thirty miles away, he could hear Fritz's enthusiastic gunners pounding away at the Canadians there. The mammoth shells caused such a racket that the men dubbed them the *Wipers Express*, after the noisy trains in London. Wes was certainly getting hell.

More bad news: Harold was missing in action! His cousin had gone over the top less than three weeks after their visit at Vimy. The Battle of Fresnoy was a mess. The CEF took 1,259 casualties to capture the village, and some of the wounded were not found for forty-eight hours. To make matters worse, the British Tommies who relieved them relinquished Fresnoy to the Germans in the first serious counterattack.

Harold's unit in the 31st Battalion got split up trying to flank a German machine gun. Last his comrades saw, he'd blundered into an enemy trench. The mopping-up party should have found him, but they'd strayed off track. Somewhere along the path to victory, Harold was lost in the chaos. Small and scrawny, he could have fallen into a patch of watery mud and disappeared forever. Lester had tread over many poor fellows on the very ground where Harold went MIA. Now he worried that his cousin lay among the forgotten corpses.

Lester needed to forget about the bombs targeting Wes. He needed to stop imagining Harold's last breaths bubbling to the surface of a swampy crater. He needed a distraction. All the troops did. Boredom was dangerous, and the officers knew it. Rest gave the infantrymen time to dwell on the madness of the war. High command's solution? Weekend sports competitions. The games occupied and entertained the men as well as relieved stress and kept them in shape. Shooting, boxing, sprinting. There was a host of events, but the main attraction was the baseball tournament.

Soldiers were tossing the ball around in the midst of a war zone. It was surreal. They were focused on hits and outs, not kills and casualties. No one cared that half of their team may soon be dead, buried under this same dirt. For those afternoons, their lives felt normal. Lester could have been back on the diamond in Saskatoon Creek—except that it was Sunday, and there were no baseball games on the sabbath at home. *C'est la guerre*, Corporal Harper told himself when he felt guilty about playing sports on the Lord's Day. At least baseball was better than a lot of queer things that the men did on Sundays in France, like going to an *estaminet* or a brothel. If there were a hierarchy of sins, surely baseball was preferable to drinking and whoring.

Any semblance of military hierarchy was cast aside at the baseball games. The level of informality reached a new low, even for the undisciplined Canadians. "He's a dud," the privates jeered a sergeant pitcher. Apparently, the worst insult they could muster was to call their superior a malfunctioning shell.

It got worse when a brigadier general stepped up to the plate. He was the highest-ranking officer in the tournament, the commander of four thousand servicemen. He was their boss's boss's boss. Did the soldiers smarten up in front of him like they would on the parade ground? Not for a second. The spectators taunted him. "He swings like a gate!" they heckled.

The British onlookers were mortified. If these were English soldiers, they probably would all have been court-martialled.

Crowds gathered to watch the 28th Battalion trounce the 5th Machine Gun Company in the first round of the tournament. Then they beat the

27th Battalion in the semi-final too. Although the Nor'westers failed to advance further, the tournament day on July 1 was a dandy. It was a hot and sunny Dominion Day—a lovely day for baseball. The engineers constructed a proper diamond in Tincques, complete with a grandstand and hand-operated scoreboard. The massed bands held a pre-game military tattoo. Everybody came out to watch. The recently promoted Lieutenant General Currie was there. Prime Minister Borden and the Duke of Connaught showed up too.

Who won the corps baseball championship? The 7th Canadian Engineer Battalion beat the 1st Divisional Ammunition Column in a low-scoring affair. No Canadian who was there ever forgot that day. Long before hockey became popular, baseball was Canada's unofficial national sport. Even Lester Pearson, the future prime minister, ranked hitting a homerun in the tournament as one of his most memorable accomplishments of the war.

The ranks of the Northwest Battalion were replenished when they were on rest. Corporal Harper was thrilled to get replacements. He was a section leader who had lost almost half of his section. Lester looked the draftees over. They had frisky can-do faces and spotless uniforms with creases still intact, just like he had at Bouvigny Huts. He put on his best Sergeant Thompson impersonation. "Aren't you as keen as mustard?" the corporal said, smirking. "Let's see how long that lasts."

The veterans treated the newbies with trained indifference. The old-timers did not scorn them on purpose. They were just seasoned soldiers who knew better than to get close to the rookies until they survived their first show. Raw recruits were usually the first to click it, and nobody wanted to get attached to a man who was about to go west.

After a month of rest, relaxation, and baseball, morale was high when the Northwest Battalion stood for inspection in front of Major

Till We Meet Again

General Harry Burstall, the general officer commanding (GOC) the 2nd Canadian Division. The "high mucky muck," as Lester termed all of their senior commanders, was most impressed with the troops. He complimented Lieutenant Colonel Ross on his soldiers' appearance, discipline, and drill. Then he sent them back into the shit.

CHAPTER FIVE

AN EXTREMELY HAZARDOUS BUSINESS

MAROC
France—July 7, 1917

THE 28TH BATTALION MOVED INTO THE BRIGADE RESERVE TO clean, repair, and strengthen the ramshackle cellars that the Canadian Corps used as billets. The underground bunkers needed a serious scrubbing. They were damp and stuffy and smelled of soot.

Lester and his friends spent their time in the quarters chatting. Stripped to the waist, they chewed the rag while each man ran his thumbnail up the seams of his uniform in search of pesky cooties.

"What a beauty!" Dan said, holding up a monster crumb.

"Darn right. He must be a sergeant," Lester replied, "'cause he has three stripes."

Dan squished the louse onto a piece of paper.

"What did you do that for?" Lester whined. "That's for my letters to Mabel."

"Sorry," Dan apologized. "But at least your wife can feel like she's here with you now."

Lester laughed. Taking out his pen, he drew a circle around the squished bug. "A louse," he wrote next to it. "There, so she knows what it is."

Corporal Harper climbed the broken stairs of the cellar. Heaving open the door, he caught a whiff of the fragrant country breeze. The scent hit him hard, a rifle butt to the nose, evoking nostalgia for Pouce Coupe Prairie. How his face used to wrinkle in disgust at the stench of fresh manure! Now the smell of shit made him homesick.

Lester stood among the piles of cracked bricks and chunks of mortar that had once made up a grand house. Thousands of pounds of masonry, countless hours of labour, the generational wealth of a family—it was all reduced to rubble in the flash of a shell.

The corporal roamed the orchards, where the peach trees were heavy with fruit. If Mabel were here, Lester thought, we would lie in the grass for hours. But Mabel was not there and the peaches were not ripe, so he headed into the village.

Maroc was picturesque, quaint, and entirely deserted. It was perfect. Corporal Harper was not looking for people—he was scavenging for food. The hungry NCO foraged through the overgrown weeds in abandoned gardens until he found a bush brimming with juicy blackberries. Lester stripped it clean.

"Blackberries on the far side of town," he told Dan upon returning to their billet.

"And strawberries hiding among the debris."

"Want to play duck on a rock with us?" a colleague asked.

"Sure." Lester picked up a brick from a ruined house and set it on a stump while the rest of the men collected rocks to knock it off. "Get your ducks ready, boys. I'll guard first," he said. "Let's see who has the arm to be the battalion's next pitcher."

After the game, he and Dan shared a casualty parcel.

"Salmon, cake, canned cherries, and maple sugar butter?" Lester remarked. "Swell dope! His wife must really love him."

"Loved," Dan corrected.

Casualty parcels were one of the rare perks of the slew of KIAs and blighties. Yet they belied a bleak reality that the survivors numbed themselves to every day. The infantrymen tried to forget the memories of their colleagues dying around them. They refused to think about their deceased friends' grieving widows and fatherless children at home.

The other perk of all the deaths? New positions became vacant. Dan was the first to opt for a safety-first job. He was leaving the battalion for a temporary position in the rear. Lester did not grudge his chum for wanting to live long enough to return to his farm, marry Myrtle, and have baby Fees. Dan had seen the real thing time and time again. The closeness to eternity had changed him, and not for the better. Gone was his chipper face and boyish charm. Now he was gaunt, hard, and sullen. Even his optimistic spirit had started to waver.

Corporal Harper didn't need to look in a mirror to know that he had changed too. Maybe Dan's right, Lester conceded. All wars ended, and he needed to consider his family as well. He was no good to them dead.

"Cigar?" his side-kicker offered.

Lester was not a smoker, but a cigar was like rum: it didn't count. He bit off the tip and pulled away on the dark tobacco with gusto.

The full moon hung over the horizon, a giant star shell in the sky, when the men headed back to their cellars. What a spectacular evening, Corporal Harper mused as he sauntered by a Frenchwoman crying on the stairs of an *estaminet*. Lester knew that she was intimately involved with one of his friends, so he stopped to help.

"Excuse me," he said in French. "What's the matter?"

"It's my husband," she sobbed. "He's sick in a military hospital, and I can't write."

"You're married?!" Lester exclaimed and stormed off.

How could he feel sorry for that unfaithful woman? Cheating on her soldier husband was an unpardonable offence. As for his friend (who will remain nameless), his actions were not befitting a Canadian serviceman on active duty.

Corporal Harper was still fuming when the Northwest Battalion marched up the line to Laurent. A whining shell soared overhead, reminding him that he had more immediate concerns. "Sounds like Fritz is putting 'em close tonight," their scout said. "We better double along now."

B Company was halfway to the front when a heavy bombardment of trench mortars, or toch emmas, rocked the lines. Pandemonium ensued. The men rushed toward the clamour of gunfire and grenades. These were their trenches. They would defend them to the death.

The soldiers arrived at the parapet to find the 26th Battalion firing wildly into the dark. A German raid, Lester figured. His section had missed it by minutes.

With the dugouts blown-in, Corporal Harper crawled into a shallow funk hole. He was fast asleep when the ripping sound of an approaching shell jerked him awake. Within seconds, Lester knew that he was done for. The high-explosive ordnance was barrelling right toward him. He was trapped. This shell had his name on it, and there was nothing that he could do. What a lousy place to die.

Lester thought of Mabel. He would never hold his wife again. He thought of Lillian. He would never even meet his daughter. The earth quaked, and an avalanche of dirt collapsed on his head. Every muscle in his body tensed. The veteran anticipated the tremendous roar, the rush of burning metal, the excruciating pain. But there was only darkness.

Lester scrambled onto the sagging duckboards. Wiping off his face, he could scarcely believe his eyes. A massive shell was lodged in the mud a few feet away from him, and it was still smoking. The corporal shook his head in disbelief. A dud.

"Christ almighty! That's a lucky stroke," a comrade declared.

A lucky stroke indeed.

After two more nights of uncomfortable sleep, the men of Platoon No. 5 packed up their gear. The Nor'westers had been ordered out of the

Laurent sector early. The mood was jubilant. No one asked why they were leaving. Who wants to know? Everyone was just happy to be out of the line sooner than expected.

It was a glorious summer evening with a balmy breeze. That was when their sentry started screaming. He was the first to spot the giant cloud creeping across no man's land. "Oh God! Gas! It's a gas attack!"

The Canadians snatched their masks as canisters whistled overhead. The Germans were lobbing gas shells at them too. The foul fog rolled over the parapet and sank to the bottom of their trenches. There was smoke and bedlam, but the troops tuned out the clanging alarms and listened for gunfire. The Germans often used gas as a smokescreen for an assault, and the Canadians had to be ready to fight off the invaders.

The soldiers took their positions. Their heads throbbed. Their lungs burned. They struggled to see through the fogged-up lenses of their goggly-eyed buggers with the tit. Were their box respirators working or were they suffocating them? The Canucks fought the urge to rip off the nasty rubber things.

What was the poison du jour? Was it chlorine? Veterans looked to see if there was a greenish tinge. Phosgene? They hoped not. That gas was trouble. You couldn't see it. You couldn't smell it. But it was eight times stronger than chlorine, so a couple of deep whiffs of a concentrated dose and you would be coughing up pints of yellow liquid until you suffered an excruciating death. Mustard gas? That was the worst. It lingered on the battlefield for days. What started as a tickle in your throat led to uncontrollable vomiting, blindness, and of course, death. Even with a box respirator, the gas would soak through your uniform and leave grotesque mustard-coloured blisters in your armpits and groin. While most of the men were not overly concerned about the appearance of their armpits, they were partial to their groins and preferred to keep them deformation-free.

Whichever gas it was, no one wanted to stay to find out. B Company was ordered to out-go, so they hurried after their scout. When the servicemen reached the support lines, they wrenched their masks off and checked the buttons on their tunics. Whew, the brass had not turned green. They hadn't been exposed to anything life-threatening for too long.

How different the real experience was from training. "The proper response to a gas attack is to calmly jog back five hundred feet to safety," the instructor at their base had stated. What a joke. Poison gas was a serious threat, but their training officers had known nothing about the reality of chemical warfare. Lester hoped that was starting to change because his old battalion commander, Lieutenant Colonel Belcher, was now in charge of a gas school in France.

The Northwest Battalion left Laurent down fifteen soldiers—all of whom were, as the CO noted, "slightly gassed." After multiple disastrous reliefs, the Canadians went into the next handover of the trenches prepared. Their gas specialists projected a dozen tons of poison into no man's land in the run-up to the exchange. If the Germans were going to ambush them this time, they would have to fight their way through toxic clouds first.

Shoving on after such a brief stint in Laurent was most unusual. Now that they were on the road, all the privates wanted to know what their next destination was.

"Where are we headed, Corporal?" one politely inquired.

While "None of your fucking business" was the typical retort, Corporal Harper was not the typical NCO. That's not to say that he lavished his men with praise or showed them much affection. Lester only ever referred to them as the same generic private. Yet he was civil and courteous, and unbelievably, he did not swear at them.

Corporal Harper nodded toward a winding trail of smoke rising from the ruins of a city. "Lens," he answered with a grunt.

Lens was a place that only a coal digger could love. Full of warehouses, tailing ponds, and slag heaps, it was hideous even before the war. But the Lensois were not troubled by the smokestacks pumping fumes into their air or the heavy metals seeping into their groundwater. The pollution was worth the price. The upper class could afford country homes with orchards and creeks and boundless blue sky thanks to the city's mines.

The Germans did not care about environmental degradation either. When they conquered the industrial centre, they made the ugly city uglier. The *soldaten* reduced the buildings to rubble and decorated the streets with the corpses of thousands of British Tommies.

A staunch believer in attrition, Field Marshal Haig did what you would expect him to do: he ordered the Canadians to launch a frontal assault on Lens in order to divert the kaiser's army away from Passchendaele, where Haig wanted to launch an even larger frontal assault. But the new commander of the Canadian Corps, Lieutenant General Arthur Currie, had a better idea. Having replaced Lieutenant General Byng, who was promoted to commander of the British Third Army in recognition of his success at Vimy, "Guts and Gaiters" (as Currie was nicknamed) was the first Canadian to hold the position. Perhaps the country's finest soldier, Currie proposed a cunning ploy as an alternative to his superior's suicidal plan. If their goal was to kill Boche, he argued, they should target Hill 70 instead. Once his corps took the high ground north of the city, the Germans would be forced to counterattack, and the Canadians could slaughter the enemy from above. Although it was not his usual hard-charging style, Field Marshal Haig approved the stratagem. Boche-killing was his passion.

Stationed in the brigade reserve at Bully-Grenay, Corporal Harper heard the earth-shattering roar of two hundred cannons pound Lens at 4.25 a.m. on August 15. The engineers added to the cacophony by propelling drums of blazing oil into the front. Cloaked in the black clouds, five thousand CEF soldiers surged up Hill 70. The speed of the attack caught the Germans by surprise, and the infantry captured many of their first-line objectives within twenty minutes.

Lieutenant General Currie used the German doctrine on counterattacks to his advantage. He masterminded the perfect death trap on Hill 70. Anticipating a lightning-quick counteroffensive, the commander sent 250 machine-gun teams forward in the initial charge. At 8.15 a.m., the first counterstrike commenced just as he'd predicted. The *soldaten* were forced to climb the narrow slope, and the Canadian Vickers and Lewis guns eradicated them. *Feldgrau* uniforms soon covered the hillside. It was a beautifully choreographed massacre. "Hill 70 Runs Red Today with Blood of German Army," proclaimed the *Calgary Daily Herald*.

Over the next three days, the Germans launched twenty more counterassaults. The troops fought in vicious hand-to-hand combat in clouds of mustard gas while shells churned the dead and dying into a bloody pulp. Warmed by the midsummer sun, the air was heavy with the sweet aroma of death. Hardened veterans turned sick at the sight and smell of the baked mush of men. The Battle of Hill 70 was a literal meat grinder. Even Hieronymus Bosch, with his paintings of grotesque torture and houses crafted out of human flesh, would have struggled to imagine a more terrifying hellscape.

Having taken the high ground on Hill 70, the Canadian Corps' guns began firing at the enemy positions in Lens, but the Germans refused to relinquish the city. Frustrated with only conquering a hill, Lieutenant General Currie ordered a probing attack on the city itself, which was where the 28th Battalion joined the melee. The Nor'westers were detailed to be in close support of the 27th and 29th Battalions, which were leading the assault. Zero hour was set for 4.35 a.m. on August 21.

The Germans struck first. Ten minutes before zero hour, they launched a heavy barrage and then charged into the Canadian lines with their rifles and bayonets. The *soldaten* drove the 29th Battalion back, and the Nor'westers were sent into the action to reinforce them.

Platoon No. 5 got stuck in fierce fighting in Nuns Alley under the direction of Lieutenant Davies. Outnumbered and pinned down, they watched their stockpile of ammunition and grenades quickly dwindle. Yet the platoon refused to abandon a single soldier. On multiple occasions, Sergeants William Eldridge and Robert Richards climbed out from the safety of their own trench to rescue a wounded private caught in hostile territory while the platoon's best sniper gave them cover. The expert rifleman topped off twenty-five *soldaten* before he was killed.

B Company was divided, the platoons isolated and cut off. Trying to seize the advantage, the Germans rushed their defensive position. But Lieutenant Davies stood his ground. He gathered together their remaining Millses and led his troops into the mayhem. Platoon No. 5 drove the enemy back with a shower of bombs, which let B Company fall back and reunite. The Northwest Battalion took 160 casualties on August 21—including Lieutenant Davies, who was shot in the ear.

The Canadians pressed on to the outskirts of Lens, where they met stiff resistance in the form of urban warfare. "The most frightful episode of warfare on the Western Front," a British correspondent labelled the siege. This was where Lieutenant General Currie made an uncharacteristic mistake. The brilliant tactician got greedy. Wanting to capture the city, he allowed his subordinates to engage in frontal assaults against Lens. Their advances were all repulsed, and the Canadian Corps took three thousand additional casualties as a result of the commander's rash decision.

What should the lieutenant general have done instead? According to military historians with the unfair advantage of hindsight, he should have stuck with his original plan. Their mission was to kill Boche, and they had taken the high ground. The Canadians could have bombarded the city at will from atop Hill 70.

On August 25, Lieutenant General Currie ended the mission. Field Marshal Haig was impressed with his storm troops. This was their most successful Boche-killing week ever. The Canucks had knocked out twenty-five thousand Germans and forced two reserve divisions to reroute from Passchendaele to Lens. "One of the finest minor operations of the war," the BEF commander declared.

When the ashes and dust of the dead finally settled, the Canadians looked down on German-occupied Lens from Hill 70. The minor operation was their hardest show to date. The ten-day diversion cost the CEF 8,677 men.

Where was Corporal Harper when his boys' bayonets were belly-deep in German peasant? He was in his own battle, fighting off Janes in small towns across France. This was the first scrap that Lester had missed, and it was a doozy. But he didn't avoid the Battle of Hill 70 on purpose. When the Northwest Battalion had stopped at the miner's village north of Loos before the fight, he was charged with a special mission.

Corporal Harper was assigned to escort duty. An officer in their battalion, Lieutenant Sinclair, was caught trying to desert. Lester was sent to collect him from prison and bring him back to face his court martial.

"Be discreet," Bill told him. "This is an ugly business and a hell of a disgrace. It gives our battalion a bad rep, you know. If it were up to some of the veterans, they would skip the bloody court martial and deliver justice themselves. That would teach the yellow bastard a lesson and discourage other cowards from shirking their responsibilities too."

As the Battle of Hill 70 raged on, Corporal Harper legged it to the closest train depot. The railyard was bustling. Rolling stock rushed into the railhead, and privates hurried to unload boxes of ammunition onto waiting lorries to supply the fighting troops. Little else remained in the slummy town. The storefronts were closed, their windows darkened.

The only businesses open were the two favourite haunts of soldiers: *estaminets* and brothels. "What a sight for sore eyes," Lester remarked. Any meal was better than bully beef, any bed better than a funk hole.

Corporal Harper longed to travel to Paris, where he could have conversations with sophisticated Parisians, but he was stuck in a stubbornly provincial town surrounded by peasants, so he ordered his favourite greasy "*oofs et freets*" at an *estaminet* and then walked the streets. The Canadian must have been pining for his homeland because the red-light district reminded him of Alexander Street in Vancouver.

The army regulated everything in France, including prostitution. To make matters simple, the military colour-coded the brothels. The blue lights were for officers. The *maisons tolérée* were refined establishments with pianos and paintings and divans. The officers sang regimental songs while scantily clad women served omelettes, champagne, melon, and other tasty treats. The red lights were for the rude soldiery. They were crude joints with queues measured in yards like golf courses. "Only five more yards to the hole," a lewd man could quip. The jokes were raunchy. The lines were long. The service was brusque. But having their own whorehouses let the Tommies avoid the awkward experience of getting their ashes hauled with their boss nearby.

Corporal Harper escorted Lieutenant Sinclair back to Marqueffles Farm. "Moo Cow Farm," the anglophones pronounced it. While the village was delightful, the trial was not. The disgraced officer was found guilty of going AWOL and ordered to be reprimanded. The sentence was duly carried out.

Thankfully, Lieutenant Sinclair avoided the charge of desertion, the penalty for which was death. Those sentences were carried out by the convicted man's comrades. Even though half of the men on the firing squad were given blanks instead of bullets—so they would never know who had killed their colleague—no one wanted any part in the execution of a Canadian. Killing Germans was bad enough.

Corporal Harper enjoyed his time at Marqueffles Farm, exploring the wooded slope of the Lorette Ridge, until his crestfallen soldiers straggled into camp. Like the rest of the battalion, Platoon No. 5 had suffered a multitude of casualties at Lens. What luck to miss that battle! Lester had dodged a bullet. Literally. The NCO who took his place was shot in the ass.

But the corporal felt guilty when his boys slunk into the dilapidated barn short their pluckiest private. Heads down and feet dragging, they stumbled in and slumbered off. Lester didn't ask what happened. Who wants to know? He just hoped that his private had not died an ugly death.

———

The Northwest Battalion spent the warm and rainy September quartered in decrepit stables in the sleepy farming village of Olhain. While the battalion received a draft of 107 reinforcements to refill their ranks, the veterans were gloomy and drenched to the skin. Lester had been in France for nine months without leave, and he was fed up with the army. The accommodations were deplorable, the wages were meagre, and the lifestyle was deadly. The only thing that he could not grouse about was their medical plan. That was stellar. There were so many doctors on staff that it was almost as if they were waiting for him to get injured.

Lester's mood improved when Dan Fee returned from his bombproof job. Hiding from the rain in the *estaminet*, the two friends whittled away their paycheques on penny cups of coffee and fried eggs at eight cents apiece. They chased the eggs down with good feeds of tomatoes, peaches, plums, and cherries. Then Lester bought two bars of chocolate, a tin of pineapples, candles, and some cigarettes.

"When did you start smoking?" Dan asked.

"They're not for me. They're for my boys. Nothing cheers them up more than a cigarette after a tough night in the trenches."

Dan could not believe it. Lester had wasted his money on presents for his privates. They were in the military. There was no need to bribe or cajole a subordinate. An order was an order. The corporal only had to tell them what to do.

"You know they call you a goody-goody behind your back, right?"

"At least they don't say it to my face like Bud does."

Shirt cleanish, stomach full, and wallet empty, Corporal Harper read a novel. Lester was an omnivorous reader who always kept a book in his pack. At the front, there was a constantly circulating library whose collection needed to be replenished frequently. In France, the soldiers shared their books freely. No one was concerned that their pages would get dog-eared or filled with marginalia. They were worried that their books would be soaked in their own blood or blown to shreds with them.

Although Corporal Harper read *The Inside of the Cup* by Winston Churchill and *Unto Caesar* by Baroness Orczy, he preferred Alexandre Dumas's tales of France. *The Three Musketeers* felt especially real because its castle was located in Olhain. The story carried Lester away to a bygone era when war was chivalrous and romantic, when it was fought honourably with swords and muskets—a time before machine guns, mustard gas, and mechanized mass murder.

While Corporal Harper yearned to experience Dumas's France, he was sorely disappointed to find the château's medieval drawbridge in disrepair and children catching frogs among the bullrushes in the moat. The storybook castle was nothing like Lester imagined when he read the book by candlelight in the stable.

The next day, Corporal Harper elbowed his way forward when the postman called his name. There was still no news from Wesley in Ypres. That was troubling. It was unlike his brother to go weeks without writing. After a fortnight, Lester would have settled for a date-stamped field service postcard with its stock greeting—"I am

THE ETERNAL QUESTION
"When the 'ell is it goin' to be strawberry?"

Lester's postcard to Mabel, entitled "The Eternal Question."

quite well"—and his brother's signature. Such proof of life was surprisingly reassuring.

"Hear about Wipers?" Dan asked. Rumours were rolling in about a large-scale Canadian offensive in Flanders.

A shell packed with fear struck Lester in the gut. Was Wes lying dead, like Harold, on a godforsaken battlefield? He pushed aside the morbid thought and ripped open the parcel from Mabel. Cake, sugar, and five francs. Priceless.

Lester owed his wife a belated birthday gift, so he hurried over to the *estaminet*. Rummaging through the souvenirs for sale in the loose joint, he found a beautiful handmade cushion designed by a lady in Olhain. It was perfect. Mabel would love it.

Alas, Corporal Harper couldn't afford the present. He had tried to save his money to get his wife a special gift—a token of his love—but then he saw the strawberry jam. The officers with cushy jobs in the rear got first pick of supplies, and they usually took all of the strawberry jam. The infantrymen up the line were stuck with the leftover apple and plum. They never got their favourite. Not this time. A jar had slipped through. So how could Lester not buy the jam the instant he saw it, even though that meant spending the cash that he had set aside for his wife?

Corporal Harper glanced around. He saw a cheap handkerchief, a typical souvenir from the front. That would do. Putting the pillow back, he purchased the handkerchief instead.

The thoughtful husband then trotted over to the YMCA and began to play *Poète et Paysan*. He made a mistake, restarted, and messed up again. After nine months on the Western Front, Lester was a better artist with a pick and shovel than a piano. Gone were the days when he masterfully played the 101st Cadet Corps band's repertoire throughout Australia and serenaded the *Zealandia*'s passengers across the Pacific too. Taking out his fountain pen, Lester sat at a table with a far-off look in his eyes.

Brandon Marriott

France
September 10th, 1917

Darling Mabel:
Now then, here goes. Compreé ink? I found a fountain pen sitting on a main road the other day, all filled with ink. Hence the blackness of this writing.

You ask if we have many casualties. You will have to judge by the lists. Some battalions catch it heavier than others; one bunch may be wiped out and another bunch right alongside may not have a casualty. That is the way it goes. Merely good luck or good fortune whether you are in the line where there is something doing or when Fritz gets sore or takes a notion.

You would like to know that the Canadian Corps has an excellent reputation out here. Anything we are given to do, we do it and hold it—which is the hardest thing. We are what is known as good "storm troops."

I have had a couple close shaves lately. Once on a work party when Fritz shelled us to hell. The other was a shell that came within a few feet of my funk hole, but it was a dud. Lucky for me. I have learned a lot, dear, but this is an extremely hazardous business, and I wish it would finish. I do not like the look of things on the Western Front.

I missed entirely the last trip in the line. I am glad I did for my section had some hand-to-hand fighting and bombing. One of my pluckiest men was killed and several wounded. The N.C.O. who took my place got a blighty in the ass. Haha. One of our platoon snipers accounted for 25 Germans before he was killed himself. A good record that.

Wesley is in Ypres, which is a very bad place, but he is pretty lucky and I hope continues so. I have not heard from him for two weeks now, and I am a bit anxious. I hope he got through this Flanders push okay. He will be lucky if he comes out with a wound. You ought to see the happy faces on the fellows with light wounds. But there are the sad cases, stretcher cases. You have no idea what these big affairs are like. It is easy to talk about it at home, but oh the work, work, work it entails.

I have not heard of Harold Empey. There is little hope. He was a new man in the regiment and not well known. I can get no particulars. There were a lot of casualties, and some of the wounded were not found for 48 hours. When we went in on that particular spot, we walked over many poor fellows.

Enough, dear. Just now I am billeted in a town a few miles back of the line. It is raining and blowing like fury. We are back away from the sound of guns, and it is a treat. Only our billets are poor, old stables in a small farming town.

I have been reading a lot of novels lately, and they somehow make me appreciate my loving wife. What I ask is that I may go back to her soon. How is Lillian, dear? I would love to kiss her sweet lips and also those of her mother. Only last night, I saw a French soldier arrive home on leave. Believe me, he was glad and did not conceal his feelings. It will be a long time before I receive leave.

The weather is beautiful this evening, and the crops look jake. Oh, to be back haying in Canada. Do you catch the kisses I send every night about 10, girlie? Of course, that would be 2 or 3 in the afternoon by you.

I received your cinq Francs with part of which I bought the enclosed "Souvenir from the Front," a token of my love.

Good bye,
Lester
xxxx

ON SEPTEMBER 17, THE NORTHWEST BATTALION MARCHED TO Villers-au-Bois, where the narrow streets were skirted with barns. The village was shitty. Literally. It lacked a modern sanitation system.

The troops lined up to pay homage to their comrades who showed exemplary valour during the Battle of Hill 70. B Company led the way with ten of the battalion's twenty medals. Lieutenant Davies was awarded the Military Cross for gallantry (even though he was recommended for the Victoria Cross), and Sergeants Eldridge and Richards were each given the Distinguished Conduct Medal (DCM) for pulling their injured privates to safety under fire.

Corporal Harper was most proud of his friend Bull. The young man was his favourite stretcher-bearer. Bull was decorated with the DCM too, and Lester believed that he deserved the medal for not flinching in a tight spot.

The DCM came with leave, but Lester was stunned when he found out Bull was on the verge of postponing his furlough. What soldier turned down time off?

"I don't know if I can resist the Janes in Paris," Bull admitted. That explained it. Like Lester, the stretcher-bearer was married with a child at home.

This was one of Corporal Harper's greatest worries too. He expected to get his own leave to Paris by Christmas. Would he be able to restrain himself from tampering with the fair sex? After all, he may never see his wife again.

They say that there are no holy days in war, but the *estaminets* did not serve booze until noon on Sundays. Making men who were bordering on alcoholism wait until midday for a drink was a small miracle. Lester relished those first few quiet hours on Sunday morning, when he read his newspaper and sipped his coffee in the loose joint.

After noon, the Lord's Day was just as rowdy as any other. "Hey,

Bull," Lester called when the stretcher-bearer walked in the door. "I can't believe you're still here. You actually cancelled your leave?"

"No, chummy. I didn't cancel it—the army did. They're cancelling Paris leave because half the men are coming back with the clap."

"At least that solves your problem," the corporal chuckled. "The pox sure is a dear price to pay for a little bit of heaven."

Lester wondered what the CEF expected from hot-blooded males living under the constant threat of death. Stuff their pockets with cash, send them to the Parisian cesspool, and expect them to stay clear of the frills, lace, and fluff of the lasses? Good luck!

Good luck, indeed. The Canadians suffered from the highest rate of venereal disease among the Allies. A total of 66,083 CEF servicemen were diagnosed with diseases like chlamydia, syphilis, and gonorrhea—that was over 15 percent of Canada's entire overseas contingent, and three times the rate of the BEF.

Nothing seemed to lower their record-setting VD level. First, the Canadian Corps tried lectures. The commanders told their soldiers about the trouble with French Janes and the consequences of the forbidden fruit. Lester found these talks very amusing, especially when the officers gave examples from among their "friends." Then the army offered free condoms. That too failed to curb the Canucks' exuberance for unprotected sex. At one point, the CEF even contacted the wives of men with VD, but the resulting suicides stopped that policy. Finally, the military instituted a new parade: the infamous and aptly named dangle parade. "Okay, you whorehounds, drop 'em," the MO would order, and groups of servicemen would obediently lower their trousers to prove that they were infection-free.

A number of the lads in the Northwest Battalion had already caught VD, and Corporal Harper wondered if his brother would be next. To use Lester's own words, Wesley was a mutt. In France, he remarked about being in well with a couple of pretty swell Janes. In the British Isles, he wrote about the fine girls in England, Ireland, and Scotland too. Wes was even thinking about the future. "I may opt for a little fat German when we get to Berlin," he said. Whenever Lester had not heard from Wes in a while, his initial thought was that his brother was embarrassed in the VD hospital. Either that or he was dead.

At least debauchery was a fun way to escape the front. Maybe that was why the VD Hospital was always crowded. It was easier to catch the clap than to acquire a bombproof job in the rear, and a diseased man got a month away from the front to recover.

While maligners went sick to evade their duty, bacchants drank themselves into a stupor to cope. Sergeant Thompson was charged multiple times for drunkenness on active duty, and he was the man who issued their rum. Bill was not the only soldier who drank to excess. More Canadians were court-martialled for drunkenness than for all other offences combined. As Prime Minister Lloyd George stated, "We are fighting Germany, Austria, and drink; and as far as I can see, the greatest of these deadly foes is drink." Even the poet Robert Graves, who'd never had a sip of whisky before the war, was on a bottle a day in the trenches.

As for Corporal Harper, he just grinned and carried on. Month after month, the reliable NCO made the best of a bad job. But even Lester wondered how much more hardship he could endure. The strain was getting on his nerves. His suffering was on par with that of the Egyptians in the Bible. The Canadian had been subjected to boils and plagues of lice, flies, and rats. He had seen rivers of blood and the sky blotted out by clouds of gas. He had withstood torrents of shells and hail and fire. His firstborn had even died. Was he being punished for the sins of his youth?

Like many veterans, Corporal Harper was beginning to feel death looming around every bend. It was wearing to never know if you would be alive the next morning. And it didn't help when their trenches had names like Peril Avenue, Doleful Post, and Suicide Corner. The longer the men were up the line, the more logic and belief blurred into superstition. Each day was a macabre lottery. A host of men in the Northwest Battalion had already had their numbers called. Who would be next? Eventually Lester's luck would run out. It was only a matter of time.

Villers-au-Bois felt especially haunted. Tricoloured medallions dangled from the crosses in the French cemetery and clinked in the breeze, reminding the living that the dead were all around them, that they too had walked these streets, that their comrades were just corpses heading irrevocably toward their graves.

Corporal Harper was having a black day, and they were becoming more frequent, so he sulked over to his platoon leader for advice. His officer saw the signs. He knew that Lester was a fine soldier, but he needed a break. Fortunately, there was a course for NCOs open at their divisional school.

The leaves were falling and the women were gathering vegetables when Corporal Harper arrived at the divisional school in Château de la Haie, a sprawling military complex home to the Canadian Corps headquarters: Camp Canada. While Lester bedded down on a lousy (literally, as in full of louse) straw floor with twenty-four other non-coms, he ate at a table with dishes and cutlery in the farmhouse next door. How luxurious!

"*Vin rouge ou vin blanc?*" the hostess inquired.

"*Vin rouge, s'il vous plaît.*" Lester wondered what his boys were eating as he took a bite of the homemade pie. Certainly not officer-quality chow like him. A twinge of guilt shot through his conscience. Had he abandoned his section? Had he left his platoon in a lurch?

Who wants to know? Lester took a sip of wine. The drink helped him ignore the moral dilemma, even if it was guaranteed to give him a thick head in the morning.

Corporal Harper was not the only NCO sent to the school on compassionate grounds because he had been out for too long and needed a rest. Unlike his comrades, however, he did not treat the course like a holiday. His perseverance paid off. When his colleagues were ordered back to their units, Lester was rewarded with a staff position drilling new drafts at the reinforcement depot. The new job came with a promotion. He was officially a sergeant.

The CEF went through soldiers like Lester went through money. When he was in Camp Canada, the infantry was thinned out (another military euphemism for death) at Passchendaele. "Rot in the mud," Lieutenant General Currie termed the Belgian swamp. There was not a single house left standing in the village. Only the charred ruins of the church remained. "Let the Germans have it," the Canadian commander pleaded with his superiors. The marshland could not be held. It wasn't worth the sacrifice. Ferdinand Foch, the French general, concurred. It was folly to take on the *"Boche & boue"* (Germans and mud) simultaneously, he insisted. The obstinate Field Marshal Haig overruled them both. His unwavering faith in suicidal headfirst attacks died hard.

Words cannot convey the gruesomeness of Passchendaele. The Allies suffered 275,000 casualties and gained no ground. "Rot in the mud" was no exaggeration. The muck was so deep that bomb holes turned into lakes and the ground became quicksand. Soldiers who passed out from injuries or slipped off the duckboards drowned. No one could help them. They would only drown too.

The watery clay swallowed forty-two thousand servicemen. Their bodies formed such a thick underlay that the survivors could not take a step without trampling on the lost. The dead pulled at their feet, the souls of the damned reaching out to drag the living into the underworld. "A thousand times worse than the Somme," one Tommy remarked.

Till We Meet Again

The 28th Battalion marched to German-occupied Belgium, where they went over the top. Although Lester's battalion was only in the line for forty-eight hours, it took a vicious battering at Passchendaele. At 6.00 a.m. on November 6, the Canadian artillery opened fire, and the Nor'westers climbed out of their trenches and advanced behind the creeping barrage. As the CO wrote in the war diary, it sounded as if every gun on the Western Front started firing at dawn. The ground was wet and boggy, and the soldiers struggled to keep up with the moving wall of death as they waded through the waist-high mud and tried to avoid the heavy and erratic German counterbarrage.

When the Nor'westers were four hundred yards from their objective, the Maschinengewehr 08s began popping off and the Canucks were gunned down. But the survivors continued to fight forward, throttling the machine guns and beating the Germans back. While they defeated the enemy and consolidated the new line, the ground was strewn with dead. The 28th Battalion lost 230 men in the assault, including three of the battalion's company commanders. With a casualty rate of almost 35 percent of the forces engaged, Passchendaele, declared Lieutenant Colonel Ross, was the graveyard of everybody.

When Sergeant Harper heard about the Third Battle of Ypres, his first thought was of his chums. Had they made it through okay? Most of them did not. Plenty were KIA or wounded, including his best friend. On November 6, Dan Fee was shot in the face. Headshots normally left a man napoo, but somehow the bullet that struck Dan spared his life. It gave him only a touch of paralysis and a droopy eyelid as a souvenir.

As Dan would later write from the hospital in the UK, he was having a hell of a time in Blighty too, thanks to the volunteer nurses in his ward. Apparently, they were a fast lot. The best part? The wound was a Canada! The lance corporal could not be profitably employed in England, so the army was sending him home. "You really should swing a blighty," his friend advised. Lester wished that getting a cushy one was that easy.

The war was ravenous, and the Canadian Corps was bleeding out. That was why Lester was pro-conscription. He was not a warmonger; he was a realist. The wastage of life was horrible. Each battalion was continually thinned out, refilled, and thinned out again. Their 100,000-man army had already lost 147,009 troops. You don't have to be a mathematician to understand that those numbers did not add up.

Canada was blood-weary, its volunteer pool exhausted. The CEF had originally sought volunteers by appealing to their love of country, honour, duty, and adventure. Then they shamed holdouts by questioning their manliness and patriotism. The Canadian Corps even used humiliation and scare tactics to coax mothers and wives to help the cause.

"To the women of Canada," one recruitment poster declared. "You read what the Germans have done in Belgium. Have you thought what they would do if they invaded this country? When the war is over and someone asks your husband or your son what he did in the Great War, is he to hang his head because you would not let him go? Won't you help and send a man to enlist today?"

Now, Lester thought, conscription was required to force the last lackadaisical boys to do their share. Was that too much to ask for? It was better to have them fighting in France than chasing Mabel and his friends' sweethearts back in Canada. No serviceman wanted to receive a Dear John letter while he was at the front.

Sergeant Harper knew that conscripts could not relieve dependable veterans, but they could reinforce them. Unfortunately, the 250 latest recruits were as unsoldierlike as could be. The quality of their draftees was deteriorating rapidly. The new lot were not even as good as those who'd arrived the year before.

Five to one. That was the rate at which the newbies were expected to die compared to the old-timers. But at Camp Canada, Lester drilled the piss out of the clumsy schoolboys anyway. He gave them a proper trench education. Hopefully that would help them survive a bit longer.

Till We Meet Again

Sergeant Harper loved catching up with the old fellas cycling through the reinforcement depot on their way back from Blighty. One of his friends brought the most extraordinary news. "When I was in England, I inquired after your cousin," he said. "Now this is only a rumour, but it's possible that Harold is a POW in Germany."

"Prisoner of war!?" An enormous grin spread across Lester's face. The sergeant did not care that the news was only hearsay. He could hardly contain his excitement. His cousin might still be alive!

The only thing more shocking than hearing that Harold might be a POW was seeing Bill return to France as a corporal. Lester stared dumbfounded when his cousin arrived from the UK. The two of them had literally swapped positions.

"I don't want to talk 'bout it," Corporal Thompson muttered, pre-empting the obvious question. His trip to Blighty had gone from bad to worse. It had started in a hospital bed and ended in a jail cell.

HASTINGS
England—June 17, 1917

SERGEANT THOMPSON STRODE DOWN THE WOODEN PIER IN the seaside town. The GSW in his right thigh had healed in the Italian Hospital in London, but the severe concussion from shellfire needed more time, so he was sent to the Canadian Convalescent Hospital on Bromley Hill in Kent.

Now Sergeant Thompson was on leave. That was the upside to getting shot: you got a brief vacation before getting shot at more. Hastings was Bill's dream destination. There were beaches and pubs and a sergeants' mess. Sun, booze, and eats—what else did he need? The Saskatchewanian was enjoying himself immensely, revelling in the sea and sand before returning to France.

Sergeant Thompson stopped to chat with a couple of acquaintances on the promenade. The night was muggy, so he ambled down to the shoreline. Taking off his boots and socks, he rolled his pants up to his knees. The waves lapped around his ankles. He lay back in the soft sand and watched the sun set over the English Channel. It was sublime. In fact, it was the perfect evening until two MPs accosted him. This was how Bill remembered the alleged incident of June 17. That was his story, and he was sticking to it.

The prosecutor at Sergeant Thompson's district court martial told a different version of the events. He agreed that Bill had enjoyed his time in Hastings. He'd enjoyed it too much. The sergeant forgot the rule for CEF servicemen on active duty in England: if you were going to drink, you needed to drink like a gentleman. Instead, Bill got blackout drunk and passed out in the wet sand. The tide rose, and his socks and boots floated out to sea.

At 9.00 p.m., a concerned citizen found Sergeant Thompson lying ten feet below the high-water mark. The stranger could not tell if Bill was dead or alive, so he ran off to find a policeman. The civilian police notified their military counterparts, and the corporal on duty dispatched two MPs to deal with the so-called dead soldier on the beach.

The MPs arrived at 10.35 p.m. to find Sergeant Thompson unconscious but alive. They shook him until he awoke in a dazed condition. Bill was too unstable to walk, so they carried him between their arms. "You would have drowned if we'd left you there," one of the MPs told him.

"Oh, I won't drown," Bill apparently said. "Where are we going?"

"You're under arrest for being drunk," the MP replied. "We're taking you to the police station."

"Oh, I won't drown," Bill kept mumbling.

The MPs escorted the sergeant to Camp Bramshott, where he was kept in military confinement for twenty-three days until his district court martial on July 10. Sergeant Thompson was charged under Section 19 of the Army Act with drunkenness on active duty. He pleaded not guilty.

While the MPs testified that the accused was intoxicated, the defence counsel presented the testimony of the two NCOs who spoke to Bill on the promenade. Sergeant Parm and Sergeant Marlowe both stated that Bill was natural and sober at 8.30 p.m. on the night in question. Thus, the defence argued, it was highly unlikely that he could have been severely inebriated by 9.00 p.m.

The defence's third witness attested to the accused's character. Sergeant Forsyth had known Bill for eight years, both before his enlistment in Canada and after, in England and France. When he heard that Sergeant Thompson had been arrested on a charge of drunkenness, he thought there must be a mistake. It could not be Bill, Sergeant Forsyth reasoned, because he had never seen him drunk in his life. In fact, he had never even heard of Bill being drunk. A good friend, that Sergeant Forsyth. One has to wonder if he was deliberately lying under oath. Everyone knew that Bill had a drinking problem. Even Lester wrote that "Bill Thompson is *just the same* [emphasis added] and can still consume beaucoup booze."

The judge presiding over the court martial, Colonel Acton, must have suspected it too. This was not Sergeant Thompson's first charge for drunkenness. Seven months earlier, he was arraigned at a field general court martial in Le Havre. When Bill was passing through the base depot in November 1916, he was found staggering down the footpath at 8.00 p.m. The MP who arrested him then testified that he was very drunk and smelled of liquor. As he would do again the following year, Bill pleaded not guilty in Le Havre. Maybe discrepancies in the testimonies at Le Havre made the prosecution's witnesses unreliable. Maybe Bill's character witness planted a seed of doubt that swayed the judge's opinion. Maybe the president of the field general court martial wanted to give him a break. Whatever the reason, Sergeant Thompson was found not guilty and released from custody.

Fool me once, Colonel Acton must have thought at the district court martial in Camp Bramshott. He wouldn't let Bill get away with the same trick twice. The colonel found Sergeant Thompson guilty on the charge of drunkenness and reduced him to the rank of corporal.

CHÂTEAU DE LA HAIE
France—November 30, 1917

SERGEANT HARPER FINISHED HIS SPELL AS AN INSTRUCTOR AT the end of November and limped back to join Platoon No. 5 in Neuville-Saint-Vaast. Everything and everyone was *pas bon*. The Northwest Battalion was at two-thirds strength, its surviving soldiers beat-up and bloodied. The town was just as battered and bruised. A solitary limestone wall stood defiantly among the rubble in the White City of Flanders. Even the headstones in the cemetery were smashed to pieces. A recently erected sign described the town best: "This *Was* Neuville St. Vaast."

Lester had fared little better. He was sporting a wonky knee, boils on his buttock, and cold sores on his lips. Even his cousin gave him grief. "Bloody hell! Sneaking off to hug a French wench, I see. Off to the doc you go now."

Despite having been reduced to corporal, Bill was made an acting sergeant major upon his return to France. He was promoted, demoted, then promoted again. The CO needed an experienced veteran to help oversee B Company, and Bill was far too valuable of an asset to be relegated to the rank of a corporal for enjoying a drink in Blighty.

The MO put Lester on rest, and he was left in charge of details at camp as the 28th Battalion marched up the line. Sergeant Harper was keeping track of his injured colleagues when he received a message from the BOR. After almost a year in France, it was finally his turn for annual leave. Guess what? Wesley was back in regular correspondence and wrote to say that he was off to England too. Let's meet at the Maple Leaf Club in London on December 11, his brother suggested.

If Wesley was such a mutt, why would he choose to stay at the Maple Leaf Club? The self-proclaimed home away from home was renowned for supplying Canadians with room, board, and socially appropriate companionship. What single soldier wanted socially appropriate companionship in London? Unlike the French Janes, the English women never responded with *"Après la guerre"* when the fellows hit them up.

Sergeant Harper stripped down and scrubbed up. His uniform was stained and rotting, so he was issued a clean one. Heaven forbid that the folks in Great Britain actually saw the sorry state of their servicemen. Then Lester went for his medical exam. Semi-presentable and free from communicable diseases, he was cleared to return to the UK. The sergeant packed his haversack, collected his pay and leave warrants, and penned a final letter to Mabel before leaving France.

France
December 5th, 1917

My Dear Gal:
You have been waiting a long time for this letter, have you not? I have no excuse. Do not put "killed in action" on the outside again. Savez? I assure you I am quite well and healthy, dear! I have not been in the line since I wrote you last, but I was taking an N.C.O.'s course at a divisional school. So, you see, I am having quite a period out of the lines.

I am still away from the battalion, and I consider myself lucky for the weather is awful (mud, mud, mud) and the Canucks are having a hard time. I missed the Passchendaele scrap in Belgium, and I'm lucky I did. It was terrible. There have been a lot of casualties lately in my unit. Gee, it makes me sore when I hear of some of our best men being killed. It makes my blood boil. And yet it goes on every day. It always seems to be the best men that go; that's why I am left, I guess!?

It is looking more like winter and, I'll tell you candidly, that I do not like to put another winter in the trenches for it is real hardship leaving out totally the element of danger. Trench for a front line, mud and slush combined with rain and cold wind make life miserable.

It is about time the world woke up to the fact that she is simply losing its manhood. You must remember that these countries are not like Canada. Here, every available man is in the army; in Canada, only those who found it convenient. Now I think it is up to Canada to give us all the reinforcements we need. If you do not, it will only take one or two shows to finish us. As Fritz said, "The Canadians came over in troop ships but will go back in a row boat!"

I received a letter from Wesley. He is off to London, and he asked me to meet him on December 11th. As I am getting my leave tomorrow, I hope to keep the date. Won't you meet me too? How I would love to spend my 14 days leave with you! Couldn't we have just the swellest time? I would sooner go with you than any other person. I think absence must make the heart grow fonder because I love you just a little bit more each and every day, girlie.

I heard from one of the old boys that Empey is possibly a prisoner of war, but he would not say for certain.

Was there a handkerchief in the last envelope? If not, then I left it at the Y.M.C.A. I was in a hurry at the time to hear a concert, and I only missed the souvenir now. Well, better luck next time.

My cold is better except for a couple of cold sores. But I am lousey *and very much so. I got a clean shirt today and that will help some. Please forgive this terrible scribble, dear. My hand is cold and cramped. Be cheerful, happy, healthy, and enjoy yourself.*

With love, dear,
R. Lester Harper Sgt.
xxxx

IT TOOK A FULL DAY OF SLUGGISH LORRIES AND TRAINS TO get to Boulogne-sur-Mer, but Sergeant Harper had a smile on his lips the entire time. Lester arrived at the port with time to spare before his ship was due to depart, so he ate two meat pies at their rest camp. He immediately regretted the impulsive decision. How could he forget about the rough passage across the English Channel? The sergeant was not the only absent-minded soldier. Scores of them lined the deck of the fast steamer, puking and moaning their way to Folkestone.

"Look—Blighty," a serviceman soon called. "It's Blighty!" Through the white foam and stinging salt water, they could see the steep cliffs of England's coastline. The chorus echoed from bow to stern. Lumps welled in throats. The soldiers could have wept with joy at the sight, except that they were men in 1917, so crying would not do. Only a Frenchman, Lester noted, did not conceal his feelings.

From Folkestone, Sergeant Harper took the train to London and disembarked in Victoria Station. In the drab winter drizzle, the city was grey and pallid, a disfigured soldier on his deathbed. London was a far cry from its glory days. The lights were dimmed, the windows shuttered. A doomy feeling hung over the capital, which was cowering from Zeppelins in the dark. Only uniforms and cripples, grey-beards and girls walked the shell-pocked streets.

Everything seemed scarce, except for the dames. Oh, churches, it was girls galore! Healthy, industrious, female war workers were everywhere. They drove buses, delivered mail, fought fires, and caught criminals. After a year at the front, Lester found them all sexy, even those who smoked cigarettes or chewed gum. Apparently, those disgusting habits were the latest fashion in England.

There was a reason why pastors preached on the lure of the city at their church parades. "If people in Canada knew of the temptations in London," one chaplain said, pounding the pulpit, "they'd think twice about sending their sons!"

Lester had left Neuville-Saint-Vaast less than twenty-four hours earlier, but he could not believe the differences between the two places. Even though London was dark and empty, everything was so neat and tidy. The littlest things, like ladies talking, gave him culture shock. After a year of dealing with French Janes who swore like soldiers, he found it queer and unnatural to hear women speaking politely in English. How was London less than 150 miles from the corpse-covered streets of Lens?

Sergeant Harper headed to his usual accommodations, but there was no room. As he was leaving the establishment, the gentleman in charge walked past. He saw Lester in his faded khaki uniform and took pity on him. "I'm sorry that we're full," he said, "but you can stay at my place tonight, if you please."

When a servant opened the three-hundred-year-old door of the wealthy bachelor's house, the aroma of rich cuisine filled the foyer.

"Would you like something to eat?" the aristocrat inquired.

"Please." Lester never turned down free food.

The Englishman showed off his eccentric collection of knick-knacks, furniture, and books assembled from a lifetime of travel while the Canadian oohed and aahed and sang for his supper. Although Lester was a would-be intellectual who longed to have stimulating conversations about literature and music, he felt painfully uneducated and out of place.

Sergeant Harper had developed a taste for tea during his training in England, but he was no longer used to drinking out of a dainty china cup. Now he slurped his tea like a soldier. Thankfully, he stopped himself before dipping the sweet biscuits as if they were hardtack. That would have mortified his host. Lester was more at home with the grunts in the trenches than the gentry in their posh abodes.

After dinner, the Canadian took a hot bath. Then a servant escorted him to his room. As the door opened, a rush of hot air from the fireplace hit him like a Jack Johnson exploding in his face. The glow of the flames illuminated the gilded paintings on the walls. They must be worth piles of money, Sergeant Harper figured. But what impressed him more was the mahogany bed. Covered in plump pillows, starched sheets, and an eiderdown quilt, that was the guest room's true masterpiece. The infantryman sank into the soft mattress and passed out. God only knew when he would sleep in such luxurious linen again.

The next morning, Lester ate herring and spuds at the Union Jack Club and then bought a pair of soft boots. His left foot was still sore, and he wanted to be comfortably outfitted to walk the city. Roving the narrow streets lined with brick tenements, the sergeant happened upon a medieval church. He milled about its graveyard. The crumbling tombstones dated back generations. The inscriptions on the memorials remembered for ages. How unlike their cemeteries in France, where wayward shells demolished the wooden crosses and resurrected the dead.

Music cascaded out of the door of the church and drew Lester inside.

"The pipe organ's fifty years old," the minister told him. "Do you play?"

Sergeant Harper nodded.

"You can try it if you like."

Lester struck a key. The note was rich and mellow. He sat down and played *Poète et Paysan*. The power and sweetness of the music flowed through the church. It filled him with awe.

Next the Canadian made his way over the Waterloo Bridge, where drunk foreign servicemen spooned English women in dark coves. Bushels of girls for the asking, he reckoned. There were even enough for the wild Australians in their silly hats and leggings. Those colonials were a rough lot with a bad reputation.

The devoted husband felt sorry for the English ladies. The best of their men were in France. Many would never have the chance to marry, so they were careless and let fellows take liberties. There was no need for flattery or courtship. All that was required was a hidden nook or cranny.

Lester met Wesley at the Maple Leaf Club. His brother looked tired and beat-up. He was recovering from a night of drinking, smoking, and whatever else young men did in wartime London (Lester felt it was unacceptable to share that with his wife).

The Harper boys toured the city on the Tube. They saw Buckingham Palace, Big Ben, and Westminster Abbey, as well as two shows at the Hippodrome. What impressed them most? The anti-aircraft guns and girls in Hyde Park, which both made fine sights.

"There's two things I've noticed on English lasses," Lester told his brother. "Poor teeth and big feet. See her?" He pointed to a gal sitting on a bench. "Her slippers could fit Burt!"

"Agreed," roared Wes. "Give me a Canadian girl and to hell with the English flappers."

The brothers stopped at a professional studio to pose for a snapshot before leaving London. As the two men stared at their portrait, neither spoke the obvious thought that was running through their minds: these might be their last moments together.

"It's rotten," Lester remarked instead.

"Nah, you don't look bad," his brother teased. "Just sozzled."

Corporal Harper went south to France. Sergeant Harper went north to Scotland.

"Be careful," Lester warned when they said goodbye. He knew that Fritz's artillery made Ypres perilous.

"You be careful too," Wesley chuckled. He knew that Edinburgh was dangerous in a markedly different way, especially for his older sibling. Lester was not proud or greedy or envious. No, those were not his vices. He had another inherent sin. "There are some fine girls all over the British Isles," Wes told him, "but the Scottish lassies beat the English girls ten ways, including the most important one: they're clean. I always wait for my bed until I get to Scotland."

Lester found that he enjoyed Scotland almost as much as his brother did. He visited Edinburgh Castle and caught a few shows, including an excellent pantomime of *Humpty Dumpty*. The married man managed to avoid all temptation until his last morning in town, when a girl from the guest house invited him to the carnival.

"Sure." Lester smiled. Who could say no to such a cutie? The Scottish women were strikingly attractive in a very unique way, with freckled fair skin, light blue eyes, and fiery red hair. No wonder Wesley loved Scotland.

All too soon, Sergeant Harper was on his way back to France. It was a bitter and foggy London morning when he boarded the train to Folkestone. The foul weather suited his melancholy mood. Lester sulked, feeling *malheureux*. The thought of returning to those god-awful trenches filled him with dread.

"It's a bloody squash in here," a chubby-cheeked Brit told his cronies.

Wait till he sees the 40 & 8 boxcars, Sergeant Harper thought. Did any of these clean-cut boys really know what was coming? Their squeaky voices and innocent laughter filled the carriages as they crowded the aisles and overflowed into the corridors. Some sat on their packs while others squatted on the floor. The compartment was a jumble of arms and legs and khaki, the future contents of a mass grave in France. Each soldier carried a round-trip ticket. Lester wondered how many would ever return.

England
December 21st, 1917

Dear Mabs:
Well, here I am on my way to France again. Excuse this scrawl, dear. The train is going like hell. It is very hard to go back now especially when everybody is getting ready for Christmas. I hope you have a happy one, even without me. Oh, I do hope I shall be home by next Christmas. I have another long year ahead in France, and I only hope I shall be as lucky this time as last.

I have not written to you for a week, and I deserve a reprimand, I suppose! Dear, you know it is hard to settle down and write when a fellow is on leave even if it is to his belle!? But I think of you a thousand times a day and long for you, so try and be contented.

Since I wrote last, I have seen a lot of Scotland as well as London. I found Wesley. We spent two days together, and we saw "Zig Zag" at the Hippodrome. I certainly had a lovely time in Edinburgh. Scotland for me after this! But I got lonely for you sometimes. You were the lacking element to make my leave complete. Other girls were alright to walk about with and take to a show, but still there was something wanting in all of them, something that only you could give!

Now, Mabs, I received some snaps that I had taken at a carnival in Edinburgh. I would like to send you one because it is good of me, but I am afraid you would take it the wrong way. I took a girl from the house where I was staying, and we went into every sideshow, merry-go-round, and photo place. Hence, we got these snaps taken together, and I do not want you to think evil of me.

Love to Lillian. Watch the papers for doings around Lens and Vimy Ridge!

Good morning,
Les
xxxx

CHAPTER SIX

PLEASE DO NOT TELL EVERYONE ABOUT THIS

SAINT-HILAIRE

France—December 25, 1917

GUSTS OF WIND RIPPED SLEET ACROSS SERGEANT HARPER'S face. Icicles dangled from his bushy moustache, and a tail of ice clung to his greatcoat. Winter on the Western Front was what Dante had envisioned in the ninth circle of his frozen hell. Lester picked up the pace. Why was he in a hurry? Eatables, of course.

Christmas dinner was on the table under the YMCA marquee at Lières. Lester licked his lips. The menu was superb. Thirteen hundred pounds of turkey accompanied by potatoes, peas, and cabbage, with plum pudding, nuts, and apples for dessert.

The battalion tucked in, and everybody got stuffed. The fellas washed down the meal with *beaucoup* beer and pure Scotch whisky, which left Bill and the rest of the boys totally pickled. What started as a grand affair deteriorated into a ruckus where the Canucks ran amok and passed out drunk.

"Some holy night," Lester complained as he crawled into bed. "The civvies must think we're mad."

"Holy enough," a comrade replied. "The men are in good *spirits*."

Sergeant Harper had pooled his money with eight other NCOs to rent a large bedroom in an elderly Frenchman's house. Although he slept on the floor in the crowded room, it was worth every franc to sit at a kitchen table under an electric light bulb and eat the tasty chips made by the owner's pretty granddaughter.

There was a south-westerly breeze with scattered shelling when the Northwest Battalion marched back up the line. Lester spent February 1 reclining in a former German cellar in the Avion sector with a jar of honey, some candy, and a new pair of socks. Mabel had sent him a beauty of a present for his twenty-fifth birthday.

Although he was under orders to shave every day, the sergeant's face was covered in a week's worth of greying whiskers because the blunt razors and gritty water rubbed his face raw. His mud-caked uniform looked almost as rough. The last year had been somewhat different from his previous twenty-four, and he did not care to repeat it.

Sergeant Harper felt like he had travelled across hell's half acre to battle Fritz in the past year. He had been at the front in Souchez, Écurie, Mont-Saint-Éloi, Thélus, Vimy Ridge, Laurent, Lens, and now Avion. In reality, however, all of the trenches were in the same ten-mile radius. Lester had simply gone back and forth, attacking and defending the same desolate patch of foreign soil.

Today was February 4, the day that he expected the war to end. There were rumours that the fighting was drawing to a close on the Eastern Front, and the Canadians hoped this would lead to the end of the war for them too. Lester went outside that evening to watch for the blue or black flares that were supposed to be the sign of peace. He was, of course, disappointed. As his CO noted in the war diary, there was nothing of importance to report that day.

As a sergeant, Lester did not have to join his men on their patrol or wiring party every night, so he hunkered down in his dingy den. With six tins of peaches, four tins of apricots, and a can of condensed milk hanging from the ceiling in a stash bag, Sergeant Harper was nicely fixed up. His quarters were homey in a dank, dark, and rat-infested kind of way. But the *beaucoup* rodents did not trouble the farm boy. As long as he slept with his greatcoat wrapped around his head, he didn't have to worry about waking up to the tickle of cold, wet paws scurrying across his face.

There was barely enough room in the cellar to stretch out, but Sergeant Harper was warm, dry, and safe from the exploding ordnance bumping their way along the street above him. The town was strewn with debris, its cobblestone road punctured by crump holes fifteen feet deep. Every few minutes, Lester heard bullets whistle overhead and shells explode in the wreckage of the town. Fritz must be blindly searching for our ammunition dump, he figured.

The walls tottered. The timbers cracked. Okay, maybe the cellar was not completely shell-proof. His candle blew out, and the stale chamber filled with dust. "Not again," Lester moaned. How many times could he survive being entombed? Hacking violently, the veteran fought the innate urge for fresh air. He needed to remain calm and stay put. Rushing outside like a panicky new recruit was the quickest way to lose your head—both figuratively and literally.

Eventually, the unsuccessful gunners got bored and moved on. Lester drove a fresh candle onto a spike, rested his feet on the plank wall, and pulled out a magazine. His quarters felt empty without Dan.

With his best friend gone, Lester was pleased to be stationed near Bud. The two men saw each other frequently and had long talks into the night. Even better, Wesley was located just two miles away. Lester would shout at his brother in line at a bathing parade or meet him for chocolate at the YMCA. Sometimes, Wesley would even drop by the cellar to while away the evening.

The surgeons had not managed to get all of the shrapnel out of his back, so he was in pain every day. On this night, Wes was awfully sore. "Life out here is just one damn thing after another," he came in ranting. "I think I've cursed everyone and everything French. If Bill Kaiser were here right now, do you know what I'd do? I'd look him straight in his little Hun face and apologize for ever disputing his right to this godforsaken country!"

Lester rolled his eyes. "What rubbish. Come on, now. Don't you have a permanent billet with regular working hours while I'm a nocturnal nomad? Don't you get beef, spuds, and bread for dinner while I eat mulligan with God knows what? How much did you win in poker last week while I sit here broke? Sounds to me like you're having a lazy good time."

Wesley's nostrils flared. His eyes filled with rage. A smile as twisted as a roll of barbed wire spread across Lester's face. Even though he agreed with every word Wes had said, he couldn't resist the urge to gaslight his brother.

Bill slipped down the stairs unannounced. "You're wanted for a rations party, Sergeant. But first, how 'bout a snort of rum? You two sound like you need it. We can hear your bickering all the way to bloody Wipers."

"To our cousin, the acting sergeant major," Wes toasted.

On February 21, the Nor'westers relieved the 46th Battalion in the corps reserve at Camp Canada. The men from Saskatchewan had left their huts in squalid shape, but no one complained. They pitied their compatriots in the Suicide Battalion. The prairie boys had seen action in every single one of Canada's bloodiest battles. No matter where they went, death followed. The Somme, Vimy Ridge, Hill 70, Ypres, and Passchendaele—the 46th Battalion was slaughtered in all of them. Of the 5,374 men who filled their ranks over the course of the war, a mere 457 walked away intact. After such monumental sacrifices, who could blame them for not tidying up?

Sergeant Harper felt punk as Platoon No. 5 cleaned the slovenly accommodations. He had been wearing the same clothes for a month, and his only shower in a fortnight had been a quick header in a dirty crump hole used by twenty-five men before him. His body showed the dismal hygiene. Lester was covered in small oily pimples and had hemorrhoids. He fingered a pus-filled boil on his neck. That needed to be lanced ASAP. I must have got a bit gassed, the filthy NCO supposed. How he wished for a good Turkish bath to sweat out the dirt.

Peckish, the sergeant unwrapped his hardtack. Hard was an understatement. Soldiers swore that the secret ingredient was cement. Lester smashed the biscuit into bite-sized morsels with the butt of his rifle and plopped a piece into his mouth. *Crack.* The hardtack was undoubtedly made from cement. His tooth crumbled. Searing pain shot up his jawline. "Damn it!" he yelped. The twenty-five-year-old was too young to be falling apart. He kicked the hardtack across the ground and set off for the nearest dentist. After seeing the old-timers with trench mouth, Lester had vowed to take care of his teeth. The thought of having cavernous cheeks, toothless grey gums, and ulcerated lesions mortified him.

"Got your mail," a friend said when he returned.

"No parcels?"

"Sorry."

The dejected sergeant took the solitary envelope. Oh, well, at least he could count on a loving letter from his wife.

Fat chance. Mabel's message made his blood boil. While Lester burned all her correspondence out of necessity, he probably destroyed this particular letter out of rage too. The sergeant did not care that his jaw was swollen and his mouth hurt like hell. He went straight to the YMCA, bought four chocolate bars, and ate them all at once. What in the blazes was she moaning about? he fumed. Didn't he tell her not to take the snap of him and the Scottish gal the wrong way? "I do not want you to think evil of me" were his exact words.

Lester overestimated his wife's tolerance. She definitely thought evil of him. Mabel was standing over him with a hymnbook of hate. His outrage festered, a wound turning gangrenous.

Brandon Marriott

Somewhere in France
February 23rd, 1918

Dear Mabel:
See here, mutt, you charge me with neglect and a whole grist of offences! You say in your last letter that you are going to have a "good time." Well, how's chances for me to have a good time over here? There are lots of French girls around these parts. It only costs a few francs, and some do it for "love!"

Maybe I should take a notion to get up some pretty European girl! I think I'll go to Germany après la guerre because they are talking of permitting a man to have two wives. Then again, I think one is enough to handle. At least judging from the tired look in the faces of those back off leave, I should think that one good healthy Jane could sap most men.

The "girl" or "good time" questions will have to wait until I return to Canada. Then you can judge me by my actions. But this much I will say: you can free your mind of a lot of rot that you have mentioned. I could have had fifty girls if I wanted, but I did not have one. I have merely been friends and taken them for a walk or to a show. I did enjoy myself and had a couple of invitations to spend the night with the fair sex. I almost wished for the moment that I was single, so that I could accept. I did not accept; what I did was just think of you. I always think of you when I am being entertained by ladies. No other girl can fill your place. I want my Mabs in preference to a whole bag full of other girls.

Well, dear, even if I am a "bad actor," I still love you until death. You are very sensitive in some respects, and I think you must do a lot of brooding or you would not have said some of the things you have done. So please forget all of the dope that you put in that letter to me. I'm going to get rid of it toute suite. You have spoken on the subject that I don't want to discuss through a letter which will be censored. I forgive you sincerely because I know you want me as I want you.

Till We Meet Again

Mabel dear, I long to be back with you. Be brave, happy, and contented as possible. Someday, I will come walking along the sidewalk. Perhaps in a row boat, at least so Heinz says. Things seem to just drag on, but there must be an end. I sincerely hope that I may have the good fortune to go back to you and be your happy and loving husband!

Good night, dear, and may God bless and protect you from harm and "temptation."

Your scape-goat husband?
L.H.
xxxx

SERGEANT HARPER WAS AGITATED AFTER QUARRELLING WITH his wife, so he went for a walk. Strolling along a stream and listening to the sweet song of the skylarks, Lester realized that he was being bullheaded. It was foolish to fight. Sending Mabel the photo of him with the Scottish girl was akin to tossing a bomb into a dugout packed with Germans. It made a bloody mess. Doubling down with an irate letter only made matters worse. Now he had to clean things up. God forbid that his head got blown off, and those were his last words to his wife.

The dying died, the wounded healed, and still the war raged on. More of Sergeant Harper's old friends from the 138th Battalion ended up in Blighty, including Hugh, who was shot in both the arm and the face. But even multiple GSWs could not stop the buff American from having fun. "Girls, girls, girls" was how he described his time in England. Lester was jealous. Bud was already away with his second blighty, and he had spent less time at the front than Lester. Some men had all the luck.

Sergeant Harper felt like he was overdue for a cushy wound. A nice blighty was definitely the best way out of France, and battle provided a welcome opportunity to get one in a limb. Lester was looking to stop two or three machine-gun bullets to send him to the UK for the remainder of the war. While getting shot may not sound pleasant, bullet wounds were clean and often sent a soldier to Blighty. Unfortunately, Lester spent most of his time in the trenches, where you were more likely to get hit in the bean by a sniper or blown up by a shell. Those wounds were messy. They usually left a man napoo. And no one wanted to stay in France to fertilize the grass.

The tide of war was shifting once again. While the Canadians had been victorious at Vimy Ridge, Fresnoy, Hill 70, and Passchendaele in 1917, their allies had suffered a series of disasters. In the west, the British had been slaughtered in failed assaults over the same few muddy miles. The French had been slaughtered too, and they mutinied. In the east, the Russians had been slaughtering each other instead of the Germans. Trained and armed at the behest of Tsar Nicholas II, the upset and malnourished soldiers had turned against their own monarch. Internal strife and revolution wreaked havoc on the country. The Bolsheviks seized control of the Winter Palace in St. Petersburg and withdrew from the war. The newly founded Russian Soviet Federative Socialist Republic signed the Treaty of Brest-Litovsk on March 3, 1918, ceding their Baltic and Caucasus provinces to the Central Powers in exchange for peace.

With newly freed troops on the Eastern Front, the German High Command redeployed fifty divisions across Europe to launch the Kaiserschlacht, or Kaiser's Battle—a do-or-die spring offensive. The US had officially entered the war, and the Germans wanted to end the conflict before the Americans arrived in strength and gave the Allies the advantage. It was a massive gamble. General Erich Ludendorff's plan hinged on Operation Michael, a complex strategy with a simple goal: drive the British forces into the sea.

Operation Michael began as an outstanding success. The Germans broke the four-year stalemate on the Western Front and conquered twelve hundred square miles, capturing the towns of Albert, Bapaume, and Pèronne. The *soldaten* were within sixty miles of Paris.

The BEF was on the verge of collapse. "Our backs are to the wall," proclaimed Field Marshal Haig in a special order of the day. "There is no other course open to us but to fight it out. Every position must be held to the last man: there must be no retirement."

With the Russians out of the war and the British defences crumbling, defeat felt like a real possibility for the Allies. The Canadians began to worry that the Germans would target them next. Their fears looked justified when, on March 26, the Nor'westers were ordered to move to Pommier immediately. They were officially on standby. There would be no more leave, and they needed to be ready to move at a moment's notice from now on.

Shoulders shivering under loaded rucksacks, the 28th Battalion set off for the gruelling eight-hour heavy march at 11.40 p.m. Although the men had marched so much that they could do it in their sleep, tonight felt different. They donned their steel helmets, fixed their bayonets, and drank from their water bottles only at halts. Strict discipline was enforced. There was no marching at ease and no stragglers. While companies were supposed to stay one hundred yards apart and keep step at all times, that was impossible in the dark. Staggering blindly after the shadowy blobs in front of them, the sleep-deprived soldiers stumbled into each other with half-closed eyes and cursed wildly until the morning light.

The situation deteriorated further when the battalion bivouacked at Pommier. The Germans started shelling the Canadians daily, and the Nor'westers were ordered to stand-to-arms at midnight.

"Something doing?" Lester asked his cousin. He already knew the answer. Nothing positive came from moving camps in the middle of the night and standing-to at 12.00 a.m.

"Heinie's coming," Bill informed him. "He could be knocking at our door any minute. Lieutenant Brown has set up a picquet line to warn us. Fight to the death and delay the advance so the Tommies can counterattack. That's the order. There's no retreat for us. We fall where we stand now."

Sergeant Harper issued each of his men an extra bandolier of ammunition and two more grenades. Then he went to his dugout to outwait Fritz's latest barrage. When he emerged, he found two privates propped up against each other. Darn useless recruits. They were sound asleep. He could not take his eyes off the new lot for a second.

"Killed by concussion," a stretcher-bearer came over and said.

"Pardon?"

"Killed by concussion," he repeated.

"Those two? There's not a scratch on either of them."

"I know. It's a freak incident. Normally they'd be full of shrapnel too. But they're not sleeping, if that's what you're thinking. They're definitely napoo." The medic walked over and touched them. The bodies toppled over. "See?" He collected their paybooks, wristwatches, and identification discs.

Lester saw a crowd of servicemen gathering together. Only one thing drew that much excitement: the mail. He joined his colleagues jostling their way closer to the canvas sack on the ground. The sergeant-cum-mailman called out the name of each soldier and flung the parcel at its gleeful recipient.

As the men dispersed with their loving letters and treats from home, Lester stepped forward. "Are you sure there isn't more?" He had not heard from his wife in some time and was overdue for a message.

The postman tipped the bag over. "No, sorry. It's napoo."

A Millsy lodged in Lester's windpipe. For the first time in eighteen months, Mabel had not written her regular letter to him. He knew that she was upset, but her silent treatment felt tantamount to divorce.

Till We Meet Again

The Nor'westers and the other battalions in the 2nd Canadian Division were sent to reinforce the British VI Corps. Their high mucky muck, Major General Burstall, wanted to gather intelligence and harass the enemy, so he approved a new tactic: deep raiding. His troops began pushing behind the front line during raids. They snuck farther into German territory and killed more unsuspecting *soldaten* hiding in dugouts. Of course, this made raids even more dangerous. The 2nd Division's casualties began to mount, and the veterans grumbled. Why were they dying while the other Canadian divisions were on rest?

Sergeant Harper was ordered to report to Captain Blackburn, the officer-in-command of B Company. The Northwest Battalion was taking part in the latest raid. Their mission was simple:

Capture the enemy when they could; kill them when they could not. Obtain any identification and other useful information.

Sergeant Harper felt a sinking sensation in his stomach. Kidnapping armed *soldaten* from their trenches was a half-baked idea. There was a reason why raids were unofficially known as "suicide clubs." He had no desire to risk his life for a shiny medal or even special leave. Who cared if people thought that he was a coward? Lester just wanted to survive the war and get home to his family in Canada. Yet the sergeant knew better than to argue with a superior.

"Yes, sir," he glumly capitulated. In the military, there was no other answer.

For two straight days, the raiders practised over a taped area that replicated the German lines. When they had memorized their roles on the mock-up of the enemy's trench system, the mission was approved. Zero hour was set for 2.30 a.m. on May 3.

On the evening of May 2, the raiders sat down for dinner. The meal was tastier than usual, and that should have made them wary. In the CEF, special provisions came at a high price, which was usually exacted in blood. Quite possibly, some German would spill the contents of their stomachs with a bayonet in a couple of hours.

Sergeant Harper ignored such concerns and wolfed down the supper. If he was going to die, he might as well die with a belly stuffed with officer-quality grub. Lester could put up with the mud, the cold, the lice, the rats, the barrages, and even the raids as long as he was well fed. Dying full was as close as he could get to dying happy.

He dressed in fighting order (less his mess tin) and collected a white armband, a smoke grenade, and a solitary Mills bomb to accompany his rifle. The raiders were expected to be in enemy territory for only twenty minutes. They should not need more weapons. Then B Company marched to the Purple Line, where, at 9.30 p.m., they snuck into no man's land in fifteen-minute intervals.

GERMAN FRONT, NEAR BRÉTENCOURT

France—May 3, 1918

I WAS ALMOST A MARKSMAN, SERGEANT HARPER REMINDED himself as he lined up the dim outline of the machine-gunner in his sights. He knew that the shot would give away his position. It would take a miracle to survive. Lester exhaled slowly and softly squeezed the trigger on his Lee-Enfield. *Crack.* The German's arms flung upward, and he tottered over.

The man's compatriot shouted. Pushing the body aside, he swung the muzzle toward the invader. *Tit-tit-tit-tit-tit.* Lester ran for the shelter of a crump hole, the machine gun ticking after him. Bullets smacked into the dirt and ricocheted off the boulders, speckling his face with pebbles.

Sergeant Harper dove headfirst into the shell hole as the bullets churned up the earth. His chest constricted in pain. Rolling over, he checked himself frantically. Whew! The Germans had missed. The awkward landing had just knocked the wind out of him.

Getting to his feet, the Canadian skulked along the side of the crater and through a bombed-out traverse. Then he shuffled up to the edge and cautiously peeked out. The sergeant could hardly believe it. He had made it within throwing distance of the machine gun without getting shot.

Time to test his luck again. Sergeant Harper waited for the fire to slacken, hoping to persuade the Germans that they had hit him. Finally, there was a lull. This was his moment. It was David versus Goliath. No, his odds were worse. David had five stones against one giant, whereas he was a lone bomber with a smoke grenade, a Millsy, and a rifle against a team wielding the world's deadliest gun.

Lester did not have many choices. In the dark, his smoke grenade was most useful to cover a withdrawal if he somehow managed to escape this predicament alive. That left him with a Mills bomb and his rifle. There was only one option: throw his Millsy and then charge the enemy. Surprise them. Shock them. Overwhelm them.

Sergeant Harper tugged the grenade loose. He pulled the pin and popped up. Fully exposed to gunfire, he challenged Fritz to a duel to the death. With a prime view of his target and the Mills bomb ready to fly, Lester knew that he could not afford to miss. If the grenade failed to take out the machine gun, he would be dead before he reached their hideout.

The sergeant chucked the two-pound bomb. The grenade arced high and landed squarely in the midst of the machine-gun crew. *Thud*. The Maschinengewehr 08 keeled over. The Germans squealed in pain.

Sergeant Harper ran toward them with his Lee-Enfield blazing. He fired in anger. He fired in vengeance. He fired for his fallen boys. He pulled and pulled the trigger, not stopping even to breathe. He was having his own mad minute.

The sergeant was almost on top of the gun pit when he remembered that he was a single fool attacking a team. Two enemy combatants were dead, but Lester was still outnumbered three to one. The Canadian jumped into their smoke-filled lair and tried to bluff the Germans into submission. "Surrender! *Aufgeben!*" he screamed. His bayonet glistened in the moonlight, and the men's eyes filled with fear. Lester levelled his rifle at one of their chests. *"Aufgeben!"* His voice boomed with the intensity of an artillery salvo threatening death and destruction.

Then Sergeant Harper heard footsteps behind him. Oh, great! I'm done for, he surmised. There's Fritz's support now. His luck had finally run out. Lester whipped his head around to decide if he should shoot or surrender. Lo and behold, the uniforms behind him were not *feldgrau*. They were khaki.

It was his team! They had followed him deep into enemy territory. They had risked their lives and gone beyond the mission's boundaries to help him. Never had he been so happy to see men disobey orders.

"*Kamerad*, mercy," the commander begged for his life. "Mercy." The three surviving Germans raised their hands in surrender.

The Canadians drove their prisoners back across no man's land by the tips of their bayonets and lugged the machine gun along too. A parachute flare burst into three red flames in the sky above them. Flawless timing—the jig was up.

The raiders returned to raucous cheers in the brigade reserve. Killing does wonders for camaraderie and esprit de corps. There were at least one hundred dead Germans, eight prisoners, and five captured machine guns. What a score! And they took only forty-four casualties.

The outstanding results were reported up the chain of command, and Lieutenant General Currie wrote to congratulate the soldiers on their splendid accomplishment.

"My Dear Ross," intoned Major Bond, reading the Canadian Corps commander's telegram aloud. "Very hearty congratulations on the fine work done by the 28th Battalion in the raid this morning. It was a real fighting raid and its success reflects the greatest credit upon yourself and the officers, N.C.O.s, and men taking part. Such enterprises are undoubtedly of the greatest value in lowering the moral [sic] of the enemy and proportionally raising it in our own troops. The gratifying result of the operation speaks for itself and bears witness to the presence of the two essentials to success in such undertakings—careful organisation and resolute execution."

Bill pulled his cousin aside after the celebration. "I heard 'bout your little out-of-bounds adventure with the machine gun," he said. "You'll be up for a DCM for that act of gallantry."

"A district court martial?" Lester asked sarcastically. "I'll finally get one like you."

"Enough wisecracks, you silly bugger. You saved a lot of lives. Damn good work."

"Thanks, but you know as well as I do that there are hundreds of men who do deeds worthy of the DCM or the Victoria Cross who never get acknowledged."

"True," Bill conceded, "but that doesn't make you less worthy."

Sure enough, the successful raid garnered a series of medals for the battalion. Captain Blackburn received the Distinguished Service Order (DSO), while two lieutenants were awarded the Military Cross. Sergeant Harper was one of six men given the Distinguished Conduct Medal.

On a glittering May morning at the divisional reserve in Bellacourt, rows of troops stood at attention in stiffly pressed tunics with polished brass buttons that shone in the sun. Lester stepped forward when his name was called and accepted the DCM. The medal was the second-highest decoration awarded to NCOs, below the coveted Victoria Cross. Out of the 430,000 Canadians sent to Europe, it was bestowed upon only 1,947 of them.

The DCM came with an acknowledgment in the UK press. "Distinguished Conduct Medal. 811729 Sgt. R.L. Harper, Infy.," proclaimed the official announcement in *The Edinburgh Gazette*. "For conspicuous gallantry and devotion to duty while one of a raiding party. He displayed great initiative and resource in searching out and discovering the enemy in the darkness, and in face of heavy fire led his men with great dash and ability. Behind the objective he rushed in alone and killed and captured the crew of an enemy machine gun about to open fire. He did fine work."

After the ceremony, there was a good old-fashioned bust-up to celebrate. Everyone got sloshed, and Lester's comrades started to josh him about the award.

"Did you pick up that tin scrap in your rations?" one asked.

Like most winners of the DCM, Sergeant Harper downplayed his heroism. There was no need for hubris. His colleagues would only mock him more.

"The stories you hear about me are greatly exaggerated," he replied. "You would have done the same. Now, Captain Blackburn deserved his DSO, I can tell you that. You know, I can't figure out the point of these raids. We lost seven of the best soldiers in our platoon, and all we found out was which one of Fritz's units we're fighting. Raids seem like a crazy, futile exercise conceived by a front office that wants to fill in the gaps on their map. They don't give a piss about us. We're just cannon fodder. How many lives are we going to sacrifice for such trivial information?"

"You're probably right, but the brass doesn't give a shit about what you think. Your intellectual rambling is pointless. It's best to keep your mouth shut and your bloody head below the parapet."

After a few drinks, Lester could not be silenced so easily. "Let's assume that the high mucky mucks actually have a master plan—that they're putting us on these suicide clubs for a reason. Even if we did find some important info, what the devil could we do with it? Look around. It takes two or three men to support every soldier at the front. We can't conduct a gigantic push for more than a few miles because we can't keep our fighting line supplied. Sure, we're beating Fritz back a little, but at a helluva cost. Every time I see the dead and wounded along the trenches, I feel sick at the awfulness of this war."

The newly decorated sergeant passed out on his rubber sheet underneath the stars. He awoke at dawn. The first rays of reddish light seeped into the night sky, streams of blood pouring out of a wounded soldier. Birdsong filled the air, and two cows grazed on the dewy grass nearby. Lester had a thick head, and his legs ached from sleeping on the stony ground. With no one else around, he leaned against the rough bark of a tall poplar, dropped his trousers, and paid his respects to a few small but troublesome lice.

France
May 27th, 1918

My Sweetheart Maybelle:
Oh girlie, you cannot know how much I miss you now. I am tired of waiting for the end of the war! I want to be home with you.

The following will be news to you, I guess. Quite a number received decorations recently in our unit, and your humble husband was among the "victims." I now have the D.C.M. Needless to say, we had a regular bust-up when the decorations came out. Bill Thompson is just the same and can still consume beaucoup booze.

I got the D.C.M. for a part I took in a raid, which we pulled off on the morning of May 3rd. Over 300 of us went over the top. We stayed twenty minutes bringing back a dozen prisoners and 5 machine guns. We killed scores. We had about 46 casualties, 6 killed. I lost 7 out of my platoon, of which 2 were killed; and they were some of the best men I had. It always seems thus, the best are taken, the "crocks" left!

Now dear, please do not tell everyone about this. There are hundreds with them, but the honour that goes with it I give to you. Anything I do out here is for you, dear, for I love you. I will not say how I got it. I mention these things to you, but do not pass them on beyond the family circle.

Quite recently I have seen a strafe or two, but I could not even get a blighty. We are working pretty hard these days but I have been lucky, extremely lucky in fact. A couple of times, I almost hoped Fritz would put two or three machine gun bullets into me or at least enough to send me to Blighty for a rest. But there is too much chance of the son of a gun putting the bullet or shrapnel through my bean and that would make me napoo. Savez? I don't relish the idea of staying here to fertilize France!

Oh, to be in dear old Canada just now. Someday in the dim future if this terrible war ever ends, which seems remote at present. There is always something doing on the Western Front now because Fritz has so many troops at his disposal. He is making a very hard try to effectively sever the Allied line. As far as I can see, both sides are about equal at present, but Fritz (realizing the Americans will be here in strength next year) is making a great effort to force a decision now.

I think that our branch of the Harper mob is doing its bit for King and Country, but to hell with patriotism. That won't get me back to Canada and you; nor will it stop a German shell. Some of these times I am going to speel a line of bull to you about what we have to stand out here, especially in the way of nerves and control of mind and body under shell fire. There is nothing harder on the spirit and morale of troops than to have to withstand enemy shell fire. I have seen a number of men killed instantly from concussion without a mark on the body. That happens when a man is very close to the shell and, through a freak, he is unhit by shrapnel. Of course, a man generally has both. Enough of that. I should not tell you these things!

Now for a reprimand. A Canadian mail came the other day, and there was no letter from you! That is the first miss you have made since I came to France. Don't let it occur again. That's all.

Please remember that I say a lot of things which I really don't mean, so have a heart. I'm full of the devil and am liable to say anything. Give Lillian a hug and kiss for me. Would you like one too, dear? There is little else to say except Je vous aime.

*With love,
Robert Lester Harper
xxxx*

p.s. Send some good-quality chocolates or candy. That is what I like. And HONEY!!!

SERGEANT HARPER WAS GLAD THAT HE STOPPED WRITING before revealing too much. Lester was no longer worried about censorship—he was concerned about protecting his wife. He told Mabel almost everything, from the stories of his friends' shenanigans to their smutty yarns and obscene jokes. He even made the mistake of mentioning his own outings with ladies. Yet the sergeant refused to write about the heinous savagery of his day-to-day existence. There were hundreds of tragedies that he could have shared with her. But what would that have accomplished? It was bad enough that he was forced to live them. Lester would never be able to forget the horror. Why should he burden her with that hell too? No, he would not. Alas, there was little else to say, except "I love you, send honey."

CHAPTER SEVEN

AND STILL THE WAR GOES ON

WAILLY WOOD

France—June 12, 1918

SERGEANT HARPER WAS CLEANING UP FOR PARADE IN THE huts five miles behind the lines when a runner approached him with a message. Report to the BOR immediately for your leave warrant, the order stated. This can't be correct, Lester thought. He was not up for leave until next year.

"What does it say?" a colleague asked.

Lester handed him the note.

"Harper," his friend declared, "you're so damn lucky. If you fell into our shithouse, I bet you'd come out smelling like a rose!"

Lester laughed hysterically. He must have never heard that joke before because he repeated it in his letters with exclamation marks to boot.

As Sergeant Harper soon discovered, his battalion had been awarded two special leave warrants for soldiers with exceptional service on a raid, and Lieutenant Colonel Ross chose him out of a thousand men, plus or (more likely) minus a few owing to recent KIAs. Unlike his friends, Lester did not need the agonizing pain of a bullet wound to get to Blighty. He only had to single-handedly take out a machine gun.

The sergeant packed his haversack and beat it for their horse line six miles away. With a cheque for eighteen pounds to cash in England and fifty francs in his pocket for transport, he scampered down the rutted road humming his favourite tune.

Just a-wearyin' for you,
All the time a-feelin' blue,
Wishin' for you, wonderin' when
You'll be comin' home again.

Twenty-four hours later, Sergeant Harper was back in London. This time, he went directly to his favourite place, Scotland, where he visited the museums, walked through the art galleries, and ate five meals a day in Glasgow and Edinburgh. He even paired the fanciest dinners with wine.

On this trip, unlike his last one, Lester made sure to see plays like *Cheating Cheaters* alone (or so he told his wife). The young Canadian cherished every moment of his special leave, and on more than one occasion, he was upgraded to prime seats at the theatre because of his DCM. Sometimes he sat close enough to the stage to make eyes at the girls.

When Lester got back to London, he saw Fortunino Matania's painting *Goodbye Old Man*. Commissioned by the Blue Cross Fund in 1916 to raise money for horses suffering during the war, the watercolour depicted a British soldier saying farewell to his dying horse in the midst of an artillery barrage. The realistic painting was violent and depressing. Lester loved it. He was so impressed by how well the artist had captured the details, especially the bursting shell, that he purchased a print and sent it home to Mabel.

The fields were overflowing with lush grass, grains, and wildflowers when Sergeant Harper returned to France. The vibrant colours of summer were a stark contrast to springtime in the line, when their trenches, duckboards, uniforms, packs, and even mud-covered skin were all various shades of brown. Little did Lester realize that this beauty had a macabre cause—the countryside was bursting with life because the soil had been enriched by the blood of the dead.

Lester found his battalion stationed in Ambrines.

"Sergeants from B Company are billeted in the peasant's house next to the château," he was told.

A house? *Trés* jake! There were advantages to being a sergeant, like sleeping in a bedroom with a window instead of on a cement floor in a stable.

Bill clapped him on the shoulder affectionately when he walked in the door. "Welcome back to the shit. We missed you. Your mail's on the desk."

Lester picked up a stack of twelve letters. Ten were from his wife.

"There was a parcel too, but it's napoo. Remember me to Mabel, will you? Her cake was delicious."

Landing back in France was an awful bump after a fantastic trip to Blighty, and Lester's buoyant mood swiftly sank into annoyance. His fourteen-day special leave felt like a dream that he longed to return to. The sergeant muddled his way through their daily grind. Everything about the military irked him. He grudged the parade dope. He grudged the donkey work. He especially grudged Bill's eating his cake.

"What's got you so glum lately?" Sergeant Major Thompson asked. "Somebody die or something?"

Lester groaned. The joke, of course, was morbid. Most of their friends were dead. Like many soldiers, his cousin had developed a twisted sense of humour in the trenches. "Gallows humour," psychologists label the phenomenon. Laughing in the face of death helped Bill cope with the absurdity of their predicament. Alcohol helped too.

"Wes!" Lester's lacklustre eyes brightened when he saw his sweaty brother dismount a bicycle.

"That's got to be twenty miles," Wes complained. "Your turn to visit me next time."

"Sounds like a lovely spin through the countryside. Don't worry, I'll make your ride worthwhile." Lester pulled out a bottle of Johnnie Walker that he'd smuggled in from Scotland.

They sat under a poplar tree, and he told Wesley about his trip. Then Wesley told him about his new position in the 2nd Canadian Infantry Works Battalion. His new unit was responsible for road, railway, and bridge maintenance and construction.

Despite having another cushy position in the rear, Wesley was trying to get out of the regiment. He was always on the lookout for a better job. "I've put in for a transfer to the Royal Flying Corps," Wes said. "I was up for my medical examinations the other day, but the doctor wouldn't pass me fit. I have to go back again in a month. The flying corps is very suspicious of anyone who has been wounded. They're afraid I might have a light touch of shell shock."

"The flying corps? Really? What kind of stunt are you trying to pull? That's a pretty dangerous job."

"Everything out here is dangerous, but flying should be interesting, and it could come in handy after the war. Plus, they practically live in luxury. You should take a stab at the flying corps too. They've put a call out for pilots and observers. Anything is better than the infantry, right?"

"I'd love to be a flyer, but it's not gonna happen. Once you're an NCO in the blessed infantry, you're SOL until you're killed or wounded."

"To a cushy one, then," Wes toasted.

"A cushy one," his brother repeated and swilled his Scotch.

Lester didn't need to join the RFC to escape the trenches. A stalwart sergeant with a DCM, he was recommended for the officer training program. As the 28th Battalion prepared to return to the front, Bill saw his cousin standing on the sidelines and motioned him over.

"If you make good in Blighty," he advised, "they'll offer you a commission. *Compreé?*"

Lester nodded.

"Oh, I almost forgot." Sergeant Major Thompson fussed about in his haversack and pulled out a German revolver. "We wanted to make sure you got a souvenir to remember your little adventure. You deserve it for taking out that machine gun."

Lester looked down the sights of the ultimate war trophy. "*Merci*," he said.

"Now good-bye-ee and fuck you!" Bill replied.

Sergeant Harper turned to his men one last time before they marched off without him. "I'll be back soon," he said. "Try not to get yourselves a little bit killed while I'm gone."

Once again, they refused to listen.

Off Lester went to Folkestone and London, where he caught a train to Bexhill-on-Sea, one of southern England's most exquisite bathing beaches. "Gee whiz," the new cadet whistled when he arrived at the Canadian Training School (CTS). He could hear the waves break from his room at the glamorous resort that served as their billets. The only thing that could make life better, he thought, was if Mabel was by his side.

Every morning, Cadet Harper rose early to swim in the sea and do PT on the promenade. Then he ate a full English breakfast before sitting through hours and hours of lectures at the CTS, which reminded him of Brandon College. The British navy, anti-submarine warfare, Turkey, the organization of different units in England and France, and so forth. The classes varied widely, but he found them all equally boring.

Cadet Harper felt like he was back at training camp. Chin up, chest out, shoulders back, stomach in. The cadets paraded in front of General Richard Turner and the Duke of Connaught, or the "funny old codger," as Lester now referred to Queen Victoria's son and Canada's governor general.

At night, the cadets donned their dress uniforms and dined with the town's elite in the hotel's winter garden while the band played in the rotunda. Although the Canadians were expected to act like gentlemen, their habits from the front were difficult to break. Lester still scratched obsessively, and all etiquette was cast aside when the waiters brought out the dishes. To the astonishment of the civilians at his table, he gorged himself on heaping helpings of roast mutton, spuds, turnips, and Sultan's pudding.

The seaside town slowly rinsed the cadets clean of the war. The daily dips, briny ocean air, and indulgent cuisine had a profound effect on Lester's physique. His rashes, boils, and lice were gradually replaced with healthy tanned skin and a layer of extra fat.

But living the high life in England had its price, which was steep and calculated in pounds. Everything was terribly dear, and Lester's pay melted away in the gorgeous summer heat. There were shows to see, sweets to buy, and weekend trips to London and Hastings. The civilians took it for granted that Canadian officers had money, and Cadet Harper got soaked at every turn. As an officer-in-training, he felt obliged to pay for first-class fares, fancy hotels, gourmet restaurants, and of course, dance lessons. *Oh, c'est la guerre!*

Lester was financially embarrassed. Saddled with debt, he owed his entire paycheque before he'd even received it. The cadet needed *l'argent* desperately to pay back his loans, so he wrote to his wife.

Bexhill-by-Sea
August 31st, 1918

Dear Sweetheart:
How are you today? I am exceedingly fine. It is hard to believe that I am back in dear old England again! Every few months, each unit in France sends several men to England to train. If they make good, they are given commissions. So, here I am at a lovely hotel by one of the most beautiful bathing beaches in Southern England. I can hear

the breakers and the surf. Now what do you think of your beau? How would you like to go bathing in a "one" piece suit? No skirt or stockings! That is the way women bathe here. How different in Canada!

We are supposed to be gentlemen now and are always spoken to as "Sir." We have to be very careful where we go and what we do and say. We cannot do things that we did when we were private soldiers, for the white band around our hats signifies what we are. We must be properly dressed and be on time, but that is all in the game. I am getting along fairly well here, and it certainly is a good change to France. The band plays in the rotunda, and we eat in the Winter Garden, which is enclosed with glass. Have a glass of wine with me, kiddo? I've just had two lovely ones!!! It costs us a lot of money here. As I am drawn up right close to date, I find it pretty hard. But I am lucky to be here at all. I won't ask you for more. That's up to you. If you can spare the dough, please send me a money order.

Have you been watching the papers lately? The Canadians have added to their laurels, for the part of the line they attacked was very difficult to handle and under bad weather conditions. I left the battalion previous to the attack, so I was fortunate because it was a hard nut to crack. I have not seen the casualty lists yet, but they must be heavy. And still the war goes on.

We are being rushed through, so don't be surprised to hear anytime that I am back in France. I have not heard from Wes lately. I hope he escapes old Fritz. He does a great deal of bombing behind our lines and makes things very disagreeable in billets even when out on rest.

I liked your last letter. It suits me fine and makes me feel that everything is going as it should at home. Say, I think you should class my letters as "The Wanderings of the Mind of a Homesick Boy" because there is no continuity in anything I say. Don't forget that through all this crazy dope of mine, I try to give my love!

Good night, darling,
Cadet R.L. Harper
xxxx

p.s. I brought a German revolver over from France with me, and I will send it home if I can arrange it. I may send other souvenirs of this place as well as of Hastings. Keep them with the rest of my collection.

AMIENS
France—August 9, 1918

WHILE LESTER WENT OFF TO ENJOY THE ENGLISH SUN, HIS battalion was having a hot time too. General Ludendorff's gamble failed to pay off, and his worst fears materialized. The Kaiserschlacht was thwarted at the Marne River (once again), and 250,000 fresh and eager Americans were arriving every month. The Germans were pushed back, outnumbered, and on the run.

Field Marshal Haig wanted to press his newfound numerical superiority. Although there were hordes of American doughboys with their youthful exuberance and fat faces at his disposal, they were inexperienced. The French *poilus* suffered from the opposite problem: they were worn out. Alas, the BEF and Dominion troops were forced to lead the attack.

The field marshal called upon the Canadians to launch an offensive from Amiens. The Northwest Battalion bravely charged across a plateau under severe enemy fire and got a bad cutting-up. The CEF took 11,822 casualties at Amiens. Yet the battle marked the turning point of the war. The Allies pushed forward seven miles and finally broke through the Hindenburg Line.

Field Marshal Haig felt vindicated. He had won the decisive battle. The Allies were now sure to triumph. So much for his critics, with their talk of costly victories and fruitless disasters. The millions of deaths from his frontal assaults had not been in vain. His strategy of attrition had ultimately proved successful. He was the man who won the war. *Quod erat demonstrandum.*

There was no time to rest and refit after Amiens because the German defences were faltering. Eager to bring the western campaign to an end, Field Marshal Haig ordered the Canadians onward to Arras. Lieutenant General Currie was given a week to plan an operation that should have taken a month. Unable to surprise the enemy, he opted for a night mission in the pouring rain. His troops went over the top at 3.00 a.m. The men could not see more than fifteen feet ahead of them. They inched forward and fought in vicious close-quarters combat. It was a helluva show. While the Canucks came through victorious at Arras and the 28th Battalion captured the village of Wancourt, the CEF lost 11,400 men in the bloodbath.

All four Canadian divisions drove east toward Berlin, liberating towns along the way. The fleeing *soldaten* decided to make a stand at Valenciennes, the last French city under their control. Surely the Allies wouldn't bombard the home of thousands of civilians, General Ludendorff reasoned. He was wrong. The artillery pounded Valenciennes mercilessly with 303 guns. But the Germans refused to capitulate, and British headquarters realized that the kaiser was not ready to accept their terms for peace. As Wesley had already figured out, "The only time anybody can talk terms with Germany is when they have beaten her on the field of battle."

Lieutenant General Currie ordered his shock troops to advance on Valenciennes. Even though the enemy was dug in with an open field of fire and outnumbered them two to one, the Canadians still crushed them. The German military was in full retreat. Smashed transports and overturned carts, discarded rifles and bombs, even dead and dying men cluttered the Nor'westers' path to Mons. The endgame was nigh. Victory felt palpable as Lieutenant General Currie addressed his overextended and depleted troops. "It has never been the spirit of the Canadian Corps to relax in their efforts in killing Boches," he told his battered and bloodied soldiers. Then he ordered them to take the city.

His servicemen were unimpressed. "What kind of rot is this?" one private grumbled. "This war's over tomorrow, and everybody knows it."

The commander was sacrificing their lives unnecessarily. Yet the infantrymen obeyed. They went over the bags on November 9, and 280 more Canadians were killed or wounded.

HAVRÉ

Belgium—November 11, 1918

AT 6.30 A.M., THE CANADIAN CORPS HEADQUARTERS RECEIVED the news that the Armistice had been signed. All hostilities would officially cease at 11.00 a.m. Signalmen and runners spread the message to the troops up the line.

The Nor'westers were the vanguard of the Allied attack, the tip of Field Marshal Haig's sword. "The Pursuit to Mons," historians have labelled the last stage of Canada's war. That term is misleading. The 28th Battalion had already passed Mons. In fact, they had charged ahead of every other unit and captured the town of Havré, five miles farther east. "The Pursuit to Havré," the history books should be corrected to read, in honour of the Northwest Battalion.

When the CO of the Nor'westers received the news, he ordered his men to stay down and not expose themselves to any danger. Private George Price was in the trenches, and he could already see the locals celebrating. A Belgian woman waved to him from the window of her home. George checked his watch. It was almost 11.00 a.m. The twenty-five-year-old was desperate to get to her before another man did. A wave was all the invitation he needed. No longer would she be able to say, *"Après la guerre."* He wanted to be the first one to kiss her on the day that peace was declared.

The impatient private from Moose Jaw poked up his head. The streets were silent. He jumped out and raced toward her house. A single shot rang out. George doubled over and collapsed. It was still a few minutes until eleven. The war was not yet over.

Private Price gasped and gurgled and writhed about the ground. A nurse ran out to help, but there was little that she could do. A German sniper had shot him right in the chest. George sputtered and died in the mud. Lester's colleague in the 28th was the last Allied soldier killed in the Great War. While his comrades toasted the end of the conflict, singing, dancing, and drinking beer, Private Price was laid to rest in the Havré Old Communal Cemetery.

BEXHILL-ON-SEA
England—November 11, 1918

NEWS OF THE ARMISTICE WAS MET WITH MIXED EMOTION IN the seaside town. At first, there was sombre quietness, tearful reflection, and bitterness. The war had spared no one. Nearly every family had lost a son, a husband, or a father. Many had lost all three.

But the sadness was soon overwhelmed by jubilation. It was not as much a victory celebration as a shared sense of relief. A great load had been lifted off the shoulders of the people, and especially, the soldiers. The cadets whooped it up like schoolboys. They hooted and hollered, hugged and backslapped each other. Their joie de vivre was contagious. Lester couldn't believe his luck. He never had to return to France. Ever.

Church bells rang. Folks poured out of the offices and into the pubs. Carloads of girls raced up and down the streets, honking their horns, waving flags, and singing lively songs. Crowds gathered around bonfires on the beach and lit fireworks into the night.

"It's over! Hurrah! The bloody war's finally over," an old Brit slurred as Cadet Harper passed him on the promenade.

No one wanted the party to end, so it continued for a week straight. There were dos and to-dos every day. The streetlights were going again, and all places of entertainment were in bounds. The cadets were great attractions, especially in the matrimonial way, and Lester was invited to every booze-up and bash. Proudly donning his dress uniform for the fifth gala in a row, he danced eighteen out of nineteen songs, to the delight of the ladies of Bexhill.

Bexhill-on-Sea
November 15th, 1918

Dearest Girlie:
Owing to the Armistice being signed, steps toward demobilization are being taken. The school here closes, and everybody returns to their reserve units. Thus, I am through.

I am anxious to see London all lighted up. How I would love to take you. What do you think, ma cherie? Won't you come and enjoy a booze-up with me? Girlie, you don't know how I long for you. You have been my "Dream Girl" for two and a half years.

I'll be coming home to you sometime in 1919. Our lucky number, Mabel. I hope it brings us good luck even after I return. I shall be home all too soon, about January 1st, I think. At least, I hope that I am fortunate enough to be in England for Christmas. Next Christmas I shall be with you for sure. I have been thinking a great deal about you and Lill and how nice it would be to be back on 107th Street! I'll get there someday, but you may not know me; I shall be a great deal different to the Lester you used to know in 1916.

Do you want to go back to Pouce Coupe or do you want me to work at something else? At any rate, I should have to get some capital. I do a lot of thinking on this subject. I am more or less a misfit but, if I could get started at something that I could use my abilities, I think I could make a happy home for you. What do you think, dear?

If we do go north, we must be independent, self-sustaining, and on our own. We will just go to our little grey home in the west where no one will bother us, for the "doos" will all be over. To hell with this wandering. I've seen enough of pomp and style and festivities. Thanks!

I close with a heart breaking with love and craving for you.

Loving kisses for Lillian and Mabs from,
Bob Harper
xxxx

THE PARTY WENT ON FOR WEEKS. THE HANGOVER LASTED FOR years. The butcher's bill from the war was staggering. The casualty lists in the newspapers kept coming out long after the Armistice. There were pages and pages of names printed in the tiniest font.

Canada had mobilized 620,000 of its 8 million citizens only to have 240,000 redden the soil of Europe. Over 61,000 of them would never return home. They would remain forever buried under the muddy fields of France. A walloping 70 percent of Canadians on the Western Front were either wounded or KIA. And these categories were not mutually exclusive. The unluckiest personnel were shot, stitched up, sent back, then killed.

The last hundred days of the war were the worst. The casualty rate was the highest in Canada's history. From the Battle of Amiens to the Armistice, the CEF suffered 45,835 casualties. The 50,000-man infantry bore the brunt of the losses. Officer training in Bexhill saved Lester's life.

The new lieutenant checked his mail one last time before leaving the CTS. Lester had not heard from his brother in a month, and he was starting to worry. He knew that things had been very rough in France near the end. Even if Wesley had avoided going over the top in the Pursuit to Havré with his bombproof job, the rear was still dangerous because of Fritz's gunners, who swept it with shells in hopes of demolishing the Allied billets, supply dumps, and road junctions.

The damsels gathered at the Bexhill train station to wish the newly fledged officers farewell. After hugging and kissing the women goodbye, Lester took his seat in the carriage. A lady he had danced with several times made her way up to his window.

"May I please have your white hatband as a token to remember you?" she asked.

Lieutenant Harper tossed the hatband out the window to her and then the train set off—not to return him to France, as he had once imagined it would, but to take him back to their training camp, where his war had really started.

It was surreal to return to Camp Bramshott after two years at the front. Their base was infuriatingly the same. It looked and smelled the way it had two years earlier: wet and dreary. Yet everything felt different. Even the biting dampness of the English winter seemed mild and muggy compared to France.

The camp was riddled with jovial memories now ruined by the war, every corner haunted by the faces of friends dead and gone. Had Lester really been so eager to make Fritz's acquaintance when they were stationed here in 1916? In retrospect, it seemed unbelievable that he had felt dejected and jealous whenever his name was not called in the draft.

Lester walked past the YMCA, where they had glibly sung "God Be with You Till We Meet Again" to the soldiers leaving for France. Most of them he would never meet again. Oh, how they sang with glory and gusto! Those poor boys knew not what was in store. How could they? Most were barely old enough to vote. They were too naive to understand that the foolhardy youth are the first to be sacrificed in battle. Lambs rejoicing on the way to their slaughter, Canada's children joyfully marched to war.

Lieutenant Harper was reassigned to his former unit. Gone were the cheery faces of his boys. Most of them were dead. He tried to remember their individual faces, but they blurred and blended together in his mind. Lester reviewed his new charges. He had a platoon full of casualties. These soldiers had survived, but at what cost? Their scars and limps accused him of betrayal, of shirking his responsibility to his men, of enjoying the pleasures of Bexhill while they fought and died in a hellish autumn campaign.

The lieutenant found life in the army better as an officer. The duties were cushy. The mess was top fare. The club was posh. He even had his own batman, who functioned as his personal servant. His greatest challenge was mixing with the other officers. In their company, Lester felt terribly small and lacking a proper education. I could have been an MD by now, he rued, if I had only had sense enough to go to McGill. Why had he been like all those silly asses who, to join the army, threw away a great opportunity?

Lieutenant Harper was playing billiards in the officers' club when an orderly from the BOR entered with a telegram. The game stopped. All eyes followed the messenger as he approached Lester. The lieutenant grimaced. The last note he'd received about Wesley in England had filled him with apprehension. His brother had been injured then. Was this message worse?

Lester took the telegram. A single glance allayed his fear. The note was not about Wesley—it was from him. Finally. His brother was all right. Better yet, he was on leave and coming to visit.

On the morning that Wesley arrived in Camp Bramshott, there was an inspection by General Richard Turner and Prime Minister Borden. Lieutenant Harper felt awful, but he was in charge of preparing his platoon. Chin up, chest out, shoulders back, stomach in. The weather was rainy and raw, and the lieutenant shivered in the cold without a coat for three hours. Then Wesley showed up, and he toughed it out again.

"Don't you look good in your new uniform, sir," Wes said. The brothers spent the afternoon together, and Lester promised to meet his younger sibling in London the following day. But the stress and excitement had fixed him for sick. He woke up the next morning sweaty and chilled with a raging fever. His head throbbed. His stomach cramped. His groin spasmed in pain.

Never in his life had Lester felt so ill. There was no way that he was going to London. This did not seem like the usual La Grippe either. Hot lemonade would not do. The lieutenant reported to the medical officer. Fortunately, the doctor on duty was competent. Recognizing the seriousness of the illness, he diagnosed Lieutenant Harper with influenza and sent him to the army hospital. Other Canadian soldiers were not so lucky. Their MOs filled them up with rum and told them to sleep it off.

Lester spent the next week bedridden in a hospital ward. He coughed and sputtered, his lungs like tanks bogged down in the mud. The pioneer lost a lot of weight, but he had survived the trenches with a dogged tenacity and refused to die from the Spanish flu. Even after his discharge, he was so debilitated that he needed ten days off to recover. Lester hoped that Mabel and Lillian had escaped the flu because it was no joke.

The lieutenant was one of forty-five thousand Canadian troops infected with the virus, which spread rapidly across the CEF. Nowhere was safe from the pandemic. Not the training camps of England. Not the trenches of France. Crowded and transient military encampments were hotbeds for the Spanish flu. Exhausted and unhygienic soldiers died swiftly. Men who woke up with a sore throat were dead from respiratory failure by lunch. Surviving the war only to die of the flu was very hard luck.

In England, life went into lockdown. The Canadian camps were quarantined, and the troops were banned from attending any gathering of more than twenty people. They weren't allowed to go to concerts, dances, or even church services. Despite such restrictions, up to four thousand CEF servicemen died from the Spanish flu. The greatest medical disaster of the twentieth century, the virus struck with a ferocity unmatched by the bullets and bombs of the Great War, killing up to fifty million people worldwide.

Mabel's co-workers at Edmonton City Dairy during the Spanish flu pandemic.

GODESBURG
Germany—December 16, 1918

WHILE LESTER WAS SICK IN THE HOSPITAL, HIS BROTHER returned to France. He took the ferry to Boulogne-sur-Mer and travelled to Belgium on the train. Then after almost three years in Europe, Wes finally entered Germany. What a beautiful country, he thought, upon his arrival in a town on the Rhine River. Unlike in France and Belgium, very few battles had been fought on German soil. The Canadian was amazed at how up to date everything was. The Germans were far ahead of the French and Belgians in terms of technology.

Wesley was billeted in the house of a wealthy family with three sons. While all three men had survived the Great War, only one had made it through safely. His two brothers had been seriously wounded. One, a private in the infantry, had been crippled in battle. The other was an aviator whose squadron had bombed London once too often, and he ended up badly injured as well.

The youngest child was a swell-looking girl of eighteen who was studying English at school. The military family was very patriotic, but they were good enough not to show their hatred. Everybody was polite, except for the old gent who skulked around the house.

"Good morning," he would say to Wesley when he woke up.
"Good night," he would say before bed.

That was it. Wes was living in the midst of the German militarism that he had signed up to fight, and the Canadian hoped he would get to stay there for Christmas.

KINMEL MILITARY CAMP
Wales—January 1919

WHEN LESTER RECOVERED FROM THE SPANISH FLU, HE WAS offered a position escorting demobilized troops back to Canada on transports. At first, he refused. The No. 5 Conducting Staff wanted officers who would stick with the job, and Lester wanted to get home to Mabel. Then he remembered that his wife had suggested working for a year in Edmonton to build capital before they went back to the Peace River Country. Why try to find a job in Alberta when he was being offered one now? He could start saving money immediately for their own little grey home in the west.

Mabel was working as a stenographer at Edmonton City Dairy, and Lester knew he needed to keep his expenses to a minimum and send her as much of his income as possible. Unfortunately, he was broke because all his belongings had gone missing and he'd had to re-equip himself, which was not cheap.

Thinking that Mabel would approve, Lester accepted the position and became a representative for the Department of Soldiers' Civil Re-establishment. His duties included informing veterans about how the government could help them reintegrate when they returned to Canada.

Lieutenant Harper relocated to the Kinmel Military Camp in Rhyl, in north Wales, where the CEF servicemen waited to embark on their journeys home. He was not impressed with the base. "A concentration camp," he called it. There were fifteen thousand bored and anxious soldiers stuck in a shanty town waiting for an open spot on the next ship. They were not impressed with the continual delays or their corrugated metal accommodations. The restless Canadians rioted thirteen times in the concentration camp.

In the mass of angry and transient men, guess who Lester ran into? His cousin Harold.

"What in the blazes happened to you?" he asked. "At first, we thought you clicked off. Then we heard you skipped out on us to vacation in Germany."

"It was far from a vacation. Heinz's Emma Gees got me at the show in Fresnoy." Harold rubbed the scars where the bullets had struck him in his buttock and legs. "I managed to crawl to an abandoned trench, where I dressed my wounds. I called for help, but no one came. When I realized that I was on my own, I tried to pull myself back to our lines. That's when Heinz spotted me. I was injured and unarmed, so he dragged me back to their hospital tent, where the docs patched me up. They kept me in a holding cell until their intelligence chaps determined that I didn't have any valuable info. Then they sent me to their rear. Back and forth across Germany, they shunted me from one muddy POW camp to another. You thought the 40 & 8 boxcars were bad—you should have seen the German railcars. Those cattle cars reeked of shit and death. We were packed in so tight that we couldn't move. Merseburg, Münster, Hamburg, and finally Friedrichsfeld. I was stuck at the last camp for fourteen months. And it was no holiday home. It was a nasty barbwire stockade with thirty-five thousand prisoners. Every morning, we were yanked out of bed at sun-up and marched out to a coal mine, where we slaved away till dusk."

"*Merde*," Lester muttered.

"*Merde* is right. It was cold, dark, and dreadfully painful work. Our only break was at night, when we slept in a wooden hut crowded with 250 POWs. We were all so weak. Man after man was cut down by cholera and typhus. I escaped the sickness, thank God, but boy, was I hungry! One slice of black bread and soup—that's it. I ate the same meal once a day for over a year. The bread tasted like sawdust and blood. The soup was just flavoured water. I barely survived."

"You didn't get any Red Cross parcels?"

"Only once a fortnight," Harold conceded. "With a bit of bacon, butter, and tea. It was hardly enough."

"Hold on," Lester said. "You had bacon and a bunkbed while I was stuck with iron rations and a barn floor? I lost a tooth to hardtack!" He opened his mouth to show him the oral casualty. "You've always been soft, cousin. First you griped about Belcher drilling us like the devil at Bramshott. Then you griped about Fritz shelling us to hell at Vimy. Now you're griping about eating bacon in Germany? You don't look any worse from your adventure. Personally, I think the experience may have done you some good."

Harold had not missed his cousin's teasing.

"Have you heard from Frank?" Lester asked.

"McAleer?" Harold exclaimed. "Wasn't he certified medically unfit and sent home?"

"That didn't stop him," Lester explained. "He re-enlisted the following month and ended up in the 5th Battalion. He even stated on his attestation form that he had no previous military experience. Apparently, no one double-checked their records. Last I heard, he was in France. Got gassed pretty bad and ended up in the hospital."

"And Bud?"

"Same old Hugh. The last letter I got from him said that he was having a helluva time in Blighty."

POSITION X.22.A
NEAR CANAL DU NORD
France—October 1, 1918

BUD WAS IN ROUGH SHAPE AFTER TWO YEARS IN THE ARMY. The recently promoted Lance Corporal Morrison had pain in his back, shoulders, and legs from bouts of pleurisy and pyrexia of unknown origin, as well as scars on his arm and face from GSWs. Soldiers often remarked that if the first two blighties did not kill a man, the third one usually did. That didn't bode well for Hugh. He had been sent to the hospital in England twice already, and now he was back in France for more.

The Canadians had been fighting for control over the Canal du Nord since September 27. The battle was intense, and every attack had been met with a German counterattack. Even Lieutenant General Currie admitted that this was some of the bitterest fighting his troops had ever experienced. Lester's friend Hopper was one of the casualties. A private in the 49th Battalion, he had been shot in the right hand on September 29.

The first morning of October was cool and misty. Hugh was thankful to be in reserve with the 31st Battalion when the 5th went over the top at 5.00 a.m. As the Canucks advanced on the canal, the Germans bombarded their lines. A series of shells howled toward the reserves, and Hugh was caught exposed. One moment, Bud was there. The next, he was gone.

"KIA," the OC of his unit reported Lance Corporal Morrison's death.

"Our positions were fairly heavily shelled and some casualties were caused," noted the commanding officer of the 31st Battalion in the war diary that day.

SAINT JOHN
New Brunswick—March 5, 1919

LIEUTENANT HARPER WAS FRUSTRATED TO BE IN HIS DEAR Canada and not going home to Mabel. But that was his job, and it had benefits. The food was excellent, the workload light, and there were plenty of opportunities to walk the streets of new cities. In Ottawa, Montreal, and Quebec City, he went to the theatre and saw professional hockey games. But Lester never truly enjoyed himself without his wife—or so he was smart enough to tell her. If only they had more money, he wished, then Mabel could have accompanied him back to England to see London all lit up.

One night in early March, Lieutenant Harper and a colleague had dinner at their hotel in New Brunswick and then retired to the drawing room, where a doctor from Edmonton was playing the piano.

"Fancy a drink?" the doctor asked after he finished the piece.

"One nightcap can't hurt, right, Doc?" Lester replied.

The men were drinking, smoking, and chewing the fat when they heard a rapping on the door. "May I join you?" a soft voice asked.

A vivacious and well-built woman entered the room. "If she had not been so nice and good looking," Lieutenant Harper later admitted, "nobody would have bothered with her."

The lady sat down across from Lester, revealing an embarrassing number of frills.

"What brings you here?" he asked.

"I'm a nurse on my way home to the US."

Lester noticed the wedding ring on her finger. "And where's your husband tonight?"

"He's still in France."

They continued to chat, and Lieutenant Harper felt the nurse's eyes on him. "Well," he said, avoiding her lingering gaze, "I'm ready for bed. It's been a helluva long day, and I'm beat."

"I'll put you to bed," the nurse replied scandalously.

Lester's eyes widened. His mouth hung agape.

"I'm knackered too," his colleague added.

"Come along, then. Are you joining us, Doctor?"

They all went up to Lester's room, where the haughty nurse began to undress his friend. When she was partially done, she started on Lieutenant Harper. His tipsy colleague was unimpressed. He grabbed the nurse by the waist and threw her on the bed.

The two officers teased the nurse, and she tantalized them in return. They started getting loud and rambunctious, and the doctor had seen enough.

"I'm going to sleep," he said with a sour look. "Watch out for her," he whispered to Lester. "She seems to be the type of woman who has to have it. It'll probably take six guys to satisfy her."

"Excuse me," the nurse replied, leaving too. "I must go and put on my pajamas."

Lester turned out the light and crawled into bed. He was almost asleep when he heard a patter of footsteps in the hall. They drew near, and the floorboards groaned. A doorknob creaked open. The footsteps disappeared.

The next morning, Lieutenant Harper headed for breakfast with another thick head. He opened his door to see the doctor across the hall. Bingo.

"Have a good slap and tickle with that nurse last night?" Lester chided.

An embarrassed smile fluttered across the doctor's lips. "You know, I thought you were going to take her on. I made up my mind not to get mixed up with her. I was sleeping soundly when my door opened, and she crawled into my bed. What could I do? How can any man resist such a fine-looking woman?"

EDMONTON
Alberta—April 1919

AFTER THREE YEARS AWAY, LESTER WAS DONE WITH THE wandering life. He left his civilian position early and headed home to his wife. The veteran was thankful that his family had miraculously survived the great calamity while most of their friends had suffered a crueller fate. He, Wesley, Harold, and Bill were the fortunate few.

Lester now knew how it ended, but the mindless butchery still vexed him. Two shells landed near funk holes. One soldier walked away. Why him? He had seen too many righteous men murdered in cold blood to believe in an all-loving God who watched over him, but was he still breathing only because of a series of lucky strokes? That was a ruthless randomness almost too absurd to fathom. The dammed-up memories and unanswerable questions came rushing back.

For the first time in history, millions of people had travelled across the world to meet in Europe. They came from every habitable continent, from the Dominions of Canada and Australia, the colonies in Africa and Asia, even the Republic of Brazil. They spoke English, French, German, Dutch, Portuguese, Arabic, Swahili, Urdu, Thai, and Cantonese. The Western Front was a modern-day Babel. Yet these men did not come together to build a tower to the heavens. They sped across the seas to murder each other. While they may not have understood one another's language, their screams all sounded the same.

How could such madness occur in the enlightened twentieth century? The marvels of modern technology were supposed to usher in an age of peace and prosperity. Cars, airplanes, and telephones were designed to unite people. But they were harnessed for the most savage and soulless mechanized slaughter. Cars became tanks. Airplanes dropped bombs. Telephones called in artillery strikes. The war was an industrial process, production and destruction on a massive scale—all compliments of modernization. Was the annihilation of a generation the promise of modernity? Was humanity's first global bloodletting a sign of progress?

Lester had celebrated the Armistice for a week, but now it seemed like a pyrrhic victory. The war was a colossal mistake. Mankind had lost far more than it could ever regain. Their lives were a modern Greek tragedy, like the story of Troy, where a minor squabble had snowballed into a massacre, with blood begetting blood ad nauseam. Sixteen million lives snuffed out over family drama—a spat among a spoiled family of monarchs, to be exact. Queen Victoria's progeny ruled the kingdoms of Europe, and an argument between three cousins (King George V, Kaiser Wilhelm II, and Tsar Nicholas II) had led to wholesale slaughter. Not even Shakespeare had envisioned a family feud erupting into such widespread carnage.

Yet the bloodshed had ended. In truth, it always did—at least temporarily. Was it different this time? Would they finally learn from their mistakes? This was the war to end all wars, after all. Could there be a lasting peace now that the high mucky mucks had signed a stack of papers at Versailles?

Fat chance. The last Treaty of Versailles, which ended the Franco-Prussian War in 1871, had already been trodden on by invading troops.

Even those who survived the war did not get away scot-free. "Some come back wounded, but few come back all right," Lester admitted. Their youth had been squandered. Their friends were dead. They were left to live with their private horrors. The crack of artillery was forever in the veterans' ears. Shells burst in their nightmares, burying them alive in their dreams.

Une génération perdue, they were dubbed. A generation of men killed before their prime. *Dulce et decorum est pro patria mori* was their great lie. Their faith in everything was shaken, from their belief in country to the goodness of humanity. Even their gods were dead.

The Lost Generation was reckless and aimless. Jaded and skeptical of traditional values, many drank themselves to death. Who could blame them? They lived in troubled times: the bloodiest war in human history, a global pandemic, the Great Depression, and then the Second World War. Their lives were forever in the crosshairs.

Many would never come to grips with the atrocities of the First World War. From the trauma of comrades dying in their arms to the horrendous hand-to-hand combat, death in the Great War was often slow, grotesque, and deeply personal. The armies had the most sophisticated weaponry, but the infantrymen slaughtered each other in the most primitive ways. Theirs was a no-holds-barred contest to the last breath. They fought with bayonets, clubs, and shovels. They punched, kicked, and bit too. Who could have anticipated such barbarity when they cheerfully volunteered in the pursuit of liberty, justice, and freedom for all?

The war had been a grim experience, but the former lieutenant had options. With his bonus and back pay, a military pension and some savings in the bank, he could afford to travel Europe with Mabel or use the government's land grant for veterans to buy a piece of property up north. The world was open before him. Yet Lester was no longer open to the world. His wanderlust had been shot up by bullets, his sense of adventure buried in mud. Gone was his desire to study French in Paris or stroll the lovers' lanes of Somerset with his wife. The war had taken that from him. The war had taken a lot from him. He was no longer the prim and proper country boy who didn't drink or swear. He was a weary twenty-six-year-old granny who wanted to be left alone with his family and a cup of tea in a little grey home in the west.

That was, if Mabel still fancied him. Had she been faithful? She had been his dream girl for almost three years. Would she wrap her arms around his neck and kiss him like he had fantasized every night, or would she recoil in horror at the change in his appearance and demeanour? He was a balding ghost of the innocent and optimistic pioneer she had married. And what about two-year-old Lillian? Would she be excited to meet her father for the first time, or would she shy away in repulsion from the stranger in their house?

The idea of home had sustained Lester through the harshest of firefights and the darkest of moods. How could his homecoming ever live up to his hopes and dreams? His mind flooded with doubt as he turned down 107th Street. He walked up the stairs, took a deep breath, and knocked on the door.

Lester and Mabel after the war.

EPILOGUE

Daddy, Did You Ever Kill a German?

LESTER AND WESLEY RETURNED TO SASKATOON CREEK IN December 1919 to find their homestead in an uproar. Their father had married a widow from Vancouver during the war, and his new bride and her children had moved in with him. Neither brother could believe that their dad had remarried in their absence, although they should have expected it. Before they left, A.W. had warned them that he was not fit to raise three boys alone.

Lester refused to embrace the hectic lifestyle of a blended family. He and Mabel rented a cabin with an outhouse in the village of Pouce Coupe for twelve dollars a month, and he took a job as the first provincial assessor of the Peace River Country. Life was not easy in the 1930s, but the Harpers survived on the government salary and a cellar stocked with potatoes, carrots, and jars of preserves. Their house was uninsulated, but the cold didn't bother them. They were pioneers.

As a surveyor, Lester travelled northern BC on horseback or by horse and buggy while Mabel tended the house, raised their daughters, and eventually wrote a book on the agricultural history of the region. Throughout her life, she never lost her sense of decorum. When she went into labour with their last daughter, Barbara, she had Lester circle the village in their car first. That way, the neighbours would think they were out on a leisurely drive, not going to the hospital to have a baby. Proper families, Mabel believed, just showed up with a new child. They didn't even allude to how or when it happened.

Now that Lester had four daughters (Lillian, May, Shirley, and Barbara), the self-proclaimed girl lover moaned about being surrounded by females. He gave each of them a nickname, just as he did his chums. To him, they were always Slim, Fat, Pickles, and Shorty.

With a career and a loving family, the veteran looked like he had successfully reintegrated into Canadian society. But the devout Methodist who went to Europe never came back. Although he rarely swore and still habitually said grace at meals, Lester spent more time drinking and playing poker at the Hart Hotel than he did in church. A cigar frequently hung from his lips, and a flask of rum was always hidden in his pocket.

Lester knew better than to smoke in the house or drink in front of his wife, though. "I'm going for a walk," he would say and wander off.

Mabel didn't complain, especially when her husband came home with a Zenith washing machine. She had a suspicion that he'd won it in a poker game, but of course, she didn't ask. Lester would only give her his usual response: Who wants to know? And that would end the discussion.

The Harpers' house was full of music. When the girls were not practising on their Heintzman piano, Lester played the sheet music that he'd brought back from London. Then his daughter May got a record player and blasted Gene Krupa's legendary jazz drumming.

Her father couldn't bear it. "Terrible," Lester remarked as he walked out the door. "Sounds like an artillery barrage."

Aside from the odd remark, the former soldier never spoke about the Great War. Whenever the subject came up in conversation, most people shared a solemn look, a nod of acknowledgment, or an obligatory moment of silence for the dead. Then they carried on. Not Lester. The

Epilogue

very mention of the conflict triggered him, and Mabel chastised anyone who brought up the war in front of her husband.

When his mother-in-law wanted to publish an account of his DCM in the local newspaper, Lester forbade her. He didn't want to see the collection of postcards, playbills, and other souvenirs that he had sent home either. He told Mabel to put them all away in her private belongings.

Even his daughters knew better than to ask about the war. Or at least three of them did. One November afternoon, shortly after a lesson on the Great War for Armistice Day, Barbara came home from school with a question.

"Daddy, did you ever kill a German?"

A thousand-yard stare crossed Lester's face, and he hid behind his newspaper.

Before Barbara could say anything else, Mabel pulled her into the yard. "Don't you ever ask your dad about the war!" she reprimanded her. "Now see here, I won't have it. Your father had nightmares every night for years after he got back. Not a word."

Although the war was unspeakable, it was omnipresent in their house. On the wall in their living room hung a painting that Barbara never liked. It was the print of Fortunino Matania's *Goodbye Old Man*, which Lester had mailed home from London.

"You see," her father had once told her. "His comrades are waving him on, saying, 'Come on, we can't stay here!'" Even decades later, there was still something about that painting that spoke to the veteran.

Underneath *Goodbye Old Man* sat his short-wave radio, earphones, and a Morse code key. As ominous reports emerged from Europe in the summer of 1939, Lester hovered over his amateur radio with a look of worried concentration on his face. He knew the impact that a war in Europe could have on their remote community in Pouce Coupe.

On September 3, 1939, Prime Minister Mackenzie King spoke to the Canadian people on a special radio broadcast on the CBC. "Unhappily

Epilogue

for the world, Herr Hitler and the Nazi regime in Germany have persisted in their attempt to extend their control over other peoples and countries," the prime minister said. "The United Kingdom has today, in the determination to honour her pledges and meet her treaty obligations, become involved in war. This morning the king, speaking to his people at home and across the seas, appealed to all to make their own the cause of freedom, which Britain has again taken up. Canada has already answered that call."

Canada was, once again, officially at war with Germany. But Lester already knew this. He had heard the news first via his short-wave radio.

The declaration of war reopened old wounds. Memories long buried bubbled up to the surface like corpses washed up by the rain. Lester's mind froze in shock. His stomach churned with disbelief. How was it possible that they had learned nothing from the bloodshed of the Great War? The loss of life felt fresh after twenty-one years.

The veteran had a flashback to Vimy Ridge. The terror was palpable. He could feel the fear as they waited to go over the top. He could see the explosions tear the Canadians apart as they struggled across no man's land. He could hear the Germans scream as his bombs exploded in their dugouts. Millions had died. Now millions more would too. The coming horror was inconceivable.

"Daddy! Daddy! Are you okay?" May asked. "Mom!" She ran to the kitchen for help. Her father sat there motionless. Lester stared through his amateur radio, tears streaming down his cheeks.

Lester continued his work as a surveyor through the Second World War, while Wesley became a successful businessman. W.O., as he now fashioned himself, had inherited his father's dreams of prosperity. Sensing an opportunity in the burgeoning town of Dawson Creek, BC, Wes used his savings to open a store located near the new terminal for the

Epilogue

Northern Alberta Railways. The trains rolled in, and business boomed. W.O. eventually sold his Harper's Department Store to the Hudson's Bay Company for a handsome profit in 1952.

Even as a successful merchant and entrepreneur, Wesley never forgot the motherly role that Mabel had played in his youth. One Christmas morning after Lester retired from his thirty-seven-year career as a civil servant, W.O. showed up with a present: keys to a new Plymouth. "To Mabel and Lester," the Christmas card read. "These keys we are sure will open up many miles of pleasure for you. One key represents our appreciation long overdue to you, Mabel, for your help during the early days when you stepped in and took the place of our mother, washing, ironing, and cooking for us. The other key is for you, Lester, as a small token of our appreciation for your help and advice over the years."

Lester never missed a Remembrance Day ceremony at the Pouce Coupe Legion, and one day, when Barbara was an adult, the legion president stopped her on the street.

"Do you know your father won a DCM medal at the famous Canadian Battle of Vimy Ridge?" he asked.

No, Barbara had never heard such a thing. She mentioned it to her mother.

"Well, I had forgotten all about that," Mabel replied.

The two women searched through the attic, where Mabel had stashed away all of the war memorabilia. There was an old khaki uniform, brass buttons, a medallion imprinted with the words "138th Battalion," and a collection of postcards from France. While one showed a serviceman flopped on his belly as a star shell bursts above him, another had a soldier opening a jar of plum and apple jam. "When the 'ell is it goin' to be strawberry?" he asks. Of course, there was also a postcard with a French Jane on it.

Among the dusty souvenirs and yellowing papers, the women came across an old newspaper from September 14, 1918. The page was titled

Epilogue

"GALLANTRY IN RAIDS &c. Deeds of N.C.O.s and Men Awarded the D.C.M." In the right-hand column, there was a single paragraph:

811729 Sgt. R.L. Harper.
He displayed great initiative and resource in searching out and discovering the enemy in the darkness [during a raid], and in face of heavy fire led his men with great dash and ability. Behind the objective he rushed in alone and killed and captured the crew of an enemy machine gun about to open fire. He did fine work.

Next to it was a handwritten notation signed by L.H. "Greatly exaggerated," Lester had written.

"Hey, Dad, what's this?" Barbara asked.

Lester looked up from his *Maclean's* magazine. "Oh, that. Where did you find that? They gave them away by the dozens, Shorty. Means nothing at all. Nothing at all."

Barbara was skeptical, and finally, fifty years after the war, Lester started talking about it.

"Wouldn't you like to go see the massive stone monument at Vimy Ridge?" his daughter inquired.

"I'd sure like to see it," the veteran replied with misty, faraway eyes. "Yes, it must be a magnificent thing. Magnificent," he sighed.

Lester never made it back to Vimy Ridge. He died peacefully at his home in 1987, at the age of ninety-four. He and Mabel were married for seventy-three years. His comrades from the legion came to the funeral to pay their respects. With no bugler among them, the veterans stood in well-worn uniforms and listened to taps play on a stereo. They sent Lester off with a final rendition of the military call for lights out. Mabel passed away seven years later, at the age of 101. The couple were survived by four daughters, eleven grandchildren, and fifteen great-grandchildren.

Some years after their parents' deaths, Barbara and Lillian returned

September 14, 1918   CANADA

GALLANTRY IN RAIDS, &c.
Deeds of N.C.O.'s and Men Awarded the D.C.M.
("London Gazette" Supplement, September 3.)

(Canadian Infantry, where not otherwise stated.)

886074 L.-Cpl. H. Baldwin.

During a raid he rushed in and captured an enemy machine-gun post, putting the gun out of action and enabling the raid to proceed. Throughout he displayed fine courage and determination under heavy fire.

112174 Pte. (Actg. Sgt.) E. B. Balfour, Cav.

This N.C.O. had located an enemy field gun about 600 yards away from some positions we had captured. He advanced about 60 yards into the open, under heavy fire of all descriptions, and engaged the enemy gun with such success that the serving detachment dispersed precipitately, leaving the gun after two of their number had been seen to fall. He maintained his position for three hours under heavy fire and prevented the enemy returning to their gun. Act. Sergt. Balfour's courageous action and initiative contributed in a marked degree to our retention of the captured position.

359 Cpl. G. E. Bayliss, Overseas Railway Cons. Troops.

For conspicuous gallantry and devotion to duty in maintaining and repairing a track, which was continuously under shell fire. It was largely due to his skill and untiring energy that nine railway mounted guns and howitzers were successfully removed. He controlled his men with great coolness, working continuously for 46 hours.

703567 Sgt. C. V. Brewer, M.M.

During an important raid on the enemy's trenches, when his officer had been wounded, Sergt. Brewer took command of the platoon. Creeping forward, under heavy rifle and machine-gun fire, he cut a gap in some fresh wire put down by the enemy, through which he led his men, being the first man into the enemy's trench. Though wounded in five different places, he fought with bomb and bayonet in most gallant fashion, inflicting heavy casualties on the enemy until, on the signal for recall, he collected his men and brought them back in good order with their casualties. In spite of his own injuries he carried out one wounded man himself, and after bestowing him in the hands of the stretcher bearers he went back and helped to carry out his officer. His behaviour throughout was an example of fine courage and devotion to duty.

748421 Sgt. A. E. Chatwin, M.M.

He bombed a hostile machine gun for fifteen minutes and then rushed up through the trench, personally accounting for four of the enemy. His splendid courage and resourcefulness set an example of the highest order to all ranks.

700792 Sgt. A. W. Cooke, M.M.

For conspicuous gallantry and devotion during a hostile attack, when in charge of a Lewis gun in the front line. A shell dropped among the crew, wounding three and burying the gun. He immediately dug it out, organised a new crew, and putting the gun into action again drove the advancing enemy back. Later, although under heavy enemy machine-gun and rifle fire, he evacuated the wounded of his crew. His fine example throughout the day was most praiseworthy.

441410 Sgt. D. E. Denmark.

For conspicuous gallantry and devotion to duty while in charge of a patrol which covered the assembly of a raiding party. Observing the raiding party in difficulties, he jumped out of the trench and under heavy fire and bombing, he got round the flank of an enemy post and succeeded in driving the enemy out, thereby enabling the attack to proceed. He has previously done fine work.

441377 Pte. F. Earl.

While the enemy were attacking one of our posts, this man, observing another party of them about 100 yards in the rear, crept out and bombed them, compelling them to retire. He then turned on the first party, engaging it from the rear, and when it also retired he followed for 125 yards in broad daylight, inflicting casualties. His energy and initiative materially assisted in foiling the enemy's plans, and he has on several other occasions shown the same qualities.

219559 Pte. S. G. Eastwood.

When the enemy were approaching on both flanks, he got his Lewis gun into action, but it immediately jammed. His section kept the enemy back with rifle fire and bombs for a short time. When the enemy managed to enter the trench, he withdrew his gun behind the parados and again came into action, when, in co-operation with his section, he forced the enemy to retire.

678309 Sgt. (C.S.-M.) C. J. Enright, M.M.

With an officer he rushed an enemy block and machine-gun post; and during a bombing fight he entered an enemy post at great personal risk and captured a machine gun which his men got away. He did fine work throughout the operations.

427161 Sgt. F. Fair, M.G. Serv.

When one of his gun's crew had all become casualties, this non-commissioned officer continued with great coolness to handle the gun, pouring belts of ammunition into the masses of the enemy as they advanced, and causing them very heavy casualties. He retired only when the enemy were so close that capture was imminent. He was severely wounded as he was walking to the new positions in the rear. The example of his deliberate courage was an inspiration to all and was worthy of the highest praise.

107323 B.S.-M. A. E. Forrest, M.G. Serv.

After his officer had been killed he took command of the motor machine-guns, and in severe fighting checked the enemy's advance. He engaged hostile cavalry at close range, and when covering the withdrawal of the infantry, and almost surrounded, fought his way out, with the loss of only two guns, after causing enormous casualties.

198145 Pte. D. France.

While one of a raiding party he rushed an enemy machine-gun post, killing three of the enemy with his revolver and capturing the machine-gun. Throughout he set a fine example of courage and determination.

45600 Sgt. J. A. D. Frechette, M.M., M.G. Serv.

When his officer was killed and the remainder of the team either killed or wounded, this N.C.O. operated a machine gun singlehanded, holding the enemy off until assistance reached him.

279653 Cpl. (Actg. Sgt.) W. G. Geron, Rly. Troops.

For conspicuous gallantry and devotion to duty in emergency work on Light Railway Lines in forward areas under intense hostile fire. On one night this N.C.O. personally supervised the repair of 42 shell breaks, requiring nearly 1,400 feet of new steel, keeping the Light Railway Lines open for traffic. He was in charge of a party working for three hours in gas masks sending forward urgently required ammunition. His courage and example in these and other instances were an inspiration to those working with him.

258709 Pte. S. Glidden.

While in charge of a section forming part of a raiding party, he rushed an enemy machine-gun post and killed three of the enemy, and was badly wounded. Notwithstanding this, he successfully carried the next objective with his section. He set a fine example of courage and determination.

811729 Sgt. R. L. Harper.

He displayed great initiative and resource in searching out and discovering the enemy in the darkness (during a raid), and in face of heavy fire led his men with great dash and ability. Behind the objective he rushed in alone and killed and captured the crew of an enemy machine-gun about to open fire. He did fine work.

679112 Sgt. A. Jamieson.

Sergt. Jamieson was in command of one half of a raiding party on the enemy trenches, and had successfully penetrated behind one of their

A LANCE-CORPORAL IN AN ALBERTA BATTALION
Who wears the Military Medal with two Bars

A MONTENEGRIN SERGEANT IN A B.C. BATTALION
Who wears the D.C.M. and M.M. with Bar.

Canadian War Records Photographs.

posts, when their reinforcements came up in rear of our party. While these were being successfully held off, Sergt. Jamieson rushed the post single-handed, killing four of the garrison and making the fifth a prisoner. In spite of the very superior numbers of the enemy reinforcements, Sergt. Jamieson successfully withdrew his men though two were severely wounded and had to be carried across "No Man's Land." Sergt. Jamieson conducted the operation with great dash, offering a very stout-hearted resistance when faced by superior numbers, and his behaviour throughout was a very fine example to his men.

18362 Pte. (Actg. Cpl.) E. H. Johnsen, M.G. Serv.

When the officer in charge of a motor machine-gun section was killed, this non-commissioned officer took command and fought hard until all his men were casualties and he himself was wounded. Nevertheless, he got a reserve gun into action, which he used with great execution against masses of the enemy until he was again wounded, this time severely. He set a splendid example of determination and fortitude.

213585 Sgt. G. Jones, M.M.

During a raid he and four others rushed a hostile post, bombed the enemy, and killed six. He then reorganised his party, and mopped up a sunken road, bayoneting what enemy remained. Though wounded, he accomplished his task and brought back his wounded. He showed fine courage and determination.

150983 Sgt. H. T. Jones.

His officer being killed, he took command of the party [during a raid], put the enemy to flight, captured a machine-gun, completely destroyed the enemy's position, and safely withdrew his party, bringing back the officer's body and the machine-gun. His courage and resourcefulness were responsible for the success of the raid.

120614 Sgt. C. Jubin.

During a raid against enemy outposts, he crept forward alone and wiped out the crew of an enemy machine-gun with a bomb and captured the gun. He then rounded up his party to come on, and in a hand-to-hand fight with an enemy post they captured one prisoner and killed the rest. He showed fine courage and promptitude.

700577 Cpl. J. H. Langtry.

When [during a raid] an enemy machine-gun opened a destructive fire on the party, after discharging a rifle grenade he rushed forward alone and leapt into the trench, bayoneting the machine gunner and killing three others. His courage on this and on all other occasions has been most outstanding.

8468 L.-Cpl. R. J. Lynch.

During an enemy raid he was in command of a Lewis gun section, all of whom were either killed or wounded during the bombardment; and although severely wounded himself, he kept his gun in action, drove back the enemy, and inflicted heavy casualties. His courage and coolness prevented the line being penetrated at this point.

2279 Pte. G. E. McManus.

During a raid, seeing an enemy machine-gun opening fire on the flank of the party, he dashed towards it, wounded one of the crew with a bomb, killed the other two with his bayonet, secured the gun and returned with it to our lines. His courage is deserving of the highest praise.

331

Newspaper article with Lester's comment.

Epilogue

to their old house in Pouce Coupe. Rummaging through the attic, they found their mother's keepsakes, still nicely organized as she had left them. Safely tucked away among a lifetime of memories was a pile of precious papers: all the letters that Lester had written to Mabel during the Great War.

AFTERWORD

I Have Really Nothing of Importance to Say

TO QUOTE LESTER ON HIS WAY HOME IN 1919: "I HAVE REALLY nothing of importance to say." As a historian, however, I feel obliged to add the following, so *caveat lector*, please. This book is, first and foremost, based upon Lester's letters. Not only do they form the basis of this history, but the italicized epistles are his and, on the rare instances, his brother's or his wife's own words. The material in each one has been lightly edited and selected from the more than seven hundred surviving pages of correspondence from the Harpers to fit the appropriate section.

This source is not without its issues. These are century-old letters written in ink or pencil during a war. Some are faded and dirty and hard to read. One even has a louse squished into it. Others are incomplete. Pages are missing or out of place (too many are similarly marked #2 with no obvious continuation). I am grateful to Lester's relations for their help in gathering, sorting, and cataloguing this archive, but the collection has holes. As for Wesley's letters, their location is not even known. Only photocopies of them have been preserved.

In terms of content, Lester was surprisingly open and candid with his wife, but he didn't tell her everything. Sometimes he chose not to. Other times, he was not allowed to. "There is much to say," he noted, "but the censor forbids it." As such, many of his stories lack details.

Afterword

The same holds true for the letters from Wesley, who wrote to both his brother in France and Mabel in Canada.

Lester preferred to use nicknames or brief descriptions and never mentioned the actual names of any of his soldiers. One was an "exceedingly nice young fellow" and another "my pluckiest private." While I have made the occasional supposition about who these people were in order to tell Lester's story, I have tried to avoid such speculation when possible and use his terms instead.

To supplement the letters, I have drawn material from conversations with the Harpers' surviving relatives, as well as the writings of Mabel, Barbara, and Wesley's son Robert. Their anecdotes are vivid and memorable, and I have tried to let these sources speak for themselves. Robert, for instance, wrote about Alfred's proposal to Gracey, while Barbara took notes on what Lester said about the war near the end of his life. These are particularly insightful, even though they rarely include names, places, and dates. It is important to remember, however, that memory is fallible, so when the oral or later sources do not align with the earlier written material, I have preferred the latter.

To put Lester's experience in its proper historical context, I have relied upon the war diaries and military records in Library and Archives Canada. While the war diaries show the specific location where he wrote many of the missives, they are useful only when he was with the battalion. The military service records similarly provide basic information on the soldiers. They give us facts about their appearances, backgrounds, movements, battle honours, court martials, and wounds. But they don't tell us how their injuries occurred. We can only surmise how each incident happened based upon the particular wound, the doctors' reports, Lester's comments, and the war diaries. I have also used academic and historical texts (most notably Tim Cook's monumental works on the CEF) to provide specific context as well as the broader history of the First World War.

Afterword

Combining all these sources has allowed me to tell Lester's story in greater detail. For example, he wrote, "The other night while on a working party Fritz turned his machine guns loose and believe me we ducked or rather flopped onto the ground." While Lester gave little other background on this incident, the 28th Battalion's war diary shows that they were wiring in Souchez and the work party was unable to go out one night because the sky was "very bright." Historical texts explain how wiring parties functioned and provide insight into what it felt like to come under fire on a work party in no man's land. I have drawn from all these sources to write the vignette in this book.

I have included dialogue in order to express the men's views and share their experiences. Much of it has been lifted from the letters. Some I have quoted directly, repeating the words verbatim, as when Lester bought the sweet biscuits from the lady at the cart. Others I have put together from what he or Wesley told Mabel at different times, such as Lester's remarks about his brother having "a lazy good time" in France. Finally, I have included some of the statements that Lester made near the end of his life. His speech about the raid during the bust-up, for instance, comes mainly from what he told Barbara fifty years later.

I have also used dialogue to provide necessary background on events, places, and people. These conversations are based on historical accounts (like the failed gas raid of March 1, 1917) or personal histories (like Lester's scar). We know, for instance, that Lester and Harold met at Kinmel, where they had a long chat about how Harold was taken prisoner and treated in Germany. Lester told Mabel that he thought his cousin was "none the worse for his adventure." I have written the dialogue based on Lester's letters, the material in Harold's military record, and the available information on the POW camps where he was kept.

The statements of historical figures, such as politicians and officers, come from archival sources and historical texts, although Prime Minister Borden's speech in Ottawa has been taken out of context. We do

Afterword

not know what the prime minister said to the troops on that day. This was what he said at another time. I have crafted the remaining dialogue through heavy research in order to present a realistic depiction of Canadians on the Western Front with the common idioms (such as "*c'est la guerre*") and slang (such as "napoo") that Lester used himself.

On occasion, the sources conflict, or worse, there is a gap in the historical record. When this occurs, I have tried to write the narratives as realistically as possible using the surviving material. In these cases, this is how I think things could have happened after carefully considering all the information available. What follows are some of the key challenges that I faced when writing this book, as well as a discussion of my treatment of sources on a chapter-by-chapter basis.

Chapter One: *Cheer Up, for the Worst Is Yet to Come.* We have surprisingly rich material on the Harpers in Canada thanks to Mabel and, later, Barbara. While I have written the account of their journey across the country based primarily on the family stories, it is important to note that this historical narrative about pioneers settling the west is, of course, outdated and fails to take into account the history of the Indigenous peoples.

While many of Wesley's statements are drawn from his letters, we don't know exactly what he told his brother when they met in the UK because Lester stated that Wes refused to tell him "very much of what he had seen—I mean the grim part." He also added that getting real information was "like pulling teeth."

Chapter Two: *Seriously Inconvenienced by the Lack of Stretchers.* We don't know when or how Mabel told Lester that she was pregnant, but judging by their limited time together before Lillian's birth, it most likely occurred in Sarcee. I have written the vignette based on this assumption,

Afterword

their love of going for walks together, and the story about his colleague's wife's affair that shocked him.

While the Northwest Battalion was in the trenches on March 1, 1917, when the failed gas raid occurred, the battalion's war diary makes no mention of being involved. It only states that preparations were being made for their proposed raid on this date after the February 28 mission was postponed.

The largest question in this chapter relates to Wesley. His medical records refer multiple times to his receiving gunshot and shrapnel wounds on September 15. Yet none of Wesley's or Lester's letters note that he was shot. They only state that Wes took thirty pieces of shrapnel in his back. Was he shot too during the charge? Or did the medical staff just use "GSW" and "shrapnel wounds" interchangeably? I have written this section based primarily on the letters, Wesley's medical reports, the battalion's war diary, and information drawn on the battle and the evacuation chain for the wounded from historical texts.

Chapter Three: *A Most Unhealthy Spot*. Lester told Barbara about the shell that buried him in mud later in life, so we don't know when this occurred or who he was with. The battalion's war diary states that the enemy shelled their camp on March 24 (resulting in eleven casualties), and Lester mentioned that he had a "close shave" around this time. As such, I have speculated that it occurred then.

Lester never said how his soldier died at Vimy Ridge, but the rest of the narrative is based on Barbara's notes as well as the war diaries and other historical works, especially Tim Cook's *Shock Troops*. I've used these sources to provide a multifaceted view of the battle, highlighting not just Lester's actions but those of Bill, their battalion, and the rest of the CEF.

While Lester located his letter on April 11 as "In the Field," parts of the 28th Battalion were on the move on this date from Vimy to their dugouts, so I'm unsure if he actually wrote to Mabel from the battlefield,

Afterword

later that day in the reserves, or perhaps both. I have added parts of later missives (such as his dated April 13) into this one to show what he said and felt about Vimy.

The story of the buggy crash on the Edson Trail was told by multiple people at different points in their lives. While the details vary in each rendition, the overall gist is the same. I have combined and summarized those accounts.

Chapter Four: *The Usual Trench Warfare.* Lester frequently wrote about airplanes in the spring of 1917, including that they strafed their lines, and the war diaries confirm that an Allied plane was brought down at Thélus on April 21; however, Lester didn't say how the soldier who had a premonition of his own death was originally injured or when this incident occurred. He just noted that the wounded man got a nice blighty and then, after a fellow close by remarked that he was lucky, claimed that he would never get out and his time had come. Lester went on to write that the serviceman was killed by a shell on his way to the dressing station, and they passed his body in the trench.

The story of the soldier who was struck by shrapnel on a mission to bury cables is also found in Barbara's notes without a date, location or name, so I have inserted it here because Lester was on loan to the engineers at this time and came under heavy shelling.

Chapter Five: *An Extremely Hazardous Business.* Lester wrote about searching for lice with his friend, but we do not know who squished the louse into his letter. An examination of the handwriting suggests that Lester labelled it. While the 28th Battalion travelled back and forth between Laurent and Lens multiple times in the summer of 1917, I have focused on the key events in this period.

Afterword

In terms of Dan's wound, his military record states that he was shot in the face on November 6, 1917; however, Lester didn't write about Dan's being wounded until the end of January 1918. Considering that Lester rejoined their battalion on November 30, 1917, and travelled to the UK himself in December of that year, it seems odd that he didn't mention it earlier in his letters or even visit his friend when he was in England. There is no record of the two men keeping in touch after Dan returned to Canada.

We do not know what happened in Scotland or what exactly Mabel said about the picture that her husband sent to her. Her letters do not survive. Judging by Lester's response, she appeared to be livid. Their argument over infidelity took place over multiple letters, and I have combined excerpts related to this issue into one.

Chapter Six: *Please Do Not Tell Everyone About This*. In May 1918, Lester wrote with shock about seeing numerous men killed by concussion blasts, so I have crafted the narrative about the soldiers dying this way to reflect his surprise at such freak incidents at a time when the battalion took casualties from frequent shelling. Lester also had repeated problems with his teeth (most likely due to trench mouth), including breaking one on hardtack, but he did not provide details, so I have included it in this chapter.

I've written the vignette about Lester taking out the machine gun based on the surviving accounts (which are presented in the text), coupled with what we know about the military tactics of the Great War, the weapons he was issued, and his orders as stated in the war diaries. While it has been suggested that he would have thrown his smoke grenade for cover before tossing his Mills bombs, such military tactics common in today's army were not necessarily used as frequently during the First World War, especially at night without modern night-vision equipment

Afterword

and in an unexpected and hurried situation. This may have happened, but we don't know. We also don't know how Lester got the German revolver or what happened to it.

Chapter Seven: *And Still the War Goes On.* There are multiple versions of the death of Private George Price. While I have incorporated details from several accounts, I've followed Tim Cook, who suggests that the private was presumably going for a kiss when he ran out from cover on November 11.

All that we know about Bud's death is found in his military record. There is a single line, by the OC of his unit, that states the date he was reported KIA. Considering that Bud was with the 31st Battalion in the trenches near the Canal du Nord when the Germans launched a barrage on that day, it seems most likely that he was killed by shellfire.

Epilogue: *Daddy, Did You Ever Kill a German?* The stories about Lester after the war come primarily from his grandchildren and from Barbara's notes and her self-published book.

ACKNOWLEDGMENTS

I WOULD LIKE TO BEGIN BY THANKING THE FAMILY OF LESTER Harper for sharing their stories and photos, helping to organize the correspondence, and answering my many questions. My wife and our son were also instrumental in encouraging me to write in a more readable style. This was not what I had envisioned when I started out, but I hope you're happy with the result.

Much has been published on the First World War, and this book would have been very difficult to write without the works of great Canadian historians, such as Margaret MacMillan and Tim Cook. In particular, Tim Cook's two-volume masterpiece on the Canadian infantry (*At the Sharp End* and *Shock Troops*) was a constant source of reference to understand and contextualize Lester's experience.

I had access to the libraries at the University of Oslo and Simon Fraser University while working there in visiting scholar and research associate positions, and I would also like to thank the South Peace Historical Society for providing material from their collection and Library and Archives Canada for digitizing the war diaries and military service records of the Canadian Expeditionary Force, allowing me to frequently revisit them. Although this book is decidedly not academic (as a colleague was quick to point out), it would be remiss of me not to

Acknowledgments

mention my former supervisors. I developed my research skills under the tutelage of Luke Clossey at Simon Fraser University, while Howard Hotson at the University of Oxford taught me the importance of writing historical vignettes in an engaging manner.

Publishing a book is a collaborative process, and I am grateful to my agent, Rick Broadhead, for his guidance and advice (especially on those long nights navigating time zones), as well as to Nicole Winstanley, Jim Gifford, Janice Weaver, and the rest of the team at Simon & Schuster Canada. This book may not have come to fruition if not for their expertise and enthusiasm. Muna Hussein, in particular, deserves credit for the title.

Lastly, I would like to thank the family, friends, and colleagues (especially those in the military and academia) who answered my queries and provided feedback. Susan Wells, Friedericke Türkheim, Keith Donaldson, Chris Hale, Paul Dempsey, Kester Aspden, Darren and Kaya Marriott, and Pat and Christine Haggerty, your thoughts were all appreciated.

ABOUT THE AUTHOR

BRANDON MARRIOTT, originally from Vancouver, received his doctorate in history from the University of Oxford. He went on to hold a postdoctoral fellowship at the University of London, then taught undergraduate history as a sessional instructor at Simon Fraser University (SFU). An avid traveller married to a Canadian diplomat, he has lived in eight countries, visited more than a hundred, and held academic positions around the world. He has been a volunteer instructor at the University of the Nouvelle Grand Anse in Haiti, a scholar-in-residence at the Newberry Library in Chicago, and a visiting scholar at the University of Oslo. Most recently, Brandon has returned to SFU as a research associate. An outdoor winter enthusiast, he can be found in the mountains in his free time with a good book and a pair of skis.